A SPUR CALLED COURAGE

A SPUR CALLED COURAGE

SOE Heroes in Italy

Alan Ogden

Bene Factum Publishing

By the same author

History

Through Hitler's Back Door: SOE operations in Hungary, Bulgaria and Romania
The Discontented: Love, War and Betrayal in Habsburg Hungary

Travel

Moons and Aurochs: Romanian Journeys
Winds of Sorrow: Journeys in and around Transylvania
Revelations of Byzantium: The Monasteries and Painted Churches of Northern Moldavia
Fortresses of Faith: The Kirchenburgen of Transylvania
Romania Revisited: On The Trail of English Travelers 1602-1941

A Spur Called Courage
SOE Heroes in Italy

First published in 2011 by
Bene Factum Publishing Ltd
PO Box 58122
London
SW8 5WZ

Email: inquiries@bene-factum.co.uk
www.bene-factum.co.uk

ISBN: 978-1-903071-35-9
Text © Alan Ogden

A CIP catalogue record of this is available from the British Library

Design and typesetting by Carnegie Publishing
Cover and book Mousemat Design Ltd
Printed and bound by Good News Digital Books

'... e questo sprone si chiama Fortezza... la quale vertute mostra lo loco dove è da fermarsi e da pungare.'

'... and this spur is called courage... a virtue which marks the place where one must take a stand and fight.'
Dante: *Convivio* IV, 26, 7

Dedicated to the memory of all SOE personnel, British, Commonwealth and Italian, who served in Italy 1943-1945 and the courageous Italian civilians who aided them.

Contents

La Resistenza Italiana

Foreword

The remarkable achievements of SOE missions in Italy have been woefully overlooked compared to those of their counterparts in France. In many ways, Italy was the forgotten battlefield of Europe and as the Allied armies advanced slowly northwards after landing at Salerno in 1943 – in many instances yard by yard – so the role of SOE and other Special Forces in support of 15th Army Group assumed both a greater strategic and tactical importance.

Operating behind enemy lines with guerrilla forces is always fraught with difficulty and in the case of Italy was particularly demanding. In these well-researched portraits of outstanding SOE officers, every conceivable challenge emerges, from the basic survival skills needed to get through an Apennine winter to the sophisticated diplomacy required to avoid internecine violence between politically opposed Partisan bands.

The personal qualities displayed by these courageous SOE officers are the benchmark for the selection of modern Special Forces – determination, ingenuity, resilience, stamina, self-reliance and a single-mindedness to close with the enemy and inflict as many casualties as possible at the least possible cost.

As the campaign in Italy came to a close, an important additional quality was demanded of SOE officers, one of intellectual rigour combined with mental agility as they planned how to manage the crucial time gap between German withdrawal from the cities and Allied occupation. Furthermore, they were charged with the remit of preventing any widespread demolition to the industrial fabric and infrastructure of Italy.

Once the Allied Military Government had taken over, SOE played a major if discrete role in overseeing the delicate process of disarming the Partisans and decommissioning the caches of arms and material that had accumulated during the war. The pursuit of war criminals and the reward of brave and loyal agents were equally important tasks allotted to them.

A Spur called Courage makes an impressive and significant contribution to the historical record of SOE and No 1 Special Force in particular and, in recalling the valour of individual SOE officers and their teams, it celebrates the tradition of leadership, teamwork and devotion to duty which British Special Forces hold so high today.

General The Lord Guthrie of Craigiebank, GCB, LVO, OBE, DL
Colonel Commandant SAS, 2001-2010

Introduction

These profiles of seventeen British and Commonwealth SOE officers do not in themselves tell the story of SOE in Italy, a subject which merits a comprehensive history in its own right.* Rather they represent its varied and multiple aspects and serve to illustrate the trials and endeavours of all members of SOE during the prolonged and difficult Italian campaign. Furthermore, it is important to remember that whereas SOE British military missions provided advice, training and supplies of arms and equipment – and in many cases that essential military asset of leadership – it was the SOE-trained Partisans and Italian missions who did the brunt of the fighting. That story has been rightly told by the Italians themselves.

The history of SOE and the Italian resistance falls into four phases. From January 1942 to September 1943, feelers were put out by SOE in London and Berne to establish contact with the Italian opposition to Mussolini. Through go-betweens who travelled between Italy and Berne, SOE kept in touch with members of the Italian Royal family, the Vatican, Army circles and left wing leaders and even neo-fascists. W/T sets were smuggled into Italy and the process eventually concluded with the successful Allied negotiations for an armistice with General Badoglio.

In the second phase from September 1943, with the signing of the armistice, the text of SOE's task had fundamentally changed. The time for political subversion was over; the aim now was to give the maximum tactical and strategic support to the advancing Allied armies. Italy, previously an enemy power, could now be regarded as an occupied country in the process of being liberated. Up to the liberation of Rome in May 1944, eighteen missions were sent into occupied Italy to make an inventory of the fledgling Partisan bands, conduct small-scale harassing raids, arrange the occasional diversion of enemy troops and assist escaping POWs, particularly aircrew.

In the third phase up to the liberation of Florence at the beginning of September 1944, a further seventeen missions were sent in as well as Italian

---

* *Mission Accomplished*, the official history of SOE and Italy 1943–45, by David Stafford (Bodley Head, London).

volunteers to arm and train Partisans, direct their attacks on specific road and rail targets and hamper enemy troop movements. At the end of this phase, there were sixty-three English and nearly 150 Italians operating behind enemy lines with thirty-three W/Ts in regular contact with SOE HQ.

The fourth phase in the winter of 1944/45 consisted of stepping up military activities, coordinating the preservation of industrial plant, harbour facilities and public utilities from demolition by a retreating German Army [Operation Anti-Scorch] and planning the establishment of civilian government during the anticipated time lag between liberation by Partisans and the arrival of Allied troops [The FREEBORN Period]. This latter brief included the potentially thorny problem of disarming the Partisan brigade. By end of March 1945, there were thirty British Missions in North Italy and eight British-sponsored Italian Missions, 140 men in all.

SOE were not alone in helping the Italian Partisan movement. After transferring its bases to the Italian mainland in late summer 1944, the American OSS began to drop supplies and operatives into the various regions on a large scale and by the spring of 1945 seventy-five OSS teams were in the field equipping and training Partisan bands. This largesse coupled with a tendency to keep its activities strictly on a 'For US Eyes Only' basis created numerous problems for the men of both organizations in the field. On a higher level, the British became increasingly alarmed about the indiscriminate arming of Communist Partisans, prompting an observation from Harold Macmillan, Minister Resident in the Mediterranean, that 'the main thing was to get a firm grip of the resistance groups before they became, as in Greece, mere instruments of Communism.'

The challenges facing the British missions throughout each of the last three phases were formidable and at times must have appeared almost insurmountable. First and foremost, they were up against a determined and experienced enemy in the Germans after September 1943. The German order of battle in Italy included unfamiliar former soldiers of the USSR, such as Turkmens and Cossacks, as well as battle- hardened infantry and panzer units, crack mountain troops and some SS battalions. German counter-Partisan tactics had rapidly evolved as a result of their experiences fighting Partisans and resistance fighters in Russia, Yugoslavia, France and Greece; transferring and adapting them to Italy was relatively straightforward except their name changed to *rastrellamenti*. As for the Italians, while officially their army had surrendered in 1943, a considerable number continued to serve Mussolini's new Republic of Salo and included the diehard fascist Brigado Nera and Decima MAS in addition to Alpini regiments and other regular units.

To stay alive behind enemy lines in Italy invariably meant keeping on the move. Lieutenant Colonel Peter McMullen, a veteran of two SOE tours in Greece, advocated 'go high and go poor and be uncomfortable' and above all 'keep moving everyday particularly in the valleys'. Mountain eyries apart, staying put for more than one night was a course fraught with risk. He recalled staying at the house of an aged Comtessa in a valley outside Piacenza which 'actually had a bath and <u>also</u> hot water and <u>also</u> sheets on the bed. I remember saying to myself as I went to sleep in luxury – "you'd better be out of here by dawn if you want to avoid being nabbed" – and I was, much to the Comtessa's consternation who had a delicious breakfast laid on.'

Aside from contact with the enemy, there were many other pitfalls that confronted SOE operatives. Even as they left the aircraft on their parachutes, it was rarely with total certainty that they would land among friends for the enemy did their best to replicate the landing signals on the DZs. When the Chariton Mission jumped into Piedmont in February 1945, they saw three landing fires, one genuine lit by the *Autonomo* Partisans, the second a German decoy and the third started by the *Garibaldi* Partisans hoping to divert supplies away from the *Autonomi*. Often there were no signals at all and the planes returned home after aborting the sortie. Once on the ground with the Partisans, the risk of betrayal by spies and informers was ever present. Stuart Hood, an escaped POW who joined up with a Partisan band, remembered waiting for an air drop when the local Partisan commander came to him with news that he had 'a man too many'. A boy was hauled before him, who on questioning said he was from Sardinia. His story, full of contradictions, did not stack up and he was taken away and shot.

Another constant threat came from the Allied side for marauding Allied aircraft were prone to attack opportunity targets and understandably found it hard to differentiate between a group of armed Partisans and Axis infantry units on the move. Ambush by own troops was also not infrequent for few Partisans had received a proper military training. Lastly, the terrain of the Ligurian and Carnic mountains of the north and the Apennines mountains of the centre provided a harsh and unforgiving battleground for guerrilla warfare, especially during the winter months when it was impossible to conceal ones tracks in the snow, no different from Serbia in 1943 when Lieutenant Colonel Jasper Rootham had observed 'winter is a bad season for guerrillas; the lack of leafy cover, the tracks left behind in the snow, and the difficulty of finding a roof at nights are all against them'.

Over and above the physical dangers of war behind enemy lines lay the mercurial and byzantine character of Partisan politics which SOE officers had to deal with on a daily basis. With a volatile mix of different political and nationalist parties dominated by the Partito Comunista Italiano [PCI] to contend with, sound judgment and a canny appreciation of human nature were essential qualities needed by individual officers. Some had the advantage of speaking fluent Italian, others had to work through interpreters but all of them had to impose their will on the Partisans through sheer force of personality and personal example. Tensions between the different strands of Partisans invariably involved SOE. In October 1944, a member of the PCI exclaimed about the rival *Autonomi*, 'we are going to have to deal with this individual [Mauri] for quite some time and we will need to show our teeth and break his teeth if necessary...Mauri has a representative of Alexander with him, Major Temple, and through him he makes reports denigrating the *Garibaldini*, painting us as bandits and looters without any military efficiency'.

Often it was their duty to deliver bad news for individual officers did not set policy. A prime example of this was Field Marshal Alexander's directive to the Partisans in the autumn of 1944 that they should cease offensive operations until the spring of 1945 when 15th Army Group would be ready to reassume its offensive. In many cases, the Partisans misconstrued this as a vote of no confidence in them and a sop to the occupying Axis forces. One officer reported that 'the directive broadcast by General Alexander.... had a very bad effect on the Partisans in my area.' Be that as it may, the reality was that Alexander had no choice other than to rest his exhausted armies.

The volume and frequency of supplies of arms and equipment was another constant contentious issue; having assured their Partisan charges that a drop was imminent, on many occasions SOE officers found themselves manning remote DZs with no sign of Allied aircraft and subsequently had to sooth the disappointment and disbelief of the Partisan bands. Furthermore, there were occasions of high embarrassment when 1,000 sets of tropical underwear were dropped instead of the promised load of Sten guns and winter clothing! Several officers like George Fielding vented their frustration on the RAF or Balkan Airforce but the reasons for the haphazard nature of aerial resupply were more complex as one mission's* log reveals: 'no reception as DZ shelled'; 'fires not lit owing to *rastrellamento*'; 'DZ

---

*   Ruina Mission

temporarily occupied by enemy'; 'too much snow on DZ to permit reception'; 'all packages dropped ...and collected by enemy'; 'whole load blew up, killing three Partisans whilst being stacked ready to cart away'. In hindsight, many would agree with John Orr-Ewing's admission that 'we in the mountains all tended to forget that clear skies overhead did not automatically mean equally favourable weather conditions at the point of take-off [and landing some hours later] and en route... Nor perhaps did we fully appreciate the navigational difficulties of finding the many mountain DZs we proposed.'

The ardent and understandable desire of the Partisans to launch attacks on German and Republican forces always invoked the prospect of immediate retaliation and savage reprisal. British SOE officers had experienced this at first hand in Greece and Yugoslavia and often found themselves in the unenviable position of advocating caution and restraint. The impact of such attacks could never seriously affect German war-fighting capability in Italy, yet the consequences were inevitably costly in terms of men and materials and more often than not resulted in the deaths of hundreds of innocent people and the decimation of their village livelihoods. A further factor at play here was the propensity of the Communist resistance to orchestrate deliberately such confrontations in order to present themselves as the true saviours of Italy, thus promoting their post-war political goals.

Yet there were occasions when SOE encouraged such risky ventures. In November 1944, Major Tommy Macpherson witnessed the aftermath of a Partisan operation to liberate several villages between the Tagliamento and Isonzo rivers on the Yugoslav border. '[The Germans] mustered a substantial mobile force backed up by garrison troops on foot, surrounded the area and proceded to rout all the Partisans, seizing a lot of valuable equipment that had been dropped to them at great risk. The result was a huge number of desertions and a massive drop in morale. Not only that, but their precipitative and foolish actions led to the total destruction of several villages by the Germans...plus reprisals that led to the deaths of numerous hostages, many by public hangings from lamp posts. The whole fiasco was the total antithesis of the way in which to pursue an effective guerilla campaign, and I found it somewhat ironic that on his return my predecessor was then taken on the staff of SOE HQ in Italy, promoted and decorated.'

The discomforts and hardships faced by SOE were probably no less or more in total than those experienced by many of the troops in the front line but there were marked differences of degree. Clothing and boots soon wore out in the harsh mountain conditions and unless quickly replaced by supply drops meant SOE personnel using locally-sourced substitutes, not always inferior as Peter McMullen's Italian boots were still serviceable twenty years later! Food was always scarce and its nutritional value often inadequate, leading to scabies and lethargy. Furthermore, theft of food was a capital offence in the Partisans' code of conduct. In winter*, the all pervading cold produced its own set of problems. Major Bob Walker-Brown of the SAS who worked with SOE's Blundell Violet mission recalled how 'we suffered a variety of ailments from the harsh cold conditions, lack of food and physical exertion which was, by this time, part of our day to day existence. We all had cuts, chapped lips, cracked knuckles and blisters which refused to heal in the cold weather, often turning septic....[some] were suffering colds, fevers or had the beginnings of flu...others had contracted dysentery or scabies, the result of a poor diet lacking nutrition...'

In their training, SOE operatives were taught how to adapt to local conditions and this was key to their survival in Italy, both in summer and winter. Stuart Hood who lived with the poor farmers of the Apennines for over a year, dubbed it a 'crude Arcadia' and 'if you strip life to its essentials they are warmth, food and somewhere to sleep. A peasant house caters for all three... We found that their enemy was authority – the landlord and his *fattore*, the state and its inspectors, the Duce and the Pope. For them Fascism meant authority. Fascism took their wheat for the communal grain pool, their copper pots for the driving bands of shells, their sons for the wars. It gave them nothing in return. Its enemies, in simple logic, must be their friends... Living with the peasants I saw the last upsurge of peasant life and of an ancient civilization – *la civiltà contadinesca*. The skills I learned, the crafts I watched, had not changed since Ambrogio Lorenzetti in the fourteenth century painted his great murals in the Town Hall of Siena.'

At times, there was almost a sense of dislocation experienced by SOE operatives. Major Richard Tolson's diary entry for 2 November 1944 gives us an insight: 'Tramonti. It is curious to reflect on the unreality of our lives; of our life as Englishmen among the Italians. One is happy enough, I suppose, in a flat sort of way; flattened by the weight of five years of war and now seeing that war through a looking glass and the fascist press. Our work room and living room is the kitchen of this old house. It is very small with two wide and deep set windows looking south and west. The atmosphere is always the same; our food cooking, our socks drying, and the harsh smell of

---

* The winter of 1944/45 was exceptionally cold, -16C° in the Po valley and much lower in the mountains.

Italian tobacco. When it is dark, an oil lamp suspended from one of the whitewashed wooden beams, gives a friendly exclusive light, dismissing in shadows the bare white walls, the stone floor, our littered arms and the wooden crucifix high upon the west wall. Outside the leaves are rushing on the wind, and the level of greyness of the sky discloses only rain. A very mourning mood fit for the dead, whose day it is, and who alone know the hopelessness of death'.

Contrary to logical expectation given the highly risky nature of their work, SOE British officer casualties in Italy were remarkably low – indeed in single figures – no doubt due in part to their superb training, fitness, resourcefulness and mental hardiness. Special mention must be made of Major Gordon Lett and Major Tony Oldham. Both were POWs who, after the Armistice of September 1943, had valiantly chosen to escape and try and reach Allied lines where they could continue the fight against the Axis enemy. They were under no obligation to do so since MI9's order P/W 87190 of 7 June 1943, instructing Senior British Officers in charge of POWs to remain 'within camp' remained in force at the time*. After being on the run for some time, both officers reassessed their chances of reaching Allied lines and concluded that they were better off continuing the fight behind enemy lines with the Partisans, an extraordinary courageous decision in the light of hindsight when it became clear that most of their fellow escaping officers had lived in hiding with peasant families until the Allied advance made going throught the lines a viable option.

Between September 1943 and April 1945, some 60,000 Allied and 50,000 German soldiers were killed in Italy. The total number of casualties on all sides including wounded and missing was very nearly one million men. Partisan losses were estimated at 44,700 killed and another 21,200 wounded or disabled. So how effective was the Partisan contribution to the Allied military campaign in Italy? General Mark Clark found them 'a great help... They were excellent at gathering information for us and often found German stragglers that our units had missed'. Field Marshal Alexander was less than effusive in his acknowledgment of their efforts; indeed he hardly referred to

---

* Of the 80,000 British POWs in Italy at the time of the Armistice, 50,000 were immediately captured by the Germans and shipped north. Of those who did escape, only 11,500 made it all the way home: 5,000 by crossing the Alps into Switzerland and 6,500 by reaching the Allied forces coming up Italy. The rest were either rounded up or shot by the Germans on the run or just faded into the countryside, settling in the mountain villages of the Apennines and never going home. Some 2,000 were never accounted for.

them other than noting 'in Italy the agent produced no information of any [military] significance'. More tellingly, Field Marshal Kesselring, whose troops had been on the receiving end of Partisan activity, acknowledged that 'Partisan bands began to be a nuisance in and on both sides of the Apennines for the first time in April 1944'. He estimated that between June and August the same year, more than 7,000 German soldiers had been killed or kidnapped by the Partisans and the same amount wounded. Much as he indignantly disapproved of Partisan guerilla tactics, going so far as to claim they were in breach of the Rules of War as laid down in the Hague Regulations, he was in no doubt about the climate of fear they created behind the front line and the demoralizing effect this had on his men.

The final word deservedly belongs to Major Bill Tilman, who had served as a regular officer in both the First and Second World Wars before joining SOE. In his perspicacious summing-up of the lot of the Italian Partisans and their British mentors, he opined that 'an Italian who became a Partisan had to suffer greater hardships and run greater risks than those incurred by regular troops. Capture almost invariably meant death, with the probability of being tortured first and hanged afterwards. If they were badly wounded their chances of getting away were slim, while for those who did get away medical care was rough and ready. A successful action usually meant reprisals during which friends or relatives might be shot, hanged or at the best imprisoned, their houses and villages burnt.

Food was monotonous, clothing was insufficient, boots bad, cleanliness nearly impossible. They could have no pay, leave, amusements or mail from home; the only newspapers they saw were Fascist; there were no canteens, cigarettes and tobacco were either scanty or unobtainable. There was no organized training or even sufficient work to counteract the long weeks of waiting and inactivity. In short, everything that makes life tolerable for the regular soldier, that sustains his morale in quiet times and in battle gives him a reasonable chance of survival, was absent from the life of the Partisans. Nor was this all. There were no periods of rest for the Partisans. They lived under the constant strain of surprise, betrayal or attack; the GAP who lived in villages never dared sleep in houses. And most serious of all, perhaps, were the political fears and jealousies, existing even in their own formations, and the suspicion that for them that the end of the war might only be the beginning of fresh political strife. It is with all this in mind that that the Partisans must be judged'.

I would like to thank all those whose assistance and enthusiasm has made this book both a pleasure and an honour to write: David McMullen for allowing me access to his father's papers and priceless photograph albums; Julia Korner for her unstinting help in fine-tuning the portrait of her father, Andrew Croft; Anna-Maria Holland for her support in telling the story of her late husband Charles; Brian Lett QC for his meticulous input into my account of his father, Gordon Lett; Oliver Barton for aiding me unlock the files concerning his most remarkable father; Sylvia Marsico, Tony Oldham's daughter, who provided me with a wealth of material about her father; Fergus Peploe whose scrutiny of his grandfather's portrait, Manfred Czernin, was invaluable; Adam Munthe who approved my entry on his father; Jane Stevens for proofing her father's entry; Richard Dallimore-Mallaby who put the family archives at my disposal; Martin Fielding, coincidentally an old school friend, for his most helpful assistance on his father, George; Jill Gardner, niece of Hugh Ballard, and Bruce Ballard, his nephew, together with Robyn Soutar of The Maitland Group, whose combined sleuthing skills enabled me to construct an accurate portrait; Anne O'Regan for her memories of her late husband Pat; Dr John Ross of the Simia Mission for his kind permission to use his photographs and for proofing my portrait of Bill Tilman; and Sir Tommy Macpherson for patiently talking me through his mission.

As always it has been a delight and a privilege to work with The National Archives, The British Library, The Imperial War Museum, The Liddell Hart Library at King's College London and the Special Forces Club. All these institutions are extraordinarily efficient and invariably courteous and helpful.

Alan Ogden
London
March 2011

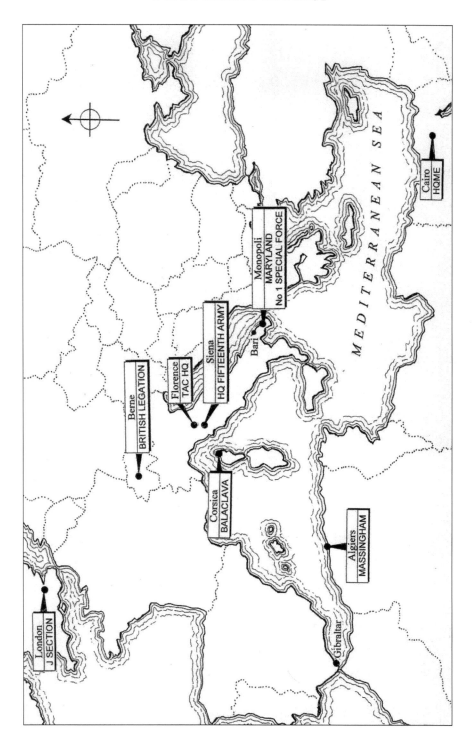

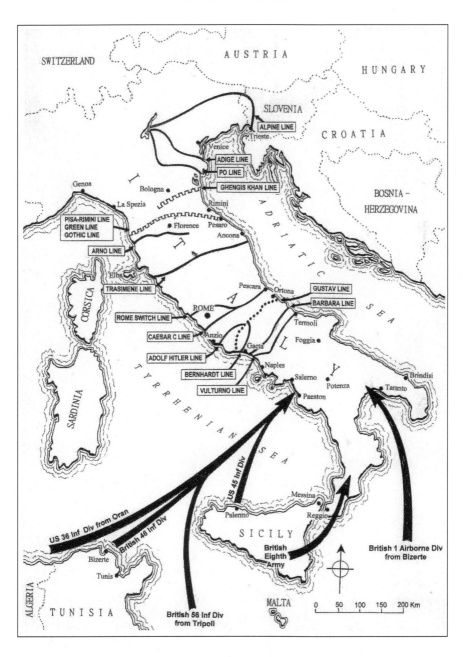

1

Major Malcolm Munthe, MC
Major Max Salvadori, DSO, MC

When twenty-nine year old Malcolm Munthe was summoned to a mysterious room in the War Office in 1939, he was acutely self-conscious that his Gordon Highlander's kilt and hobnail boots were somewhat out of place; everyone else was wearing service dress or suits, and all sported shoes. However, his appearance was of no concern for his interviewers' interest lay in his command of foreign languages and Swedish social connections. The second son of the second marriage of the world famous Swedish physician and philanthropist Dr Axel Munthe, author of the best-selling *The Story of San Michele,*[*] Munthe had been brought up between the Swedish court [where his father was the Royal Physician], Italy, and Britain, where his mother, Hilda Pennington-Mellor, owned two large houses, Hellens in Herefordshire and Southside House in Wimbledon.

After obtaining a degree in politics at the London School of Economics at the same time as running a boys' club in a deprived quarter of Southwark, Munthe joined the office of the High Commissioner for German Refugees[†], Major-General Sir Neill Malcolm, who had been chairman of the Council of the Royal Institute for International Affairs from 1926 to 1935. Sir Neill's elder brother, Sir Ian Malcolm, was a senior figure in the Conservative Party, having been assistant private secretary to Lord Salisbury in 1895-1900, parliamentary private secretary to George Wyndham, the Chief Secretary for Ireland, in 1901-1903, and private secretary to Balfour in the United States in 1917 and at the Peace Conference in 1919. With such good connections, it was not surprising that Munthe was offered the comparatively safe Tory seat of East Ham South.

Alarmed by Mussolini's invasion of Albania, Munthe presented himself to a recruiting office in Buckingham Gate and on the basis of his Scottish

---

[*]   Published by John Murray in 1929, by 1930 there had been twelve editions of the English version alone, and Munthe added a second preface.

[†]   The High commission for Refugees coming from Germany was established in October, 1933, by the League of Nations and incorporated into the League in 1936. By 1938, over 150,000 Jews had fled from persecution in Nazi Germany.

Christian name was told to report to the Gordon Highlanders in Chelsea Barracks. After recruit training, he was sent to Weedon Cavalry School for Officer Training rather to his annoyance as 'on the whole...it was preferable to be shouted at than to shout at others". It was at this point that MI[R] requested his services and after a short interview with the DMI and a crash course in blowing up railway lines, he made his way with fellow student Andrew Croft to Bergen to convey equipment to the Swedish Volunteer Corps for use by the Finnish Army which was under attack by the Russians.

Soon the two British officers were on their way to Tornio, a town that straddled the border between Sweden and Finland. At the Finnish head-quarters, the General asked Munthe whether he liked Molotov cocktails. He replied in all innocence that he had done very well on the *misemaria*, the sticky liqueur he had been drinking! That evening, they were summoned to dine at Swedish HQ where the Swedish General instructed Munthe in the art of rolling cigarettes. Such niceties continued as both the Finns and Swedes courted their guests for shipment of arms. When Croft was ordered back to Bergen to sort out various delays, Munthe set out with a Finnish ski patrol to put his recently acquired knowledge of explosives into practice. After booby trapping an abandoned tank, he selected a spot on the railway to plant the camouflet device he had brought out from England. Two hours later, a mighty explosion shook the forest as thirty pounds of plastic explosive detonated prematurely, triggered by a Russian shell falling nearby. As it turned out, there was no need to lay another mine since the railway was subsequently captured by the Finns. Instead Munthe was directed back to Tornio to greet General Sir Ormond de L'Épée Winter and the first contingent of British volunteers. The chain-smoking General, master of five Russo-Slavic languages, promptly developed a high fever and took to his bed. In the event it did not matter since an Armistice between Finland and Russia was proclaimed a few days later.

Such were the needs and necessities of the War Office in April 1940 that it sent Munthe as Liaison Officer to the Norwegian Army in south Norway, irrespective of the fact he had never even visited the country; Scandinavia was, after all, composed of Finland, Sweden and Norway, so the thinking was that they were all more or less the same. Arriving in Stavanger with his W/T Operator, Munthe made contact with the British Consular shipping adviser, Commander Platt RN. By now the Germans began to arrive and after burning as many confidential papers as they could, Munthe's party

---

* Sweet is War p24

MAJOR MALCOLM MUNTHE, MC

which consisted of eleven men and one woman extricated itself in dribs and drabs from enemy occupied Stavanger, eventually ending up in a fisherman's cottage on the Fordefjord. Short of food, Munthe set off for help and after walking for several days reached Norwegian lines. Shot in the leg during a German attack, he was captured and sent to Stavanger Hospital from where he escaped with help from Norwegian patriots and after recuperating in a safe house, set off to find a fishing boat to rescue his abandoned companions. After a series of close shaves with German intelligence, Munthe finally arranged for a boat to take the English party to the Shetlands but he himself remained behind as his leg would have betrayed them if they were intercepted by a German patrol boat. Several weeks later, with courageous help from Norwegian friends and patriots, he made his way to Sweden on foot and at 6.30 a.m. one morning rang the doorbell of Brigadier Reginald Sutton-Pratt, the British Military Attaché, who greeted him with the words: "Mary, guess who's here!"

News soon followed of a Mention in Dispatches and promotion to Major in line with his new job of Assistant Military Attaché. However, his stint in Sweden was to prove controversial to the authorities there, for far from carrying out the normal duties of an Attaché, Munthe was busy organizing volunteers for the Norwegian resistance, providing them with training, explosives and weapons. One operation resulted in the blowing up of the Oslo-Bergen railway; another, codenamed Barbara, designed to disrupt the movement of German guns being smuggled through Sweden to Norway, failed when the Swedes arrested his Norwegian agent on the frontier. Both incidents were blamed by the Swedes on Munthe. This prompted him to concoct a more secure network which he christened 'the Red Horse' after Grane, the horse of the goddess Brynilda in Norse mythology. A team of four Norwegians and a Swede was dispatched to make a reconnaissance of the railway at Trondheim and then by sea to Aberdeen* and the clandestine supply of Finnish arms to Norway resumed. An aborted attempt by members of the Norwegian resistance orchestrated by Munthe to kill Himmler on his visit to Oslo was brought to the attention of the Swedish Government by the Germans and thus Munthe's time was finally up. Perhaps it was just as well since an attempt had been made on his life on the quayside and after a desperate struggle with his assailant, Munthe had managed to drag himself out of the water, left with just his shirt and trousers. There was no sign of his attacker beneath the inky surface.

---

* They safely arrived and successfully returned to Norway where they blew up the railway.

From the autumn of 1941 through to the end of 1942, Munthe continued his work for the Norwegian resistance out of the SOE offices in Baker Street, training agents and planning raids. Then with the Allied poised to invade Sicily, Colonel Roseberry, the head of SOE Italy in London, was given carte blanche to recruit Italian speakers from within SOE and Munthe, anxious to be back in the field, volunteered and was accepted. Picked to lead a small unit*, codename Brow, to land with the first wave of Eighth Army, they attached themselves to the Cameron Highlanders. After safely disembarking in Sicily, Munthe's team spent their first night at Syracuse, mulling over their orders which were to get in touch with anti-Fascist elements behind enemy lines, with a view to encouraging revolt against the Fascist forces and to form guerrilla bands which they would then supply by parachute. Soon they had a number of volunteers on their books and started to plan anti-Fascist insurrections in Catania and Palermo which were some way behind enemy lines.

Operation Lowbrow was one such mission and its SOE officer and two Italian guides crossed the lines dressed as peasant evacuees, carrying explosives hidden in hollowed out melons. Contact with this party was immediately lost and two more missions were aborted, including a proposal by Munthe to cross the lines, dressed as an aged, sick peasant woman on a donkey, his W/T set hidden under his black skirt. When Messina fell on 17 August, the work of his unit in Sicily came to an end. On balance, given its tiny resources, it had been a success, with a number of very promising contacts on the mainland on its books and a modus operandi established. Sadly, it later transpired that the young officer in charge of Lowbrow had been caught by the Germans and after being made to dig his own grave, shot at close range†.

Lieutenant Adrian Gallegos RNVR of the Advanced Naval Section of No.1 Special Force remembered working closely with Munthe at the time. 'His expression was boyish and he looked younger than his age. He had a finely formed head which clearly showed its bone structure, his tilted-up nose was intelligent and enquiring and his light blue-grey eyes were unable to hide what went on in his mind and were always ready to smile. One could at once see what a genuine, sincere and painstaking person he was. He had slender hands, with long tapering fingers and his manner was specially

---

*   Innocuously called G [Topographical] Liaison Unit 15th Army Group
†   Testimony of Sergeant Morro, Royal Carabinieri Regiment. He later joined Munthe's unit and was killed in action.

gentle and sympathetic. All about him denoted a busy, artistic mind full of imagination, and conscientious to a degree; in short, a very fine character, full of idealism.'

On 25 July, two officers had arrived as reinforcements, thirty-five year old Massimo Salvadori known as Captain 'Max Sylvester', and Captain Dick Cooper*, who had recently escaped from Vichy France. Born in England to an aristocratic Protestant family, Max Salvadori had been involved in the anti-Fascist movement in Italy since the 1920s when he and his father were both beaten up by the Blackshirts. Completing his education in Geneva, Max returned to Italy aged twenty-one as the secret representative of the exiled politician, Alberto Tarchiani, one of the founders of the *Giustizia e Liberta* party in Paris in 1929. For three years he carried out underground activities until he was arrested by the Fascist secret police in 1933. Imprisoned and tortured on the island of Ponza, his release was obtained after the intervention of a British cousin and he emigrated to Kenya to farm. On the outbreak of war, Salvadori was sent by British Intelligence to the United States to contact Italians who might be sympathetic to the Allied cause and be prepared to go to Italy at a later date. It was while he was in Mexico City in 1943 that he learnt his own application to join the British Army had been approved and he returned to Italy for the first time in ten years as an SOE officer. Cooper who had originally been inserted into North Africa as a solo operator was under strict orders not to cross the enemy line as the Gestapo had a voluminous file on him.

Allied strategy now focused on the invasion of Italy proper. Codenamed Vigilant, Munthe's unit joined British X Corps, part of the US Fifth Army, and sailed for Salerno on 6 September. The landing was far from easy and SOE arrived in the town while it was still in German hands. Couriers were nonetheless sent through the lines to anti-fascist contacts in Naples and soon two excellent opportunities to raise the standard of anti-fascism arose. First, the arrival of the famous leader of the *Arditi* in the First World War, General Pavone, at Munthe's HQ in Salerno presented SOE with the ideal military figurehead to rally the resistance. Second, ten miles to the north in Sorrento lived Benedetto Croce, the greatest living opponent of Fascist philosophy, who could provide the intellectual leadership to galvanize Italy out of its moral stupor. The problem was that he was still in enemy territory.

By now the island of Capri had fallen, a symbolic moment for Munthe given his father's long association with it. Rear Admiral Morse, whose task

---

* Also see Chapter 2

was to re-open the ports of western Italy, had established his temporary HQ on the island while waiting for the fall of Naples. As well as British MTBs and American PT boats, his resources included a flotilla of high speed Italian MAS boats and it was on one of these that Munthe dispatched Gallegos to Sorrento to locate Croce. He found him at his house, the Villa Tritone, working by candlelight late into the night. Conscious that time was short as the Germans were already on their way to arrest him, Croce agreed to leave with two of his daughters and landed in Capri shortly after midnight. Munthe himself went to the Villa the next night along with Alberto Tarchiani to collect Croce's wife and remaining daughter. Realizing that Signora Croce was most reluctant to leave without her newly hung out washing, he swept her into his arms and ran back to the boat under the very noses of the Germans. Meanwhile, Gallegos had set off on another mission and failed to return. Later SOE learnt that his MAS boat had hit a mine and he had been captured on landing. Imprisoned in Germany, he escaped and reached Allied lines almost a year to the day after setting out on his ill-fated voyage.

When Naples fell on 2 October, Munthe moved his unit into the city and then established a training base on the Island of Ischia, where he moored their two newly acquired motor torpedo boats. Captain Edward Renton of the Black Watch was now second in command, Michael Gubbins, the twenty-two year old son of SOE chief General Sir Colin Gubbins, operations officer and Captain Dick Cooper acting Quartermaster. All in all No.1 Special Force now numbered some fifty men. Despite a certain friction with the OSS, epitomized by a meeting General Donovan arranged with SIM without inviting SOE*, throughout the autumn 'coup de main' raids were successfully carried out behind enemy lines, couriers passed across the lines and contacts established with would be resistance fighters. Over seventy operations were mounted but as the Allied advance ground to a halt around Monte Cassino, conditions became increasingly more difficult.

An example of how dangerous the front had become was when Salavdori and Cooper took two agents to the lines to infiltrate them to Rome from where they were to make their way north to organize Partisans. Having made a detailed reconnaissance the previous night, they left them in a deserted farmhouse to prepare for their crossing and set off to return to the American lines. Suddenly they heard a tremendous explosion and having checked that it was not Allied mortar fire, they returned to the farm where they found the senior agent half-lying, half-sitting against a tree. It was clear he was dead and

---

*   Munthe got wind of it and turned up uninvited!

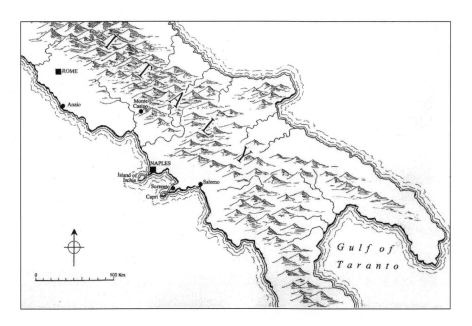

on closer inspection, they realized that they had all walked through a German minefield. As they carefully extricated themselves, they came under fire from German machine guns and were both lucky to get out alive. It was only then that they realized how lucky they had been when all four of them had walked through the minefield the night before without stepping on a device.

Finally Munthe's force was absorbed into the new SOE HQ set up at Monopoli near Brindisi and re-formed as a small advance party to move with forward units. It was in this mode that it landed at Anzio on the night of 22 January 1944. Sergeant Will Pickering remembered the disembarkation as 'artillery and mortar shells were falling all over the place as we drove down the occasionally cratered road...Munthe overshot our front line and headed for a farmhouse in No-Man's-Land...By now the Germans seemed to be concentrating their fire on us but this failed to impress Munthe. He strolled around the farmyard wearing his green Gordon Highlander's kilt and seemed completely oblivious to the shells which were raining down all around him. Captain Gubbins, in the predominantly red tartan of the Cameron Highlanders, was equally unmoved by the mayhem'. Munthe and his colleagues expected to be in Rome within the week. His initial plan was to drive to Rome through the enemy lines in a German-marked ambulance, wearing German uniforms and then coordinate the Partisan resistance groups. However, after some days, they were no longer in wireless communications with Rome and thus it was imperative to get a reliable messenger to and from the city to report on what was going on. Information was trickling in about mass arrests following the initial wave of sabotage and disruption by anti-fascist resistance groups who had been urged by SOE to 'do their damnest'.

With Salvadori down with jaundice and evacuated to Naples, it was left to Munthe and Gubbins to find a suitable evacuee and they soon identified an Italian who had arrived from the city two days earlier. In order to verify the route he claimed to have taken, the two officers made their way to the front line to collect their courier who was being held by the Irish Guards in a cave. En route, they were caught in the open by a German mortar barrage and the slit trench they took cover in received a direct hit. Gubbins was killed outright, Munthe badly wounded in the head, chest and hands by shrapnel splinters. It was the end of his war.

In later life, Munthe was to become a pacifist, more by a philosophical inclination than by his experience of war. His personal courage exemplified by an utter disregard for his own safety masked a deep sensitivity which meant that the deaths of men under his command weighted heavily on him and remained with him throughout his long life.

Anzio beach head

Major Malcolm Munthe: 28 April 1944: recommendation for MC

Major Munthe has on three occasions during the last nine months commanded a small special force in the field with great gallantry and distinction, and with complete and utter disregard for his own personal safety.

Throughout the Sicilian campaign, he commanded G [Topographical] Liaison Unit; he landed at Salerno on D day in command of Special Force, Fifth Army; and he led a small force at Anzio until he received a severe head wound and had to be evacuated.

On each of these occasions, Major Munthe was attached to the senior Army formation, but because of the special nature of his duties and because he was working independently, being neither under command nor in support of a nearby formation, most of his work passed unnoticed by local commanders.

He was, however, engaged throughout on highly dangerous work. His principal task was to infiltrate agents through the enemy lines; and he did this successfully, on many occasions leading them personally and at considerable risk deep into the enemy positions. Several times he came under deliberate small arms fire; many times his duties took him into heavily shelled areas. But he always persisted and never failed to distinguish himself whether by his conduct or by his achievement.

All those who served with him testify to his inspired leadership and to his contempt for danger. Many isolated acts of gallantry have been quoted by them, many of them meriting individual distinction; but because of the circumstances in which he served it was never possible to advance his name for an immediate award.

Awarded

Major Max Salvadori: 25 April 1945: recommendation for immediate DSO.

At the end of 1944 a delegation was sent to the HQ of Field Marshal Alexander by the CLNAI. Before leaving, the delegates requested that an Allied officer should be sent to Milan to maintain contact between them and the Allies. The task of finding this officer was committed to No1 Special Force and Major Salvadori immediately volunteered for the work.

Max Salvadori

He was dropped by parachute into Southern Piedmont in January 1945 and straightway made contact with resistance leaders in Piedmont. During his journeys at this time he was twice ambushed and on both occasions managed to make daring escapes. After establishing a forward W/T base in Partisan territory, he himself moved into Turin in civilian clothes and was successful in contacting the leaders of the underground movement in the city and in passing to them the various directives of AFHQ and 15th Army Group.

At this time, the situation in Turin, and more especially Milan, had become critical. Daily arrests were taking place by the enemy of prominent organizers of resistance in both cities and two of the CLNAI delegates to SACMED, who by this time had returned to Milan, were captured with them. Major Salvadori's British assistant, Captain Keany, was also killed while attempting to reach the Milan rea.

In view of these serious developments, we immediately warned Major Salvadori against entering Milan until the situation was quieter. Major Salvadori, however, preferred to enter the city to investigate the situation there and to assist the remaining members of the CLNAI in maintaining their organization and developing their work. He has now been in Milan for more than two months, living clandestinely; and, during this time, he has maintained constant contact with Bari and passed intelligence reports of extreme importance to RESMIN, AFHQ, 15th Army Group and Allied Commission.

This officer is in constant danger of capture in civilian clothes as daily arrests are still taking place, and his courage and determination in these circumstances are of the highest order, and he is most strongly recommended for the immediate award of the DSO.

Awarded

Major Max Salvadori: 2 March 1945: recommendation for immediate MC.

Major Salvadori has served with SOE, both in North Africa and Italy, for the last fifteen months. During this period he has three times been the member of a small mission, carrying out independent tasks in forward areas and behind enemy lines: with G [Topographical] Liaison Unit in Sicily, with Special Force Fifth Army at Salerno on D day, and with a small force at Anzio.

In addition to these three campaigns, Major Salvadori has on several occasions performed special missions based on this HQ [No.1 Special Force], usually involving his infiltration behind enemy lines for the purposed of guiding an agent across. He has performed these duties always with the greatest calmness, cheerfulness, and contempt for danger, and his leadership has been a source of encouragement to all those who served with him.

Major Salvadori is now standing by to undertake a particularly hazardous task. Once more his leadership and indifference to his own personal safety are evident. A recognition of his continuously gallant service is most strongly recommended.

Awarded

2

Colonel Andrew Croft, DSO, OBE
Captain Dick Cooper
Captain Ken Carson, MC

By the time he was thirty, Andrew Croft had achieved more than more people aspire to in a lifetime. When he was seventeen, his father introduced him to mountaineering, taking him to Bel Alp above Brigue in the Rhone Valley. What impressed him most was the Aletsch Glacier, the largest and longest glacier in the Alps, and when he found himself some years later in the presence of the great Fridjof Nansen, whose Arctic achievements included the first crossing of Greenland in 1888, the seed of polar exploration was firmly planted. After a brief career as a cotton trader was brought to a premature end owing to the depression which followed the Wall Street crash of 1929, Croft perfected his fluency in German and French and then took a teaching post at Ferndown Preparatory School. It was during the summer holidays in 1933 that he received a telegram from his old Oxford friend, the cartoonist Roger Pettiward*, "Would you consider proceeding Greenland fortnight's time?"

Arriving in Greenland on 12 October, Croft spent the next seven months mastering the art of dog-sledging and acclimatizing to the harsh conditions. It was not until June 1934 that he met up with the expedition leader, Captain Martin Lindsay of the Scots Fusiliers, and the other member, Daniel Godfrey of The Royal Engineers. On the evening of 18 June, the British Trans-Greenland Expedition finally set off and 103 days later, after an epic journey, it safely reached its destination, the coastal settlement at Angmagssalik. A stint in India at the court of the exotic Maharani of Cooch Behar filled in time before the Arctic beckoned once more and Croft joined twenty-three year old Sandy Glen's† Oxford University Arctic Expedition to the North East Land situated to the north-east of Spitsbergen. Four months of winter darkness mainly spent in subterranean 'stations' constructed beneath the

---

* He was killed while leading his commando troop against German coastal guns during the Allied attack on Dieppe in August 1942.
† Later Sir Alexander Glen, KBE, DSC and bar

ice cap gave way to daylight at the end of February and after some rest and reorganization, on 12 May 1936 the Expedition set off by sledge for a five week circumnavigation of North East Land. This was followed by more sledging and mountaineering adventures in Spitsbergen before returning to England that autumn.

Croft settled down in Cambridge where he had been offered the position of secretary to Louis Clarke, who doubled up as the Curator of the Museum of Archaeology and Anthropology and Director of the Fitzwilliam Museum, but spent his spare time planning a crossing of the Antarctic with his friend John Rymill. In January 1938, Croft accompanied the anthropologist Ethel Lindgren to Norbottens Län, the most northerly province in Sweden, to study the reindeer herding techniques of the Laplanders. However, with war looming ever closer, Croft shelved his Antarctic plans and learnt to fly de Havilland Moths in the Civil Air Guard. On the outbreak of war in 1939, he reported to the RAF who pronounced him too old, at thirty-three, to be a fighter pilot. Never one to take no for an answer, Croft approached the Fleet Air Arm but, given his Arctic credentials and knowledge of languages, it was not long before both naval and military intelligence vied for his services.

British Military Intelligence [MI(R)] duly recruited Croft and despatched him in December along with Malcolm Munthe on a mission to ferry arms to the Finns who had been attacked at the end of November by the Russians, at that stage of the war allies of Nazi Germany through their mutual Non-Aggression Pact*. Prior to their departure, the two trainee agents were instructed how to sabotage the Murmansk strategic railway by means of an eight foot pipe stuffed with explosives. After working in Bergen harbour for a few days supervising the transfer of 'farm implements' from ships to trains, they made their way by train to the Finnish frontier town of Tornio to await the arrival of the arms consignment, dining on alternative nights with the Finnish and Swedish generals. It proved to be a lively assignment. Munthe managed to blow up the railway only to be told it had been captured by the Finns and then greeted a group of British volunteers under the aptly named General Sir Ormond de L'Épée Winter; Croft meanwhile had returned to Bergen to sort out a blockage in the supply lines. Both of them were soon back in England, Munthe to

---

* The Soviet Union had signed a non-aggression pact with Finland in 1932 and a similar pact with Nazi Germany in August 1939. A secret protocol in the latter included the 'political rearrangement' of the Baltic States, Finland and Poland.

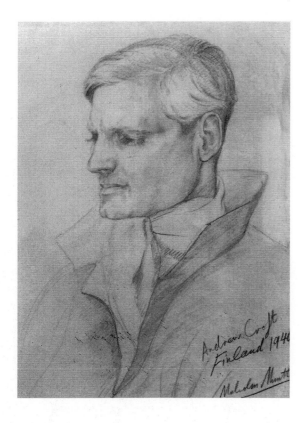

Andrew Croft
by Malcolm Munthe

attend a parachute course and Croft to take charge of equipping an 11,000 strong British Army expeditionary force earmarked for Finland with arctic clothing and equipment.

After the Swedish brokered armistice of 13 March 1940, Croft and Munthe were both redirected to Norway, just in time to get caught up in the German invasion. After an exhausting trek to the coast, Croft was picked by a destroyer and reported to the War Office on 24 April. Twenty-four hours later he was on his way back to Norway as Chief Intelligence Officer to Brigadier Gubbin's Independent Companies, the forerunners of the Commandos. He soon teamed up with fellow polar explorer and later brother-in-law, Lieutenant-Commander Quentin Riley RNVR, and submariner Commander Bill Fell RN, and the three of them launched a series of daring small-scale raids along the coast to harass the enemy's lines of communication. Yet again, Croft ended up leaving Norway in a hurry and resurfaced at Bill Stirling's Guerrilla Warfare School at Invernailort Castle in Invernesshire.

Within a week, he was on his way south to assist Brigadier Gubbins in creating a series of secret stay-behind patrols in the event of a German invasion; his fellow officers included the explorer and travel writer, Peter Fleming, and the actor, Anthony Quayle. After setting up twenty-four such patrols in Essex and Suffolk, Croft joined the Combined Operations Directorate under Admiral Sir Roger Keyes with the brief to test new designs of landing craft which were under development. Gubbins, who had moved to SOE, put in a request for Croft's transfer but in the meantime a counter order had been issued by MI[R], summoning him to Stockholm as Assistant Military Attaché to replace Malcolm Munthe* who had been declared persona non grata after blowing up the Oslo-Bergen railway and being implicated in running the Red Horse network which supported the Norwegian resistance.

Relations with Sweden as a neutral country were critical throughout the war, especially given its strategic location, metallurgical industry and natural resources. On the surface, Croft mixed comfortably with the international community but on another level was deeply involved in clandestine activities like helping George Binney of British Steel smuggle a year's supply of ball bearings to England in five chartered Norwegian ships. Two stolen German briefcases which had been handed to Croft by Norwegian agents turned out to contain details of German meteorological bases in the Arctic and so in June 1942, Croft was reunited with Sandy Glen and the two of them conducted a lengthy air reconnaissance of the sites from the vantage of a Catalina flying boat.

Released by MI[R] to active service, Croft returned to Combined Operations and took charge of No.1 Troop 14 Commando who had been tasked to infiltrate the fjords and islands of Norway by canoe and sink enemy ships by attaching limpet mines to them. In mid-winter, the troop trained in the stormy seas off Balta sound on the edge of the Shetland Islands before moving to Loch Carron on the West coast of Scotland. Under Croft's instruction, their progress was remarkable given that they had no battle experience and little knowledge of canoeing; an exercise involving putting dummy limpets on Allied shipping in the Kyle of Lochalsh was a resounding success. Then, out of the blue, Croft was forbidden by Combined Operations to take part in any offensive operations in Scandinavia because of his privileged work in Sweden as Assistant Military Attaché. Fortunately

---

* Munthe had remained in Norway and after some hair-raising escapades and narrow escapes, managed to cross the border into Sweden.

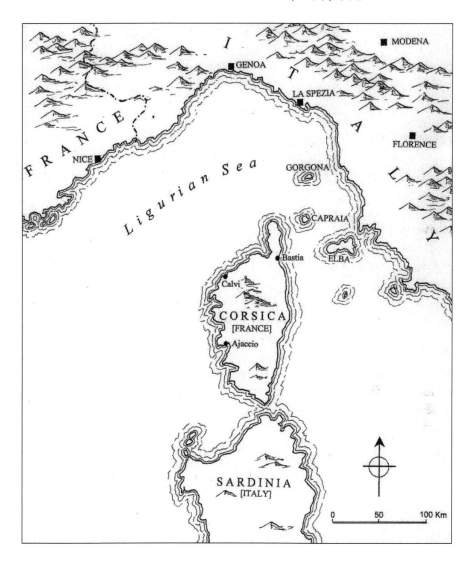

Mountbatten's loss was Gubbins's gain and on 2 April 1943, Captain Croft flew out to Algiers to join SOE's Massingham station.

Having loaded up a high-powered car with urgently needed stores, Croft drove 500 miles on his own along poor roads to report to Special Forces Unit in Tunisia. After conducting two patrols behind enemy lines when he collected some useful information about German troop dispositions and movements, the North African war ended for Croft when the Axis powers surrendered in Tunis on 13 May and he moved to Mahouna in eastern

Algeria when he met up with Commander Gerry Holdsworth RNVR, the SOE officer in charge of the Massingham Naval section, and his deputy, Lieutenant Brooks Richards RNVR. These two officers, who had pioneered the early cross-Channel clandestine operations to France, immediately recognised a kindred spirit and put Croft in charge of small boat training for SIS and SOE agents.

In mid-August, a chance arose to take a number of clandestine radio sets to the Italian mainland and Croft set off on a three week voyage on HMS Seraph under the command of the submarine ace, Lieutenant Commander Jewell. At Portofino, he went ashore in an inflatable rubber boat in a heavy swell and then cached the sets under some foliage, making a note of their precise whereabouts to pass on to the Italian resistance. Mission accomplished, the submarine headed for home but the pugnacious Jewell was unable to resist firing torpedoes at an enemy ship off Bastia, boarding an Italian merchant ship steaming towards Genoa and sinking a number of German landing craft off the Italian coast with his surface gun. It was an eventful journey, made even more memorable for Croft when Jewell allowed him to navigate the submarine home.

By early September 1943, when Italy was clearly out of the war following the Armistice, Brooks Richards despatched Croft to Corsica to set up the Balaclava Mission, a joint naval/military enterprise to land agents and their equipment on the enemy-held coasts of France and Italy. For Croft, 'the fun of running my own show to a large extent unsupervised" was the high spot of his war. Arriving in Ajaccio on the Brittany trawler *Serinini* with a crew of eleven, Croft persuaded various French officials the value of his mission and then sailed north to Calvi which he reached on 3 October. Almost immediately he arranged for Ignace Bianconi, a resourceful bar owner and deputy of the Front Nationale, to join the mission and soon they had their own quay, storeroom and apartment. Although Nice was only ninety-one miles from Calvi, Bastia on the east of the island was better placed for operations on the Italian mainland, so Croft moved his headquarters to the Villa des Pins about a mile out of the town on the St Florent road. Lieutenant John 'Bunny' Newton RNVR had arrived as skipper of the *Serinini*, shortly followed by the twenty-two year old Paddy Davies from 30 Commando, a fellow Stoic who had served with Croft in 14 Commando. His role was to set up a joint intelligence bureau co-located with the Balaclava Mission.

---

* A Talent for Adventure p177

On 30 December, Balaclava was augmented by one of SOE's more colourful characters, forty-four year old Captain Adolphus 'Dick' Cooper, who was posted in as Conducting Officer responsible for supplying, training and briefing agents. Fluent in six languages as a result of an eccentric upbringing in the Diplomatic Service, Cooper had joined the French Foreign Legion when he was only fifteen and a half and won a Croix de Guerre at the Dardanelles as a Legionnaire. Subsequently he transferred to the British Army and after service in Italy and France, rejoined the Legion in 1919, finally leaving it as a sergeant in 1930. His adventures are immortalized in *The Man who Liked Hell: Twelve Years in the French Foreign Legion,* published by Jarrolds in 1933. However, despite having done 'a little intelligence work in Italy in the First World War" and having served with the Spaniards as a French agent in the Second Moroccan War in the 1920s, all this counted for nought when war broke out since his job as a civil servant with the GPO's Continental Telephone Exchange in London was classified as a reserved occupation.

After a barrage of letters to the War Office, he was finally interviewed by SOE in February 1941 and assessed as 'a man with a definite and colourful personality' and 'a very good type of *débrouillard* tough' though one interviewer remarked 'I cannot quite look upon him as the officer type and am sure that the battledress of a private soldier is more suited to him'. Duly selected to work for MI, after intensive training Second Lieutenant Cooper was put ashore in Algeria as a solo agent in July; inauspiciously, his W/T fell into the sea as he disembarked. Within minutes of landing, he was challenged by a gendarme who he promptly threw over a cliff before setting off for Oran. It was not long before the Deuxième Bureau, France's external military intelligence agency, caught up with him and having lured him to a meeting with 'Polish' officers, arrested him on charges of endangering the security of the state.

After four very tough months in prison, Cooper arrived on Christmas Eve 1941 at Laghouat, the British internment camp on the edge of the Sahara run by the Vichy French. The following June, he was one of twenty-seven prisoners who escaped through a tunnel, only to be recaptured within days and sentenced to sixty days solitary confinement. Such was his notoriety by this stage that the Vichy authorities shipped him to mainland France where he was interned in the Camp de Chambaran in the Isère. Released by the French a month later, Cooper ingratiated himself with an Italian military convoy and hitched a life to Marseilles where after making contact with Pat

---

* The Adventures of a Secret Agent p17

O'Leary's* underground escape organization 'Pat Line', he was spirited through Spain and arrived back in England at the end of January 1943, somewhat chastened by his experiences. In a Personal Note attached to his debriefing statement, he frankly admitted that 'I have met with grave difficulties and several dangerous situations and although in physically good health, I cannot deny that my nervous system has suffered from the strain and do not feel the confidence in myself that would be necessary if I were to be sent again to an enemy country.' Rejoining SOE in Sicily in July, Cooper's front line war continued as an agent runner, first through the American lines and then the British. It was in this capacity that he arrived in Corsica with four Italian agents to infiltrate onto the mainland.

At the end of 1943, Balaclava carried out its first operation. Codenamed Valentine, the plan was to land two SIS agents on the Italian coast north of La Spetzia but from the start it was dogged by hitches; initially, one of the agents was delayed reaching the embarkation point, resulting in its postponement. Then when they finally put to sea, two hours out of Bastia, bad weather forced the ML to return to harbour. On the third attempt, the ML was replaced by a 45-knot Italian built MAS and on the night of 2 December, Croft and Lieutenant Geoffrey Arnold rowed the two agents shore. Lifting them clear of the surf to give them a dry start, the SOE team returned to the MAS, none the wiser about the agents' identity or mission†. This was to be the form on all future operations.

Although responsible for the entire administration, training, recruitment and operational performance of Balaclava, Andrew Croft was a great believer in leading from the front. His journal records with gusto the excitement of landing agents in enemy held territory: '12 June: Ops party successful! AC back in Bastia at 0530 hours having landed three agents east coast of Elba – this operation gives all a great feeling of satisfaction as in opinion of SIS it was impossible – AC and party sneaked in the "bodies" right under the defences...27 June: Ops party back at 0730 hours unsuccessful – arriving at pin-point they found three E-boats waiting for them – two of the E-boats opened fire at range of 250 yards and MAS boat, having no escort, compelled to run for home – flat out!'

Demand for the services of Balaclava exponentially increased as the Allied

---

* Belgian-born Albert-Marie Guérisse

† Years later, Croft found out that they were called Paolo Risso and Sylvio de Fiori, both members of the Genoa-based Otto organization. De Fiori was later arrested and did not survive the war.

*Captured Italian MAS,
Corsica 1944*

war effort gathered pace. Requests came from the French Deuxième Bureau and Battaillon de Choc, the American OSS and the British SOE and SIS. It was the latter organization that was threatening to swamp the mission with its growing list of requirements submitted by its representative, Lieutenant Commander Pat Whinney, and early in 1944, Admiral Dickinson, Senior Naval Officer Corsica, ruled that while Croft and his men could continue to help SIS and indeed the Americans and French when asked, they were an independent organization and must remain so. At the same time, Croft was anxious to search for alternative landing sites as beaches were becoming increasingly dangerous due to landmines and booby traps.

One idea was to use unexpected places such as jetties and piers and to test it Croft and Whinney set off to land a party of agents [Tail Lamp II] on Voltri Pier on the western side of Genoa harbour. No night landing in enemy held territory was ever straightforward but on this occasion, having reached the landing point in two rubber boats at 0300 hours, Croft could not find the reception committee although he could hear the German sentries talking in their machine gun posts and see the glows of their cigarettes. To make matters worse, an old woman emerged from her cottage and placed a lamp on the ground in front of her. She then went back inside. Croft flashed the pre-arranged signal at her but there was no reply. He then tried the password but other than a gruff male voice in response, nothing came back. Despite the confusion, the three agents were safely sent on their way and the landing team returned to the MTBs for the journey back to Corsica. This was by no means the only occasion when there was no reception committee. Of the five operations carried out for Captain Peter Fowler of A Force [IS 9], on three occasions the reception committee failed to turn up.

On the night of 19/20 June, an operation for A Force was launched [Ferret] and the shore party consisting of Sergeant Bernard Jones and

Corporal Basil Bourne-Newton successfully put three agents ashore. It was while they were investigating a light on the shore which they thought could have been an A-Force party of escaped POWs waiting to be picked up that a German E-boat suddenly appeared, causing their American P 403 to slip silently away. Faced with the silhouette of a new unknown vessel, Jones and Bourne-Newton immediately rowed out to sea, determined to protect the location of the landing place. It was the last heard of them until they landed in Capraia in Corsica and contacted Bastia four days later. They had rowed a distance of ninety-five miles in approximately eighty-six hours, a performance in a rubber boat unsurpassed at that time, and their voyage had been by no means uneventful as the ship's log humourously noted: '21 June: During the day a swordfish made a reconnaissance of the rubber boat circling three times two foot off at a depth of two to three feet. Offensive action was taken and the fish shot between the eyes with a .45 automatic and in the body with a Sten. Unfortunately carcass sank. 22 June: During the day two whales surfaced and cruised slowly past at thirty yards distance. No action was taken.'

The final sortie of Balaclava took place on the night of 29 July 1944 when four agents were successfully landed. The tally over its nine month existence had been impressive. Croft wrote "since our first operation on 1 December, eight months previously, twenty-four had been successful out of fifty-two sorties; I had personally taken part in twenty-four sorties. In addition to radios, armaments and couriers we had landed eighty agents and brought out twenty-four during a period of the war when few agents were being dropped by air into the occupied territories of Northern Italy, Elba and Southern France." Analysing the reasons for the twenty-eight unsuccessful sorties, Croft identified seven caused by bad weather, seven by hostile craft, six by faulty navigation, four by no reception committees and four by unexpected complications including truck loads of Germans suddenly swarming down onto a beach landing site. It was a resounding achievement and rightly marked by gallantry and meritorious service awards to ten of its members. On 6 August, Croft left Corsica for parachute training at Massingham in Algiers and ten days later jumped into the area west of Montpellier in the South of France as head of a nine-man operation Snow White tasked with disrupting enemy lines of communications in the Carcassonne-Beziers-Narbonne-Montpelier area.

Linking up with the French resistance, Croft set about organizing ambushes and demolitions on the enemy's lines of communication, interdicting convoys and collecting intelligence on German troop movements;

his friend, Peter Fowler of A Force who had jumped with him, was killed during one of these actions. Croft's diary entry of Tuesday 22 August reads: 'Peter Fowler was buried in the churchyard at Moureze at a beautiful ceremony attended by the *maquis* here and indeed the whole village. The two gendarmes [who had been killed with him] were buried on either side of him'. Following the liberation of Montpellier on the evening of Friday 25 August, when 'the Britishers were not exactly assaulted but kissed hundreds of times by both sexes', Croft returned to England where he was put on standby in March 1945 to command a group of parachutists who were to be dropped into different areas of Denmark. His own objective was General Oberst Lindemann's headquarters in Jutland and it was with some relief that this dangerous mission was superseded by the end of the war in Europe; instead, Croft's final duty was to act as liaison officer in Copenhagen between the GOC General Dewing, the Danish resistance and the Germans.

Andrew Croft's wartime service had been extraordinary. Fearless and determined, he imposed the highest standards on himself and others to ensure success and to reduce risk whenever possible. Utterly unafraid of putting himself in danger to carry out his mission, his devotion to duty throughout the many adventures he underwent was exemplary – and his labours did not go unrewarded.

Lieutenant Colonel Andrew Croft: the citation for his DSO which was awarded on 13 March 1945 is not available. Croft attended an investiture at Buckingham Palace in July 1945 when he was made an officer of the Distinguished Service Order and also awarded the Polar Medal by HM George VI.

Captain Ken Carson: 13 March 1945; recommendation for MC

This officer was filling the appointment of Second in Command of the base operating small craft landing agents by sea on the Mediterranean coasts of enemy occupied France and Italy. In nine months, twenty-four completely successful operations were carried out, of which four were under the personal command of Captain Carson.

On the night of 18 February 1944, three men were landed on the mined coast of Elba in exceptionally heavy seas. The success of this operation was entirely due to the resolution and fine judgment of Captain Carson. Four days later, messages were received that the men were being hunted by the Germans and in desperate straits. Although the period during which such operations are normally attempted was over, the importance of the task was such that their recovery was undertaken. At the pre-arranged pinpoint, no light signals were visible, but Captain Carson calculated that the German patrols had prevented the agents reaching the spot. He accordingly requested the ship to be navigated further south and here the lights were seen. When Captain Carson's party reached the shore in the rubber boat, the three agents and a guide were found in a state of complete exhaustion, and German patrols could be heard searching the vicinity. Great care

'Bunny' Newton and Peter Fowler

Dick Cooper

had accordingly to be taken in embarking the exhausted men and paddling out again to the fast craft. As a result of these operations, not only were the lives of the agents saved, but in addition vital and comprehensive intelligence was secured of enemy dispositions, which materially assisted the capture of the island.

On the night of 19 March 1944, the Italian MAS boat containing a shore party and the agents to be landed arrived two hours late in the area of the pinpoint, owing to encountering hostile craft, and the moon was already rising when the operational party left the ship's side. As the shore party returned, an E-boat, 200 yards away, approached the MAS boat which she had seen and challenged. The MAS boat at once got under way and altered course towards the rubber boat. Meanwhile two other E-boats appeared to seaward and immediately opened fire. Captain Carson and his men succeeded in dragging aboard the two occupants of the rubber boat as well as the boat itself, thus avoiding any material evidence being left behind in the area as to the nature of the night's operation.

The landing of two agents on the south coast of France on 28 April 1944 was a perfect example of this type of operation. The shore party covered the 1,000 yards to the shore, established contact with the reception committee, and returned with important documents within forty-five minutes of the first sighting of the signal light.

Captain Carson is cool-headed and resolute. His judgment, confidence and good humour were admired alike by all those with whom he worked. The many detailed preparations which are so essential to special operations, were carried out by him with meticulous efficiency on all occasions.

I recommend this officer for the award of the MC.

Awarded

3

Major Dick Dallimore-Mallaby, MC

There is no better way to introduce Dick Mallaby than to quote from the eulogy written by Lieutenant Colonel Richard Hewitt, No.1 Special Force Chief of Staff, and published in the Special Forces Club Newsletter in 1987. '... Dick's two missions demonstrate sufficiently aspects of his character which his easy-going nature did not always suggest to those who knew him only casually; his quiet but almost reckless courage, his initiative, his determination, his loyalty and his natural probity. He was most certainly one of those who, even by the exacting standards of SOE, served honourably and beyond the call of duty to the very end'.

Dick Mallaby had first arrived in Italy from Ceylon in 1925, aged six. His father had been a planter at Nuwara Elyia, the quintessential British colonial hill station in the heart of Sri Lanka's tea country, but after his wife died in 1920, he had moved to Italy a few years later where he remarried to Maria [Marion] Bargagli-Stoffi, herself half-English, and settled in Asciano, a small hill town about twenty-five kilometres outside Sienna. Young Dick was educated initially in Asciano and then aged nine sent to the Franciscan College and Friary at Panton Hall in Lincolnshire for two years before returning to Italy to complete his education, first in Asciano, then in Siena and finally at the Liceo Scientifico in Modena. Apart from his blue eyes and fair hair, in all other respects Mallaby was an authentic Tuscan.

With perfect Italian, fluent German and passable French, he reached England on 3 September from Italy* and joined the signals section of the 8th Battalion The Devonshire Regiment in October 1939, then volunteered for the Parachute Regiment in November 1940 and as so often happened in wartime actually ended up with No.8 Commando [Layforce] in the Middle East in March 1941 when he saw action at Tobruk. From there, Mallaby transferred to SOE in January 1942 and after completing his training, became a signals instructor with SOE in Jerusalem with the rank of Sergeant.

In 1942, SOE had managed to smuggle a W/T set into Trieste, the key transport hub for German forces in western Yugoslavia and Italy. That done,

---

* His father followed two months later.

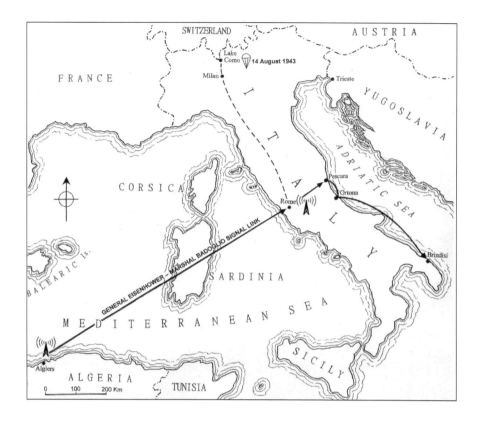

there was now a need for a W/T operator and an Italian agent codename Kelly was identified as a suitable candidate in October, the idea being to drop him into Yugoslavia from where he would make his way on a Trieste-bound steamer in the guise of a sailor. His brief was to act as W/T link between two resistance groups [PSI and 900] and to communicate their requirements to SOE in Algiers and to notify details of all courier arrangements. He was also charged with collecting military and political information which he might deem useful to SOE. The problem was that Kelly proved to be a slow learner and as a last resort, he was given Mallaby in November as his personal instructor to get his Morse and signals procedure up to speed. After a series of cancelled and postponed flights, Kelly, already short on confidence, finally lost his nerve; when Mallaby heard about it, he immediately volunteered to take his place.

Meanwhile the brief for Operation Neck had been changed. Mallaby, now designated agent DH 449 codename Olaf, was first tasked with making contact with an Italian resistance group in Como, then to set up a W/T link to

Algiers and arrange supply drops and finally to instruct the Partisans in the finer arts of sabotage. Plans to drop him into Yugoslavia were postponed due to a lack of aircraft and likewise a submarine landing on the coast near Trieste never materialized. Instead, after making a single practice water jump into the sea off Algiers, he parachuted into the Lake Como area at 0400 hours on 14 August 1943, an act that bestowed on him the distinction of being the first British SOE agent to be infiltrated into Italy, a belligerent country. His mission was clandestine in every respect; if caught, he was unequivocally a spy.

His plan was as follows. On reaching the water, he would inflate his dinghy and paddle to the eastern shore. There he would dispose of his [waterproof] suit, Mae West and dinghy by cutting them up and sinking them. He would then hide his waterproof bag containing compromising documents and crystals and make a note of the exact spot where he had hidden it. He would then make his way inland away from the lake and hide up until about 0700 hours when he would continue his journey to the safe house. So much for the theory; the practice turned out to be somewhat different.

Heavy RAF raids over Turin and Milan the night before had made the enemy air defences extremely jittery and as Mallaby's aircraft approached, the air raid sirens were sounded. Moreover, evacuees from the cities had been heading north to the safety of the lakes, looking for accommodation and camping sites, so 'villages along lake were all lit up' as Mallaby's pilot later reported. Signori Borghi and Abate, the Rural Guard of Carate Commune, had both heard the aircraft and spotted the descending parachute, so they rushed to the town square and with two others in tow, set out in a rowing boat to investigate; 'after a few minutes of hard rowing, having arrived more than half way along the lake, they made out an individual in a small rubber boat, to whom they shouted to stop. This individual replied "Friend".'[*] They hauled him on board together with his kit and equipment, which later proved to be very incriminating, including three forged ID cards, various permits, a driving licence, discharge papers, 113,000 Italian Lire in Lire 1,000 notes, crystals for a wireless set and cryptographic negatives[†]. The Mallaby case was now a cause célèbre, both in Italy and England. The FO telegrammed Osborne, their man in the Holy See, explaining the situation and stating 'we are most anxious to ensure that he [Mallaby] is not shot out of hand. Unless you see strong objection, please intervene unoffi-

---

[*] UPI report 16 August 1944. In a later account, Mallaby told them he was a shot-down Caproni pilot.
[†] For three signals plans – Maraschino Orange, Maraschino and Pallinode

cially in any way you think most effective, letting be known that we are contemplating offering an appropriate Italian in exchange.'

Meanwhile, Colonel Roseberry of SOE's J Section in London, having got word to Mallaby in prison that plans were afoot to spring him, departed for Lisbon to meet the mission sent by the anti-Nazi Italian Chief of Staff, Marshal Badoglio, to facilitate a peace deal with the Allies*. The overriding priority for him was to work out how to establish direct communications between Marshal Badoglio in Rome and General Eisenhower in Algiers. The communications system had to be completely secure, so the first piece that Roseberry put in place was to provide the Italian mission with one of SOE's portable sets rather than risk using an Italian army W/T. Then came the question of the operator and Roseberry stressed how important it was to follow the correct security procedures once on air and the necessity to sticking to the scheduled times. The Italians were duly impressed by this argument and according to Roseberry, the conversation then went as follows:

'We cannot get such an operator.'

'I can give you one.'

'Where is he?'

'In Italy.'

'An Italian?'

'No. A British officer who entered your country by parachute so as to be available for just such an emergency.'

'Will he work for us?'

'Definitely no, unless he receives from you in original certain messages which he will know could not have emanated from anybody but me.'

'Where is he now?'

'In prison in Como; you captured him two days ago.'

'How shall we know him?'

'Your official description of him reads as follows.....'

It was a gamble, for would the Italians buy into using a man who had already been publicly arraigned as a British spy? And in the meantime, how long should SOE stand down their other rescue plans? One thing was certain: if tried by military tribunal, Mallaby would be shot. Having impressed on the mission before they left for Rome that although Mallaby was a British subject, he was born in Italy, loved Italy and was prepared to risk his life in an attempt to fight against Fascism, it was a huge relief to

---

* A War Cabinet Minute dated 14 Janaury 1943 records that SOE had been in touch with Badoglio 'for some time'.

Roseberry that the unmistakable signals 'print' of Mallaby came on air two days later and from thereon in, Mallaby handled all the clandestine traffic between Rome and Algiers right up to 3 September when he left with Marshal Badoglio and King Umberto for Brindisi. Three days later the new Italian government declared war on Germany.

Celebrity status for Mallaby was now over and he resumed his more prosaic duties as a W/T instructor, this time with No.1 Special Force, teaching trainee Italians agents provided by the Italian military authorities. By now, he was a Lieutenant for on 24 August 1943 his Emergency commission had been gazetted which was gratifying since Army bureaucracy had turned his name down due to procedural rules when it had originally been put forward in January. Then on 10 December 1943, he was deservedly recommended for an immediate DSO for his extraordinary courage and devotion to duty; with no explanation, the award was reduced to a MC.

In early 1945, SOE came up with a new mission for Mallaby, Edenton Blue; he was to join up with the Partisans north of Brescia, open up W/T communications and arrange the reception of further British military missions. After that, he was go down to Milan and control all W/T communications in North Italy. The mission was composed of Mallaby, Anselmo the W/T operator, Don Giovanni, a priest and chaplain to the Green Flames, and another priest, Don Zanin. After leaving Tac HQ I Special Force in Siena, Mallaby made his way to Berne via Rome, Lyons and Lausanne and stayed at the British legation there until 13 February when he travelled to Lugano and met up with the other members of his mission. The next night, having been dropped off at the border by two smuggler guides, the party, all wearing civilian clothes, started the climb across the mountains. Despite wearing ordinary shoes which caused many a slip on the snow-covered grass, they reached Carlazzo early in the morning of 15 February. After two and a half hours rest, they set off again, and on reaching Menaggio after an eight mile walk, they hired a boat and crossed Lake Como to Varenna. From here, having failed to find a secure way to hire a car, they hitched a lift on a lorry to Lecco where they finally managed to locate a car. However, since it would not be ready until two that afternoon, they retired to a restaurant. Most probably betrayed by a young man who had also been a passenger on the lorry, it was not long before two NCOs of the Brigate Nere entered the restaurant and carried out identity checks on them.

Giovanni was found to be carrying Swiss money, the other priest had Swiss cigarettes and Nescafe on his person and although Mallaby and Anselmo were 'clean', they were taken to the local Brigate Nero HQ at

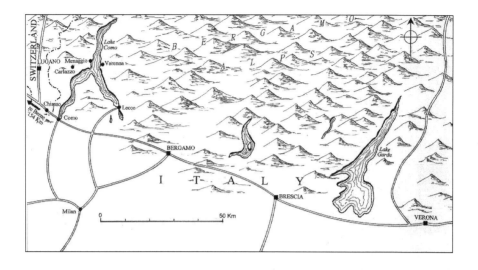

Lecco where to their horror it transpired that, despite their story of being complete strangers until they had met on the lorry to Lecco, all their ID cards had been made out to the same address in Milan which had been destroyed in an air raid in 1943! At this point, an Allied air raid over head caused some confusion and in the gathering darkness Don Zanin managed to escape; Mallaby reached the courtyard without being seen but realizing that the chances of escaping were nil, returned to his cell. He now decided to try and bluff his way out and stated that he was a British officer called Captain Tucker on a secret mission to contact Marshal Graziani, Minister of the Armed Forces of the Republic of Salo. It worked and Mallaby was whisked off to Como and then to Lake Garda, where he was interviewed by Colonel de Leo, the head of Counter-Espionage in Graziani's Intelligence Service.

By now, Mallaby had had time to work up his story and he told De Leo that in late December Field Marshal Alexander had personally briefed him to make contact with the Marshal through Cardinal Schuster in Milan and if successful, to convey the following ideas. First, in the event of a German withdrawal, the Republican forces should do everything in their power to avoid the destruction of industry and infrastructure. They were also to do whatever they could to maintain order and public safety. Secondly, Partisan forces would be expected to contribute to the anti-scorch operations and to the maintenance of law and order but this activity would be directed by Field Marshal Alexander himself. These measures were all designed to avert unnecessary bloodshed between

Allied and Republican forces and in the event of the Republicans being unable to maintain order, Alexander would send in police forces by air to the trouble spots. Finally, should the Marshal like to enter into negotiations with the Allies, Alexander was ready to send a plane to take him to AFHQ with all the necessary guarantees; he was equally happy if the Marshal wished to take his own plane. De Leo agreed to convey Mallaby's statement to the Marshal, though he remarked that he found the lack of secrecy in the way the mission had been carried out to be regretful.

Nevertheless, there had been a meeting of minds, especially on the subject of the Partisans. De Leo told Mallaby that there was a very real fear that the Partisans would come down from the hills and fight everyone, so that utter chaos would ensue. Mallaby responded by reassuring the colonel that the Allies had also evaluated such a scenario and that plans were in hand to counter irresponsible behaviour and chaos. Nothing more was heard until the morning of 26 February when suddenly a German SS captain came for Mallaby and took him to the Palazzo delle Assicurazloni in Verona. He repeated his story to the Germans and was quickly taken to a villa on Lake Garda to meet SS General Karl Wolff, commander of all troops in Italy not in the front line. After being persuaded by Mallaby to take his identity on trust, Wolff discussed the prevailing military and political situation with him and ending by offering to act as an official or unofficial link between the Allies and those members of the German leadership with whom he was friends, including Kesselring, Himmler and even the Fuhrer himself. Mallaby picked up on this offer and said that Alexander would be willing to send a plane for him to go to Southern Italy or indeed Wolff could take a German plane to an Allied airbase. Wolff went on to table a specific proposal: if Alexander would undertake to stop supplying Partisan communist bands in the North of Italy, he, Wolff, would allow all other bands and armed groups to pass freely through the lines to the south if they wished to do so.

Their meeting finished on a cordial and friendly note, with a request from Wolff that if he returned Mallaby to Switzerland to solicit a response from Alexander, in return Mallaby would undertake not to give away the various locations he had been brought to. To this he agreed and was then taken back to Verona. From there he was escorted to the frontier by the Germans and on the night of 28 February crossed it near Chiasso. Using the name Bernardo Francini, which he had previously arranged with the Swiss security services, he handed himself over to the Swiss frontier guards, who to his horror could find no record of his cover name. A lengthy delay thus resulted with Mallaby processed for internment as a political refugee and it was not until 11 March that he finally arrived back at the British Legation in Berne. Meanwhile, Mallaby's initiative had caused some consternation in SIS HQ in London. McCafferty in Berne received a curt signal from Roseberry: '"C" here has been told of these developments. Please put "C" man your end in picture and keep him there.'

Mallaby had given his parole to General Wolff that he would return to continue negotiations but by the time he had made contact with the British Mission in Berne, events had overtaken him and he was specifically released from this undertaking. Roseberry explained in a letter dated 23 March to Sir Orme Sargent of the FO that "the OSS were subsequently approached directly by General Wolff and, so as to avoid duplication, our representative [Mallaby] was told not to pursue the contact and to leave everything to OSS unless he was asked by them to take a hand." The discussions that ensued were drily nicknamed The Wolf and Little Red Riding Hood [Allen Dulles].

The intriguing question remains: was Mallaby trying to bluff his way out or was he in fact an emissary of Field Marshal Alexander? Whatever his real role may have been, Dick Mallaby was certainly remarkably well informed when he sat down opposite Wolff on 26 February. Since late 1944, when it was apparent that Germany was losing the war in Western Europe, there had been a numerous approaches to the Allies, some official, others unofficial. Albrecht von Kessel, a diplomat working for Baron von Weiszächer, the German ambassador to the Vatican, had contacted the British with a proposal to prevent 'the complete ruin of Germany' as had Franco Marinotti, an Italian industrialist, in league with Wilhelm Harster, commander of the security police and SD in Italy. In November, the Vatican sponsored Cardinal Schuster of Milan to send his secretary Don Guiseppe Bicchierai to Switzerland with a five-page plan outlining a deal whereby the Germans would abstain from destroying Italian industry in exchange for the Partisans ceasing all acts of sabotage and other attacks on German troops. The RHSA foreign intelligence chief, Walter Schellenberg, engineered a meeting between SS officer Hans Wilhelm Eggen and an American diplomat Frederick Loofborough to relay the message that Europe was in imminent danger of being subsumed in Bolshevism and evidence of Soviet duplicity with the Allies was readily available. In February 1945, Baron Alexander von Neurath, the German Consul at Lugano and the son of the former German foreign minister, proposed to the OSS in Berne* that he would form a triumvirate of Kesselring, Wolff and Rudolph von Rahn [the German ambassador to the Republic of Salò] and they in turn would approach Field Marshal von Runstedt, C-in-C Army Group West, with a view to suing for peace in the West. Wolff himself visited Himmler on 4 February and had an audience with Hitler two days later from which he came away with the understanding that the Fuhrer had given his tacit consent to put out feelers to the British and Americans in the hope of splitting the alliance with Russia.

Following his unscripted but encouraging encounter with Mallaby and acting on what in reality was little more than a perceived nudge from Hitler, Wolff sent Baron Luigi Parrilli, formerly the representative of the Kelvinator and Nash companies in Italy and a man with good contacts with the Italian Partisans, to Switzerland to set up a meeting [Operation Wool] and after an initial session involving SS Hauptsturmführer Guido Zimmer, Standardtenführer Eugen Dollmann and Paul Blum of the OSS in Lugano on 2 March, Wolff crossed the border on 8 March and met with the OSS's Allen Dulles in a Zurich apartment. Now known as Operation Sunrise, it was as a result of this meeting that Field Marshal Alexander sent two senior representatives, Major General Terence Airey, his chief intelligence officer, and Major General Lyman Lemnitzer, his deputy chief of staff, to meet with Wolff at Ascona on 19 March. Although the Russians had been informed about the preliminary nature of these negotiations on 12 March, their request to have three of their own representatives present was declined and a major row ensued, culminating in a tense exchange of letters between Roosevelt and Stalin. It proved impossible to arrange a meeting between Alexander and Wolff in these circumstances, and with Airey and Lemnitzer withdrawn on 4 April, no further progress was made until the actual surrender of Italy on 29 April with cessation of hostilities on 2 May, a mere five days before VE day.

---

* Colonel Prince Alois Auersperg, Air Attaché at the German Consulate in Berne, had been in touch with the OSS as early as 10 November 1944 and told them that von Neurath had Himmler's approval to bring an 'important SS personality stationed at present in Italy' to Switzerland.

Major Dick Mallaby: 23 October 1943: recommendation for DSO

This officer was dropped alone into Lake Como by parachute on 14 August 1943 in conditions of unexpected difficulty which were a severe test of his courage; but his descent was observed and he was taken prisoner. Though kept in handcuffs and beaten, he refused to divulge the names of those in Italy with whom he was to work, but tried to persuade his interrogators to use him as the means of communication in planning a coup against the Germans.

After a time, an Italian General, who had been to Lisbon to approach the Allies, was persuaded to use Lieutenant Mallaby to operate a secret wireless link between Rome and Algiers. He was taken from prison and made contact with Algiers at the first attempt, keeping the link open until negotiations had gone far enough to allow operators of the Allied Armies to take over.

The wireless contact he provided was for some time the only link between General Eisenhower and Marshal Badoglio. Had it not been for his exceptional coolness, perseverance and devotion to duty, an Armistice might not have been concluded in time for 'D' day.

He is therefore recommended for an immediate award of the Companionship of the Distinguished Service Order.

Downgraded to MC

Mallaby and friends on VE day

4

Lieutenant Colonel Charles Macintosh, DSO

A chance meeting in Gibraltar with Commander Gerry Holdsworth, then commander designate of No.1 Special Force, over dinner with the governor, General Mason MacFarlane, took Charles Macintosh to Italy via Algeria where, as Operations Officer, he was instrumental along with Holdsworth in establishing Maryland, SOE's headquarters at Monopoli just outside Brindisi. Later, as a mission commander and then officer commanding Tac HQ in Florence, he participated in and directed many of SOE's operations in Reggio Emilia through to the end of the war in April 1945.

Born in Montevideo, Uruguay, of New Zealand parents, Macintosh was educated at the Dollar Academy in Scotland and then Cambridge. He was working for the Shell oil company in Venezuela when war broke out and was told by the British Embassy that since oil production counted as a reserve occupation, he would have to stay put. However, there was an appeal process and before long, he was interviewed in Maracaibo by a British colonel ostensibly working for the War Office. His release from reserved status soon followed and after completing his officers' training course, he was commissioned into the Intelligence Corps and posted to the Inter Services Research Bureau, an early cover name for SOE. Having completed a number of specialist SOE courses, Macintosh embarked for Gibraltar in March 1942, hoping to put his fluent Spanish to good use.

The principal SOE office in Gibraltar was the Villa Lourdes, originally set up by Hugh Quenell, a partner in the City law firm of Slaughter and May, and then run by Edward Wharton-Tigar and Barbara Salt. To all appearances a Captain in the Royal Engineers, Macintosh joined H Section whose job was to look after SOE activities in the extreme west of the Mediterranean area. He carried out a variety of tasks, from defending shipping against Italian frogmen to tunnelling into the Rock to prepare against attack. At one point, he trained two OSS officers in sabotage techniques.

After the Allied invasion of North Africa got underway in late 1942, SOE needed to reorganize its operations in the Mediterranean theatre and in February 1943 established a base near Algiers, codename Massingham. Macintosh arrived there soon after and, together with the OSS, ran small groups of locally recruited anti-fascists behind enemy lines in south Tunisia who were tasked with disrupting enemy communications. When Tunis fell in May 1943, he passed the time parachuting until called late in July to Sicily where he was put in charge of refurbishing captured enemy weapons and recycling them to Partisans in Italy and the Balkans.

As soon as the Allies landed on the Salerno beaches south of Rome on 9 September, the rapidly evolving political situation threw up a whole host of challenges for SOE. In touch with Italian underground parties long before the Armistice of 8 September, it was clear to SOE that no early stable political change could be achieved since many of the main players were still underground in German-occupied Northern Italy. Macintosh wrote that 'politics was not our business but the close link between politics and Resistance meant we were bound to become involved."

A tremendous task now confronted SOE in Italy, namely how to persuade the Allied military high command of the possibilities offered by the Italian resistance movements and the use which could be made of the Italian armed forces which had come over to the Allied side. A further factor was the number of Allied prisoners who had escaped or been set free in Italy. While well resourced with people and weapons, the Maryland HQ mission was desperately short of transport and one of Macintosh's major roles as Operations Officer was to rectify this. However, life as a staff officer had its limitations and when news came of the death of Michael Gubbins and serious injuries to Malcolm Munthe at Anzio, Macintosh asked to become operational again. Despite serious and very valid objections by the Security Officer that Macintosh knew far too much about the organization to risk capture, he entered Rome on 4 June 1944 with a five-man team.

The Allies did not have to fight for Rome street by street nor was there an uprising; so the team's job was limited to contacting friends and seeking out the few enemies that had been unwise enough to stay behind. The result of the Rome mission was that it was considered a success although Macintosh himself felt that it had achieved very little. Infiltration routes through enemy lines to the north had proved impossible due to the skilful German defence in the area and the site he selected for a future SOE headquarters in Rome –ironically the German Art School – turned out to be a protected building and hence not available. However, he was pleased that he had recruited Captain Tom Roworth, a POW who had been hiding out in the Vatican.

---

* *From Cloak to Dagger* p28

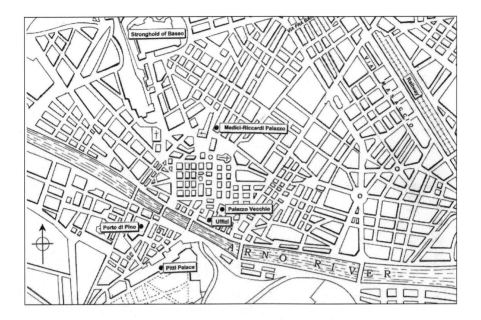

His next mission was to lead a party of six operatives* to Florence at the beginning of August 1944. The city formed an important part of the German defensive system known as the Arno Line and there was every likelihood that this time the Wehrmacht would defend the city street by street. Facing the Allies were the 4th Parachute Division, about 1,000 SS storm troopers and dozens of armoured and scout cars. By the time Allied troops entered the outskirts on 3 August, four bridges across the Arno had already been blown and a fifth, the world famous Ponte Vecchio, prepared for demolition.

The immediate task for Macintosh's unit was to make contact with the Partisans with whom contact had been lost in early June when 'Radio Cora', a W/T set operating in the southern half of the city had been located by German detector vans and its operators killed. In the city itself, the GAP were especially active, operating in small groups of five men supported by SAP intelligence squads. Florence attracted particular attention from the Axis anti-Partisan experts as it was the HQ of the CLN for the whole of Tuscany and of the Comando Marte, the unified military committee composed of the military leaders of all resistance political parties.

---

*   Second Lieutenant Norris, an Italian officer, the W/T Corporal, Gunner Hunt and Driver O'Neil.

Arriving at Poggibonsi in their American 'White' scout car, bedecked with a Vickers Machine gun, two Bren Guns and three Tommy guns, the team was just in time to hear the bridges being blown before it set off in the direction of the city on 4 August. The first Partisan unit they came into contact with was the Roselli Brigata [belonging to the Arno Communist Division] which was engaged in hunting down enemy snipers. From reports provided by Italian intelligence officers, it was clear that the river was to be used as a major obstacle to barr the Allied advance. Heavy artillery and mortars were ranged in the hill to the north of the city and fire controllers had clear line of sight to many of the registered targets. The question for the Allies was whether the Germans would treat Florence, like Rome, as an open city. This was not just from the point of view of protecting the exquisite built heritage but also in safeguarding the lives of the civilian population, now swollen to 400,000 due to an influx of refugees, who were confined to their houses with no food or essential services. Scabies and typhoid were on the increase, rubbish was not collected and corpses remained unburied.

Macintosh set up a meeting with Brigadier Mould, the commander of 21st Indian Brigade[*] which was the main Allied formation in the south of the city and warned him that Partisan activity was likely to increase and to expect a general uprising which would in all probability trigger a major response from the Germans. Mould acknowledged this appreciation but said it was most unlikely that the Allies would authorize an advance into the city proper as it would create heavy civilian casualties which would play straight into the hands of German propagandists. However, he was all for Macintosh studying the feasibility of putting a small reconnaissance force across the river.

Providentially, on the morning of 5 August, an Italian officer in civilian clothes sought Macintosh out and introduced himself as Henry Fisher[†], commander of 3 Rosselli Brigata in the north of the city. His story was somewhat incredible. Dodging German tanks and patrols he had made his way to the Palazzo Vecchio, the headquarters of the forward SS commander, Colonel Fuchs. A patriotic policeman had let him into the Palazzo and once inside he made his way along the complicated system of interconnecting galleries, corridors and bridges which the Medici rulers of the city had devised in the fifteenth century to allow then to move between the Palazzo Vecchio and the Pitti Palace without using the streets. Progress was far from easy; at times he had to crawl on his hands and knees past unexploded

---

*   Part of XIII Corps

†   Real name Enrico Fischer

demolition charges, pick his way through minefields and at one point using a ten metre rope he had to lower himself down to ground level.

Once his Comando Marte credentials had been established, Macintosh asked Fisher to return to the north of the city and bring two of the Partisan leaders back with him for a conference. Recognizing the necessity to keep the use of Fisher's secret passageway to the minimum, Macintosh quickly procured a field telephone and 500 yards of line which conveniently fitted into a medium-sized suitcase. That afternoon, they both went back to the river and after Fisher had climbed back up the rope, Macintosh attached the case to it and Fisher hauled it up. A few hours later, SOE was talking on the telephone to Partisan officers hidden in the SS headquarters.

On the afternoon of 6 August, Fisher returned with Carlo Ragghianti and Colonel 'Nello' Niccoli of Comando Marte. At a meeting with 21st Indian brigade, the Brigade Major explained that the Allies still hoped that Florence would be treated as an open city and hence he wanted Florence to be kept as quiet as possible; it was left unsaid that he did not want guerrilla troops disturbing the situation in his area. Separately, Macintosh discussed broad plans with Nello, covering guidelines for avoiding engagements with enemy units to early relief of the problems affecting the civilian population. The next day Nello made his way back across the river while Ragghianti stayed on for talks about a future civilian administration. The stand-off between the opposing armies continued and it was after a dinner with General Kirkman, XIII Corps Commander, that Macintosh received permission to evaluate the possibility of making an undetected crossing of the river in battalion strength. Crossing the bridge, he concluded that it would not be practical to attempt a crossing even in company strength; even if a small force reached the Uffizi, it would be at the mercy of the German guns.

The period from 4 to 10 August had been characterized by sniping, sporadic machine gun fire and indirect fire by mortars aimed at opportunity targets in the south of the city. Joint operations between British units and the Partisans to flush out snipers had only limited success. Just before 0400 hours on 11 August, Macintosh received news that the Germans were starting to withdraw from the Palazzo Vecchio. He quickly collected Ragghianti, Norris, Fisher and Gunner Hunt and pulling themselves up on the rope made their way across the Ponte Vecchio into the labyrinth of corridors in the Uffizi. When they reached the Palazzo, news came that the CLN were in session at the Medici-Riccardi Palazzo, so after sending Norris back to Brigade with a short report, Macintosh set off with the others to attend the meeting. By this time, a Partisan uprising was in full swing; some 3,000 men organised into military units were on the offensive in three zones, Zone 1 in the south and the other two in the north. This was exactly the situation that Macintosh had urged the Partisans to avoid for the Allies had made it clear that they were not prepared to act in support of any unauthorised uprising.

Macintosh crossed the river to report to Brigade who repeated that there would be no early crossing by the army. At Corps HQ, the view was more flexible and Macintosh re-crossed the Arno to talk to the Partisan leaders, instructing them to establish themselves on the canal line but to go no further. Meanwhile they should clear out any enemy between the canal and the river and await an Allied crossing. By the evening of 12 August, the Partisan effort was all but spent; heavy casualties, lack of ammunition, the regaining of the initiative by the Germans and the failure of the Allies to cross the river made their position precarious in the extreme.

Early on the morning of 14 August, three British rifle companies crossed the Arno and by the evening, 21 Indian Brigade was firmly established on the north bank. Quick to respond to this positive change in circumstances, the Comando Marte reorganised their forces and relocated their front. From now until 31 August, the position in Florence was one of stalemate; the Indian Brigade on the canal line, the Germans on the outskirts and the

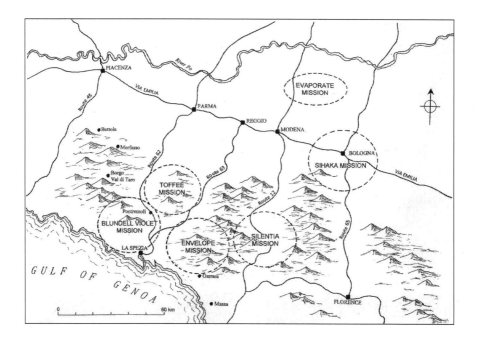

Partisans between them. Bitter fighting continued day after day in the vicinity of the tobacco factory, Porto di Pino, the railway, the Fortezza da Basso and between Via Masaccio and Via Fra Bartolomeo, where most of the Republican forces were concentrated.

The advance by Allied armour on 1 September heralded the end of the battle. Partisan casualties amounted to 205 killed and over 700 wounded. Nearly 3,000 Partisans marched past General Kirkman in the victory parade on 7 September. Macintosh was sent on leave to England; in his absence, the faithful Gunner Hunt returned to Monopoli where he installed himself on the roof of the main SOE office and took pot shots at the staff arriving for work. When a raid was mounted to dislodge him, no trace was found of him and legend has it he vanished into the Italian countryside never to be seen again.

In October 1944, Macintosh attended a series of meetings with Holdsworth in Monopoli to discuss the role of SOE during the expected advance of the Allied armies. Depending on the speed of the advance, its role could vary from large scale sabotage and resistance operations to smaller hit and run tactics. What was clear was that as the Partisan bands came within range of front line troops, SOE would need to coordinate its activities at Army level, so Macintosh took charge of the newly formed Tactical Headquarters of No.1 Special Force in Florence.

Structurally, it was to be commanded and administered by 1 Special Force but operationally controlled by Fifth Army with a small mobile HQ attached to Fifth Army HQ with SOE representatives at all formations down to divisional level. A comprehensive signals net was to be established between Tac HQ, field missions and Monopoli. Its remit was wide ranging, including assistance and advice to Fifth Army on all matters concerning the resistance in enemy occupied territory, operational control of all British and Italian missions within the Army TAOR, including delivery of supplies to all such missions, the provision of intelligence on bombing targets, the organization of courier services through the lines and the provision of mobile forces for special reconnaissance tasks as required by field commanders.

After a visit to the front, Macintosh concluded that with the Eighth Army stuck in the mud some fifty miles from Bologna and the US Fifth Army in no condition to force a breakthrough, Tac HQ would need to establish firmly a headquarters in Florence and become a more static organization. To effect this, it had to take over the radio links of the missions behind the lines and start to supply Fifth Army HQ with good intelligence. As the severe winter intensified, the front remained static and inevitable frustration occurred when the Partisans saw little sign of Allied activity. Macintosh meanwhile put together a small air wing which was able to deliver small scale stores and also infiltrate and extricate key personnel.

By now installed in a villa in Via delle Forbici high on the road between Florence and Fiesole, Tac HQ's special Intelligence Reviews and Monthly Reports started to find favour with the staff at Fifth Army. By mid-January 1945, the basic organization of Tac HQ's principal areas of interest had been established, the Apennines having been divided into zones, each with its own mission manned by British and Italian officers. In turn, the missions began to strengthen their own organization and those of the Partisan units to which they were attached, stock up on supplies and extend their intelligence gathering. Sabotage operations continued but on a scale designed to avoid the Germans reacting in strength. Over the course of the coming months, Macintosh got to know nearly all the BLOs in his area and indeed formed valuable arms length relationships with highly effective escaped POW Partisan commanders like Major Tony Oldham and Major Gordon Lett.

In the last phase of the Italian campaign, Macintosh went forward with the advancing armies to Bologna and then with jeep and driver to Modena Reggio, Parma and on to Milan. For three years, Macintosh had been involved in SOE's secret war in Italy, both as a staff officer and as a field commander, from the first landings in Sicily to the surrender of the Axis armies. It was a unique achievement and the esteem in which he was held after the war by the Partisans made for a fitting tribute.

Lieutenant Colonel Charles Macintosh: 4 September 1944: recommendation for DSO

On the morning of 12 August 1944 21 Indian Brigade took over the original Florence Garrison including Partisans in the city. Major Macintosh with one officer assistant was the only means of liaison with the Partisans. At the time of the arrival of the brigade, the enemy were counterattacking the Partisans in the centre of the city with tanks and infantry and reports were received that of the four *Garibaldi* Brigades two had been cut off and probably destroyed, and that behind the Partisans and down to the River Arno about 200 Fascist snipers were practically in control of the streets. This situation appeared critical. Major Macintosh and his assistant crossed the River Arno alone in circumstances requiring the greatest cool nerve and courage. His assistant was wounded by a sniper, but Major Macintosh succeeded in conveying the plan and orders to the Partisan leaders. As a direct result of his gallant action, when British and Indian troops crossed the river next day they were met by

Above: Indian Brigade sapper in Florence

Above left: Macintosh's view of the Ponte Vecchio

Left: Air photograph of the Ponte Vecchio

Partisan guides, and a Partisan screen cleared snipers from their path as they penetrated the city. Throughout 13 and 14 August, Major Macintosh moved through sniper infested streets conveying orders and information with complete disregard for his own safety. On the night of 14/15 August when the ANC HQ behind the British lines was attacked by a Fascist gang, Major Macintosh immediately proceeded to the spot, assumed command of the Partisans and Carabinieri and quickly restored the situation.

Throughout a very difficult period this officer displayed qualities of leadership and gallantry of the highest order. It was principally due to his actions that two thirds of the city was occupied smoothly and with very few British casualties.

Awarded

5

Captain Michael Lees

Having just left Ampleforth School, Michael Lees was only eighteen when war came. After a spell in the Queen's Own Dorset Yeomanry, he was drafted to India where he wrangled his way into the Parachute Brigade, eventually ending up in the Canal Zone in Egypt on notice to return to England. Far from happy with this outcome and by now champing at the bit for some action, Lees's curiosity was aroused during a chance encounter at the bar in Shepheards Hotel in Cairo in early 1943 with a garrulous officer who had recently joined the staff of a highly secret department of GHQ. Intrigued, he managed to secure an interview with a Colonel Lonsdale and then cajoled his way into seeing two other officers, one of whom sent him to Major Basil Davidson on the SOE Balkan Desk, who welcomed him to the organization and gave him a Serbo-Croat grammar to read. At twenty-one, Lees had managed to join SOE, four years under the official joining age and with no specialist qualifications.

After completing his training, Lees was dropped into the mountains south of Skoplje in Macedonia in territory annexed by Bulgaria in 1941 where he joined Major John Sehmer's mission attached to Major Djuric's Četniks, Partisans loyal to the exiled Serbian King. With him jumped two Royal Engineers, Lieutenants Tomlinson and Smith, and W/T Operator Thompson. Within days, the nine members of the two SOE missions found themselves caught in a deadly pincer movement of German and Bulgarian troops. Under constant attack, they moved across country, skirmishing as they went until forced to split up. When the missions next met, they were down to four men; Smith had died of wounds, Thompson killed outright, Lindstrom, a member of Sehmer's mission, executed in cold blood by Bulgar troops and another of Sehmer's men, Corporal Blackmore, also died of his wounds; Tomlinson was missing*. Having lost over half their effective strengths, the missions were re-tasked by Cairo: Sehmer was to remain with Djuric while Lees was to move fifty miles to the north as BLO of Fugue Mission to three Četnik brigades in the area between Mount Kukavica and

---

* He was later found with a bullet wound in his arm and remained with Sehmer.

Lescovacs town to prepare to attack enemy road and rail communications.

Over the next seven months, Lees found himself immersed himself in the particular politics of the Serbian resistance, each brigade vying with the other to achieve pride of place. His job was not made easier by the scant

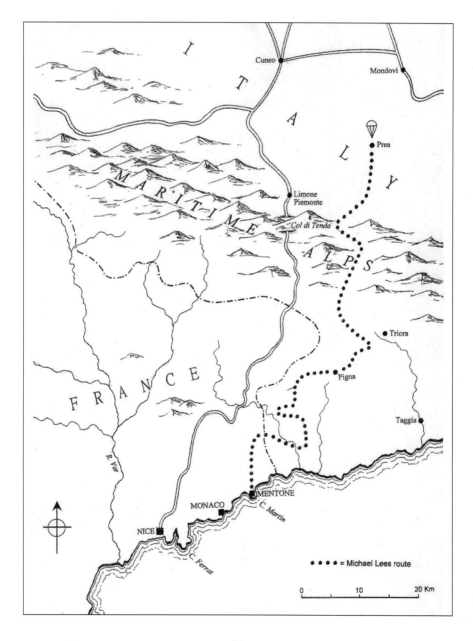

supplies he received; sufficient arms for 300 men were dropped over the period, a paltry amount when shared between the three brigades and a pittance compared to those received by Tito and his Communist Partisans. Often hindered by local rivalries, Lees nevertheless managed to mount several daring sabotage attacks on the Nis-Skoplje railway and it came as a bitter disappointment when, along with all the other BLOs attached to General Mihailović's Četniks, he received the order to pull out.

As Lees flew out of Serbia in April 1944, sitting opposite Major John Sehmer of Skoplje days, the long forgotten words of his mentor Basil Davidson echoed in his ears: 'Your job is to help the Yugoslavs to fight the enemy and not to take part in their civil war and, if it should come your way, you must do everything in your power to stop it. The Partisans are getting stronger and though the plan at present is to support Mihailović in Serbia, you may find that this is no longer possible and that you have to change sides. At all costs keep an open mind.'

On return to Bari, Lees was earmarked for Hungary but after meeting with Major Neville Temple who was headed for Liguria in Northern Italy, it was agreed that he should join him. At the end of August, Lees's mission consisting of him, a reporter called Paul Morton, the artist Geoffrey Long and an Italian codenamed Roberto were inadvertently dropped to a band of Communist Partisans rather than to Temple's *Badogliani*. It was an inauspicious start, followed by news that Morton had sprained his ankle on landing and more seriously Roberto had fractured his thigh. Soon the party was on the run from Fascist patrols and in the course of trying to contact Temple, a maverick Scots Guards escaped POW William McClelland collected them by car and took them to the headquarters of Nani, the leader of the *Garibaldi* division, who in turn passed them on to Major Enrico Mauri [Martini], the charismatic *Badogliani* commander to whom the mission should have been dropped in the first place. At last, Lees rendezvoused with Temple, who told him that his mission had been posted missing!

Merging his mission with that of Temple, whose second-in-command Captain Arne Flygt had recently been captured, Lees set about training the Partisans in weapons and explosives and doubling up for Temple when he was away in Turin. It was on returning from one such meeting that Temple asked Lees to take two members of the Turin CLN through the lines to France as they had vital intelligence to impart to the Allies. Two days later, he set off at the head of a sixteen-strong group of a distinct international character; in addition to the two Italians, Paul Morton, Geoffrey Long and two downed American pilots who had been working as cipher clerks for

Neville, there were an Australian, two British and a French escaped POWs and another American pilot, together with three local guides and the redoubtable Guardsman McClelland. Having warned the American Army in the South of France to expect them in four days time around 2 October, the party marched for three days, reaching Pigna about fifteen miles from the coast. With many of the group on their last legs*, Lees went ahead with a five-man advance party including the two CLN members. Successfully dodging German patrols although at one point they stumbled across a German artillery observation party and exchanged fire with them, Lees led his team safely across the lines and delivered them to Brigade HQ in Mentone. It had been an epic journey, safely completed due to Michael Lees's inspirational leadership.

In August 1944, Lees married Gwendolen Johnson who was serving as a FANY in Bari and in December, after a few weeks leave in London, he was sent back to Italy and reported to Monopoli on Christmas Eve. Here he bumped into Bert Farrimond, Temple's W/T operator, who told him how after Lees had left, Neville had ordered an attack on Alba and during the fighting which followed had been accidentally killed by a Partisan lorry. Farrimond had managed to get out by plane from Major Mauri's newly completed airstrip hours before the Germans overran it. Impressed by Farrimond's dogged determination to get through on the airwaves irrespective of the technical difficulties, Lees promptly recruited him as his W/T Operator for his new mission, 'Envelope', which was directed to organize and supply the Reggiani Partisan Division in the mountains west of Bologna. In early January 1945, the mission dropped near Gova and was met by Major Wilky Wilcockson, the BLO to the Modenesi Partisans, whose area marched with that of the Reggiani Division. Lees told him he had come to take over the Envelope Mission from Captain Johnny Johnston; Wilkcockson informed him this was not the case and that he was only 're-inforcing it', which prompted an altercation between the two resulting an an exasperated letter from Lees to Macintosh at Tac HQ bemoaning the confusion. It was an inauspicious start and almost immediately they were snowed in by a ferocious blizzard but the following day reached the headquarters of the Reggiani commander, Colonel Augusto Monti. His 2,000 strong Division consisted of three *Garibaldi* Brigades and one Green Flame Brigata, an unusual alliance especially since the latter was commanded by a Roman Catholic priest, Don Domenico Orlandini. After meeting all the principal players, Lees was puzzled, summing up his unease that 'these men

---

*   Morton, Long and four others reached Mentone by boat in November 1944.

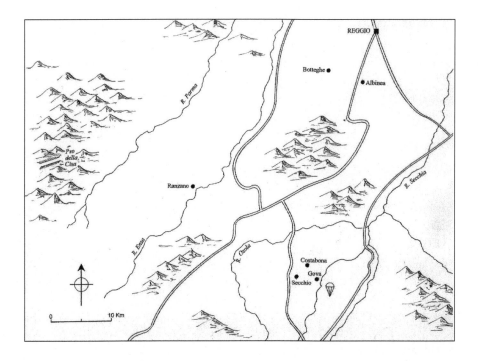

were living in the mountains, not fighting in them'. That was all about to change.

On his way back to Gova, he came across Wilcockson in Costabona with all his mission's equipments packed on two mules. During the night, Wilkockson told him, the Germans had attacked the Modenesi Division which had split up and gone into hiding. Gova had been captured that morning. Panic set in and soon Monti's Reggiani Division disintegrated and dispersed like the Modenesi, leaving Lees's mission unprotected. A gruelling twenty hour march across the mountains through deep soft snow brought Lees and his men safely to Ranzano where they met up with the abashed Colonel Monti and his dejected staff. From Lees's perspective, the disaster presented an opportunity to rebuild the Reggiani from scratch and he persuaded Monti to agree to allow him to play a major role.

Soon, Lees had organized a sabotage squad under Glauco Monducci known as the Black Owls or *Goufo Nero* and an Intelligence Cell under a Partisan called Kiss [Guilio Davioli] which enabled him to run his own couriers and to test Partisan intelligence reports against his own sources. One of his innovations was the introduction of the half-way house, whereby mountain couriers would meet their city-based counterparts, thereby not compromising their security on account of their lack of knowledge of each other's area. After moving his headquarters to Secchio, a small hamlet near to Gova and Costabona, Lees supervised supply drops, ensuring that their distribution between brigades was equitable, and having reorganized the deployment and administration of the Partisans, set his sabotage squad, now forty strong, to work. In his February monthly report, he proudly reported seven road and two railway bridges destroyed and forty units of rolling stock rendered useless. Enemy casualties were put at 123 German killed, seventy three 'possibles' and 169 wounded. The Lees effect had begun to work.

In a characteristic memo to Major Charles Macintosh at Tac HQ in Florence on 7 February 1945, Lees asked for an assistant as 'things are getting almost beyond us from sheer weight of work. As you know we're handling a lot of W/T traffic, about ten messages most days. These all have to be deciphered! Then there's intelligence, all the other stuff...and odd things which a mission has to do, dropping grounds and God knows what before one can even start to get around detachments, commands, recces etc...Personally I'm far more interested and far better at the more active side of the job...Your very welcome drops of explosive have opened up new fields of fun which I'm aching to get at but at the moment I'm tied to an office stool.' Being a bureaucrat 'sat on his arse' behind enemy lines was not Lees's idea of fighting a war.

One of the mission's new recruits, an Austrian deserter from 4 Fallschirmjäger Division near Bologna, volunteered to Lees that he was convinced that somewhere in the vicinity there was an important German headquarters, possibly even an Army command. Putting Kiss on the case, it transpired that this was indeed true for his network discovered that the headquarters of LI Mountain Corps was located at the Villa Rossi in Botteghe. Furthermore it served as forward headquarters of the German Fourteenth Army and had recently been visited by Marshal Graziani, commander of Italian Republican forces. It so happened that at the same time, Lees was asked by Bari whether there were any opportunities for SAS raids in his area. The answer as far as Lees was concerned was self-evident and the seed of Operation Tombola began to germinate.

Lees now completed an arm's length reconnaissance of the Villa, only to discover from Smith, his new second in command who had dropped during his absence, that the SAS were not expected in the immediate future. As it transpired, this was a blessing since Lees's Partisans captured the telephonist of the General's private exchange at the Villa Rossi who provided valuable additional information, including news of the changeover of

Lieutenant-General Feurstein by Lieutenant-General Hauk. The very next day, 6 March, six Dakotas arrived over Secchio and dropped four aircraft loads of stores and ten SAS parachutists, commanded by the twenty-three year old Major Roy Farran.

Commissioned into the 3rd Carabiniers (Prince of Wales's) Dragoon Guards, Farran had first seen action when attached to 3rd The King's Own Hussars in Egypt during the December 1940 to February 1941 battle of Sidi Barrani, when Commonwealth forces defeated the Italian army. He then took part in the battle for Crete but while leading a tank attack he was wounded and captured. For these actions he received his first MC. After several attempts, he escaped under the perimeter fence from the Athens POW hospital and, with Greek help, secured a *caique* and, with a group of British and Australians, sailed for Egypt. After a stormy nine-day passage, when they ran out of water, the party was picked up by a destroyer north of Alexandria and Farran received a bar to his MC. By January 1942, he was ADC to Major General Jock Campbell, commander of 7th Armoured Division. On February 26, shortly after Campbell's VC was gazetted, Farran was driving him when the car overturned and Campbell was killed.

Wounded again later that year, Farran returned to England, but was back in North Africa in early 1943. Here, after parachute training, he joined 2nd SAS. After leading a raid on Cape Passero lighthouse in Sicily, he then carried out reconnaissance and sabotage patrols on the Italian mainland, of which one of the most spectacular was in October 1943 when he dropped with a SAS detachment north of the River Tronto behind German lines. In five days his force destroyed transport, cut communications and blew up railway lines – a third MC followed. On 19 August 1944, Farran landed by Dakota transport at the American-held Rennes airfield in Brittany with sixty SAS men and twenty Jeeps and penetrated some 200 miles through enemy lines in four days, joining the base set up by the earlier SAS Operation Hardy near Chatillon, north of Dijon. Operation Wallace ended on 17 September, having resulted in 500 enemy casualties, the destruction of 95 vehicles, a train and 100,000 gallons of petrol. For his outstanding leadership during this period Farran was awarded a DSO.

Operation Tombola had finally arrived. Farran had ostensibly gone along with the flight to check that all went well; in fact, he had every intention of jumping himself and closing with the enemy, so he 'accidentally' fell out of the aircraft, conveniently with a parachute strapped to his back. Between 7 and 23 March, Farran oversaw the equipping and training of a new 300 strong Partisan *Battaglione Alleata* commanded by himself and reporting to Colonel Monti; it was a far from straightforward task for when he first addressed the new battalion at Quarra on 6 March, 'it looked like a picture of Wat Tyler's rebellion and I was very shaken indeed by the appearance of the raw material'. A further twenty-four SAS officers and men jumped safely on 9 March, including a piper from the Highland Light Infantry, who unpacked his instrument and gave a quick rendering of 'Highland Laddie' to the assembled and rather bemused Italians.

The new equipment dropped in six sorties included a 75 mm Howitzer, 3 inch mortars and Browning heavy machine guns; these weapon enabled Farran to design a defensive position centred on the Cisa, Torricella and Penna mountains, strong enough to resist the initial thrust of any *rastrellamento*. In the event of being overrun, a precipitous escape route across the summit of Monte Cisa was successfully recced by Lieutenant David Eyton-Jones. Tombola was now ready for action and its first operation was Lees's long-dreamed of attack on the German HQ at Albinea. Both Farran and Lees were well aware that the three week lull in enemy counter-Partisan activities must be coming to an end at any moment. Indeed a strong German patrol had already engaged the Green Flame outpost to the east and had only withdrawn under heavy fire from the SAS .5 Browning MG.

On 21 March, the planned attack on Villa Rossi was given the green light by 15th Army Group and a Mustang dropped up-to-date air photographs of the target as at 18 March to the Secchio Partisan HQ. The strike force consisted of twenty–four SAS soldiers, thirty Russians deserters from 162 Turkoman Division commanded by Victor Pirogov ['Modena'] and forty Partisans, half of them from the *Garibaldini* and half from Monducci's

B 24 Stores drop

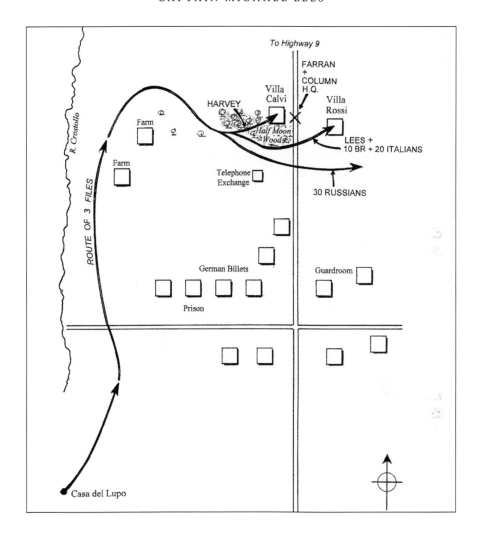

Goufo Nero. The plan was simple: after marching for two nights, the attackers would assemble at the Casa del Lupo, a remote farmhouse out of sight from the enemy. From there, ten SAS and the *Goufo Nero* would attack the Villa Rossi where hopefully the German general would be sleeping; another ten SAS and the *Garibaldini* would storm the next door Villa Calvi, which was used as an office by chief of staff Colonel Lemelsen and quarters for his staff; the Russians would throw a ring round the whole areas to prevent interference.

Despite suffering from a bout of recurring malaria which he had contracted in Yugoslavia, Lees dosed himself up with quinine and grappa

*Members of the SAS raiding force:
Ken Harvey [top right]*

and dealt with last minute arrangements. A signal came in from No.1
Special Force warning of an imminent *rastrellamento*, to which Lees
replied 'rastrellamento balls', stating that their positions were strong
enough. Tact with headquarters was not Lees's strong suite and his admi-
rable spirit of aggression did not sit comfortably with the understandable
concern of Major Macintosh in Florence, who was still picking up the
pieces after the devastating July *rastrellamento* of the Herman Goering
Division in the Montefiori area. Tac HQ at Florence then told a neighbouring BLO, Major Jim Davies, to get in touch with Lees and Farran and
order them not to go ahead. Since he was unable to make radio contact,
Davies cycled and walked to Secchio but on arrival found no one there.
Farran was receiving similar messages from Major Bob Walker-Brown on
the SAS net. At a meeting with General Clarke, commander of the US
Fifth Army, Walker-Brown had been told to delay the attack, so that it
could be coordinated with the date of the Fifth Army offensive. He fired
off a signal to Farran, urging him to postpone operations for ten days if at
all possible. By now a day's march from the start line, Farran 'resolved to
pretend the signal failed to reach him (sic) in time'; Lees, who was still
running a high temperature, wholeheartedly agreed.

After a text book approach march to Casa del Lupo and the observance
of strict security including the detention of five peasants who wandered
into the farm, the three columns set off to the objective on the night of 27
March. Arriving undetected, nineteen year old Lieutenant Harvey* of the
SAS led the attack on the Villa Calvi, mowing down four sentries with his
Bren gun and after the door was blown in by a bazooka, he charged in with
his troopers. Four Germans were killed on the ground floor including the

---

*   Awarded a DSO for his leadership on this mission.

Lees's air ambulance:
a captured Fieseler Storck

Staff Colonel. Then as the remaining Germans became rolling grenades down the stairs, Harvey ordered him men to set fire to the building, and taking their two wounded comrades with them, withdrew under a hail of covering fire.

With surprise now lost, the assault went in on the Villa Rossi. A furious battle raged on the upper floor as the British stormed up the spiral staircase. Lieutenant Riccomini and Sergeant Truscott of the SAS were both shot dead and Lees was seriously wounded by three bullets in the chest and leg as he fought his way upstairs in search of the General. A third SAS soldier, Corporal Bolden, was killed as the fire fight intensified. Having evacuated their wounded, the SAS set fire to the building and as soon as he saw the flames, Farran fired three red Verey lights to signal the withdrawal. After rallying, the attackers withdrew, slowed down by the two wounded SAS men, one of whom, Corporal Mulvey, had to be left in a farm house along the way. Excluding an eight-hour halt at Casa del Lupo, the retiring Tombola troops marched for twenty-two hours without a halt until they reached Secchio where they received a tumultuous welcome.

Carried on a ladder by two SAS men* to a barn two miles away, Lees lay up for three days with Glauco Monducci, the Black Owls' commander who had also been shot in the leg. A visiting doctor was unable to assist, exclaiming 'I can do nothing to help; you should be in hospital!' Hidden in the bottom of a manure cart, the two were smuggled into the outskirts of Reggio where Lees was seen by another doctor. His prognosis was dire, telling Lees that unless the severed nerve in his leg was repaired within ten days, he would lose it. SOE

---

* Burke and Ramos were later awarded the MM for their courageous and selfless actions.

Bari mounted a daring rescue operation and Lees was successfully picked up from a small field near Ranzano by a captured German Fieseler Storch aircraft flown by Furio Lauri; the next day Lauri returned for Monducci. The raid had been partially successful. Both buildings were destroyed and over thirty Germans killed or captured, many of them officers. Allied losses were three SAS killed and three wounded, six Russians captured and two wounded and three Italian Partisans wounded.

Despite his Nelsonian breach of the rules, Farran was allowed to remain in the field to continue to attack German communications and narrowly avoided a courts martial on his return. However, Lees met with official displeasure on his return to Florence on the grounds that he had blatantly disobeyed orders. The full fury of senior SOE staff officers, sore from the rasping criticism levelled at them by 15th Army Group, fell on the hapless young officer; Hewitt dubbed him 'troublesome, insubordinated, unreasonable, tactless, irresponsible and highhanded' and another reported in May 1945 that 'this officer gave considerable trouble from the time he was infiltrated. He was resentful of all orders issued to him by HQ No.1 SF or Tac HQ and his attitude is typified by the extracts from letters* written by him in the Field'. He returned to England to recover from his wounds and was replaced in Secchio by Captain John Lees, no relation. Yet the vendetta by SOE senior officers continued.

As Lees's on-the-spot commander, Farran had witnessed his extraordinary courage during the attack on the villa and the immense fortitude he had shown afterwards. He therefore recommended him for an immediate MC:

'During March 1945, Captain M Lees was commanding a British Mission to the Partisans in the Province of Reggio del Emilia, Italy. He organized his partisan division into an efficient guerilla force and by his courageous example inspired the Italians to attacks on the enemy which they would not otherwise have performed.

On 4 March he conceived a plan for attacking the German Corps HQ which controlled the whole [German] Fifth Army front from Bologna to the sea. With great skill and courage he carried out a preliminary reconnaissance which revealed all the details of the HQ.

On 26 March the HQ was attacked with great success by a mixed force of British parachutists and partisans. Captain Lees led his own band of

---

* This refers to the increasingly acrimonious correspondence between Lees and Macintosh. They ended the war not on speaking terms.

partisans into the Corps Commander's villa with such dash that the ground floor and the first landing on a spiral staircase were taken in the first rush in spite of intense fire from the enemy. When his men hesitated in the face of such intense MG fire, with complete disregard for his own safety he stood on the staircase and waved them on inspiring them to further efforts. Eventually he was seriously wounded but continued to shout inspiring orders to hi men from the ground. When the order was given for the force to withdraw, Lees was carried through enemy territory on the plains for two days by two British parachutists and finally left in a safe house by Reggio.

After ten days arrangements were made for Lees to be picked up by an aircraft but it was found impossible to transport him from the plains which were thickly populated by Germans to the improvised Landing Strip in the Apennines. Lees took the matter into his own hands and although in great pain organized the capture of a German ambulance which transferred him to the mountains.

It is considered that the success of this attack on the German LI Corps HQ, which had a great effect on the outcome of the final battle in Italy, was largely due to the gallantry, initiative and unequalled courage of Captain Lees.'

This stirring recommendation was dismissively quashed by SOE who stated that since Farran was a SAS officer, Lees was neither under his command nor seconded to him and hence his recommendation was ineligible. They also made it clear that if Lees had not been wounded, he would have been the subject of a very serious investigation in regard to his alleged non-compliance with orders. Still in hospital, Lees raised a question regarding his pay for he was under the impression that he had been granted the temporary rank of Major once he had assumed command of a BMM. The answer was a derogatory 'no'; the SOE chain of command denied all knowledge of the matter. Not surprisingly, his request to join SIS as a career officer after the war was not followed up.

In his obituary in the Special Forces Club Newsletter of Spring 1993, the final paragraph reads: 'Sadly he did not receive the recognition he deserved – a dismal finale to the career of a very brave man.' In hindsight, Lees would probably have been more suited to the single-minded military ethos of the SAS rather than to SOE, that strange hybrid of politics, diplomacy and the profession of arms. Indeed his Confidential Report of October 1944 read 'he is not, however, recommended for work involving intricate political negotiations'. It was left unsaid that this equally applied to the internal politics of SOE. Determined never to be brow beaten by officialdom, late in life Lees conducted a passionate and eloquent defence of General Draza Mihailović, whom the British had so abruptly and perfidiously disowned in late 1943; if his extraordinary bravery in the field went unrecognized, Michael Lees's courage with words did not.

Lieutenant Ken Harvey, SAS: 1945: recommendation for a gallantry award

On the night of 26/27 March 1945, Lieutenant Harvey was in command of a party of ten British parachutists which attacked a villa containing the documents in the HQ of the German LI Corps at Albinea, ten miles south of Reggio nel'Emilia.

Having approached his target unseen, Lieutenant Harvey shot the four sentries with his tommy gun. He then led his party into the house, having shot his way in through the door. Intense opposition was encountered inside, the Germans firing down a spiral staircase. Harvey, with great courage, gallantry and complete disregard of personal safety, inspired his little band to fighting fury. The ground floor was taken and many Germans were killed,

Major Roy Farran

including the Chief of Staff. Realizing that he could not force the staircase, Harvey lit a big fire in the documents room and kept the Germans inside by machine gun fire until the villa was well ablaze. Although the whole area was now in a state of alarm and machine gun bullets were flying everywhere, Harvey guided his party safely back to the mountains, infiltrating through large German concentrations. The party also carried its two wounded men back with it to safety.

Throughout this action, Harvey was remarkable for his gallantry and cool, clear decisive thinking. The damage he did to the German Army from Bologna to Massa was grievous. His behaviour inspired his men to follow anywhere an officer they love and trust.

Awarded a DSO

6

Major 'John' Bernard James Barton, DSO and bar, MC

John Barton initially enlisted in the Grenadier Guards in November 1938 and after obtaining a commission in The Buffs in May 1940, he was rebadged to the 44th Reconnaissance Regiment of the Royal Armoured Corps, which had been formed as part of the 44th (Home Counties) Division in early 1941. It arrived in Egypt with the rest of the 44th Division in mid-1942 and during preparations for El Alamein was especially trained for mine clearing. Working closely with the 11th Hussars, the Regiment successfully cleared the way for 7th Armoured Division through the German minefields but during the course of this action suffered heavy casualties. On 8 March 1943, it joined 56th (London) Division in Iraq, seeing service in Iraq, Palestine, Egypt until the Division moved to Libya at the end of May 1943. The regiment then landed with the rest of the 56th Division in Italy on 9 September 1943, where it served for the remainder of the war, transferring to the Royal Armoured Corps on 1 January 1944. During his time with 44th Reconnaissance Regiment, John Barton was awarded an MC, which was announced in the London Gazette on 19 August 1943.

In December 1943, Barton transferred to No. 2 Commando, which had taken part in the Sicily and Salerno landings and was now based on the Island of Vis off the coast of Yugoslavia as part of 2 Special Service Brigade in support of Tito's Partisans. In mid-February 1944, he was sent to reconnoitre the German-occupied Island of Brac. As soon as he had made contact with the local Partisans, one of them was captured and admitted that a British patrol was in the vicinity. This prompted the 200-strong German garrison to threaten retaliation on the local inhabitants and in response Barton proposed to assassinate the German commandant. Once the Partisans had given him details of the commandant's house in Nerezisce village, Barton dismantled his silenced Sten gun and sent it ahead, hidden in a bundle of faggots carried by a donkey. After slipping into the village disguised as a shepherd, Barton, accompanied by two Partisans, reached the commandant's house and killed him with two bursts from his Sten. Beating a hasty retreat pursued by barking dogs and the sound of shots, he lay up in the hills until being safely extracted three days later. At the end of the month Barton returned to Brac and led a successful night attack on a German outpost, bringing back eight prisoners with valuable information about enemy troop deployments. For these two actions, he was awarded the DSO. A later report written by Barton concerned the efficacy of his silenced Sten gun. He noted that 'this operation could have been done with any automatic weapon, but is doubtful if we could have made a successful retreat if we hadn't used a silent Sten.'

Promoted Captain and placed in command of 5 Troop No.2 Commando, Barton inadvertently found himself in trouble. One former commando remembered that 'about this time Jack (Churchill) banished to Italy Lieutenant Barton who had operated some weeks before at Nerezisce on Brac on patrol, shot and killed the local German Commandant before returning to Vis with five prisoners. It seemed that he had conducted this business in civilian attire, which the Germans pointed out was a 'no-no' in the rules of war, and that further, if captured Lieutenant Barton would be shot. Jack could not be moved on the matter even though this officer had been awarded the DSO for his actions.' Another commentator stated that on 20 July 1944 Barton was no longer allowed to operate (in Yugoslavia) since his name and exploits had been published in the UK newspapers, a view confirmed by SOE's Lieutenant Colonel John Beevor in May 1945[*].

No.2 Commando's loss was SOE's gain and having transferred to SOE, Barton's first mission was to kill or capture the distinguished and very able Generaloberst Heinrich von Vietinghoff[†], referred to a General 'x' in his post-operational report. None other than Field Marshal Alexander himself had personally requested this special mission. From December 1941 to August 1943 von Vietinghoff was Commander-in-Chief of the German Fifteenth Army in France. From 1943 onwards he commanded the German Tenth Army in Italy, and was largely responsible for the highly effective delaying actions based on the successive defensive lines built across the country, such as the Winter Line from November 1943 to May 1944 and then the Gothic Line in the autumn of 1944. In October 1944 he was temporarily raised to overall command in Italy (Army Group C) when Field Marshall Albert Kesselring was seriously injured in a car crash returning from a General Staff meeting[‡] when his vehicle collided with a long-barrelled

---

[*]   Letter to A/DH London from JGB Ref SD/33 dated 18 May 1945

[†]   Hewitt's recommendation for the bar to his DSO confirms this.

[‡]   In January 1945, on Kesselring's return, he left Italy to command Army Group Courland in East Prussia but returned as the supreme German commander in Italy when Kesselring was moved in March 1945 to command German Army Group West in France.

Von Veitlinghoff

gun coming out of a side turning on the Bologna-Forli road. Not surprisingly, Field Marshal Alexander took a personal interest in Barton's mission. After the war, he wrote that 'von Vietinghoff, like most of the senior German generals, was an able commander who reacted with speed and determination when faced with a dangerous situation.'

The twenty-four year old Barton left Brindisi on the night of 3 November and was dropped to the Silentia Mission where he was met by Major Wilcockson, the BLO, and taken to a house in Gova, forty miles west of Bologna. Wilcockson was in a poor humour since hundreds of sandbags had been dropped instead of the boots, socks and greatcoats which he had asked for. Two days later Barton rode over to Major Johnston's mission at Ligonchio where he collected an interpreter, an Italian paratrooper and a German-Italian who could pass muster as a German. On the day they left Ligonchio, another air drop took place with many of the stores falling into German hands, and the luckless Wilkockson this time received a consignment of antique Italian rifles, more dangerous to the user than to the target. After a three day march, Barton's team

---

*   Memo J/3440 Major de Haan to Lieutenant Colonel Pleydell-Bouverie 14 January 1945

reached German-Fascisti territory and with bicycles provided by the Partisans, rode into the centre of Reggio. At one point they met a patrol of German cyclists who ordered them to dismount; pedalling for all they were worth, they miraculously escaped despite a hail of rifle and Schmeisser fire.

After staying in the town for three days, they left for Modena, cycling along the Via Emilia. Barton had a silenced Sten gun over his shoulder 'which made him (sic) feel rather conspicuous' when passing long horse-drawn and vehicle convoys, fortunately using no lights for fear of attack. While in Modena, Barton had to change houses every night; during the day, he regularly passed Germans in the street who looked him up and down with suspicion. Still on bicycles, the team left Modena for Miran-dola but there were German reprisals going on in the area so they had to make a wide detour and reached Concordia where they finally made contact with Partisans from the East and 'started out, moving a short distance each night, living in holes in walls, under haystacks, in barns and stables and all manner of peculiar hide-outs.' On one occasion, they were hidden in a hole in a barn with the entrance to their hide covered with hay.

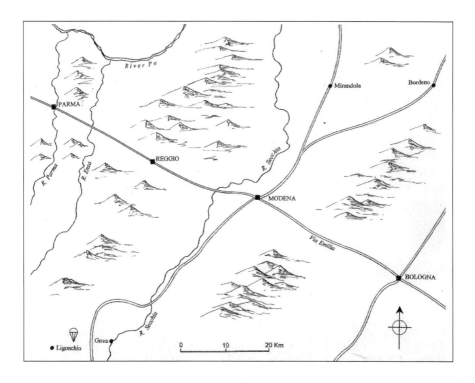

This worked well until the cow which had been asleep woke up and ate the hay just as a German patrol entered the barn. Fortunately, they did not notice it.

The whole of the next month was spent in the Bordino-Ferrara area where life was 'possible but not pleasant'. The area was under continuous search and many Partisans were captured and immediately shot. Barton finally contacted the Partisan commandant and told him the information he required about von Vietinghoff's whereabouts but despite interrogating German prisoners, deserters, Russians and Poles, and Partisans, no one could tell him where the General was. Strangely enough, everyone seemed to know where General Kesselring was, irrespective of the fact that he was in hospital in Germany recovering from a car accident. One promising contact was a Fascist Captain of the Milizia who was a good Fascist by day and an even better Partisan by night. He thought the General was in the Verona-Brescia area and agreed to go and check it out. The next day, using the Milizia Captain's home as his base, Barton looked through the shutters and saw three trucks of Fascists approach. There was no time to hang about so the mission jumped out of the window and hid in a pile of sugar beet in a shed. The tempo of searches increased and Barton was forced to leave the village and hide out in the open fields. The house where they had stayed was burnt down by German troops. While this was going on, Barton's interpreter walked out, leaving him on his own for ten days, moving from house to house trying to make contact with the Partisans, most of whom had been captured or shot. To make matters worse, he was lousy and had developed scabies.

Just before Christmas, Barton decided that in all probability the General was north of the River Po but before he set out for the Verona-Venice area, he asked the Partisan commandant of the Modena area to collect and collate all available intelligence from Milan, Verona and Venice to try to ascertain exactly the General was. Having been told that this would take six to eight weeks, Barton decided to return to base and reached Wilcockson at Gova on 29 December. A forty-seven hour march took him to Catigliano from where he crossed the lines in early January 1945 and made contact with American troops. He was depressed by the failure of his mission but determined to go back. He had learnt some valuable lessons 'living in the plains', one of which was 'cycle about with a pistol in your pocket and, if challenged, ride up to the sentry and shoot first.'

He therefore proposed to No.1 Special Force that given the fact that the Partisan movement on the plains in the Carpi area was well organized, a British mission could successfully act as a link between it and Fifth Army.

This would rectify the absence of any liaison between the two which was the current situation. Bari agreed and Barton started preparations to operate in the plain, having first established a secure mountain base. Major MacDermot was briefed to follow him in if the mission proved successful. Meanwhile, in between missions, he had gone back to the UK on leave and married Miss Mary Stone on 29 January at Henley-on-Thames.

On 10 February 1945, Captain Neil Oughtred and Corporal Ted Fry of the Cisco Mission dropped to the Asta DZ where Captain Michael Lees was waiting for them. Their brief was to establish a secure base for Barton in the mountains and then act as a supply and communications centre for him. They were also tasked with setting up a secure courier system. After spending a week with Lees and liaising with Major Jim Davies of the Silentia Mission and a local OSS team, Oughtred began to contact the local resistance and soon had couriers lines to the SAP and GAP HQs in Reggio, Modena and Carpi. However, it was apparent that his base at Costabona was too far from the plain, so when he received news that Barton was dropping on 12 March, Oughtred moved his HQ to Monte Largo in the Valestra area. Almost immediately he had to move due to the presence of a strong enemy patrol and he withdrew to Cavola but it was not to be for long for no sooner had the mission reached it that an enemy drive forced them to retreat to Percola di Cavola. Throughout this period, no news had been heard of Barton and other than receiving one plane load of supplies in the Valestra area, little was achieved. On 22 March, another enemy *rastrellamento* got underway and after retiring to their base at Percola, they were attacked in their safe house by an enemy patrol on the night of 31 March and quickly withdrew to Qara where they buried their W/T set. On 9 April Oughtred was ordered to close down his mission and to join up with Major Charles Holland in the Parma region. He reached him on 14 April, having never made contact with Major Barton.

Meanwhile, Barton's team consisting of himself, Sergeant Barratt and two Italian brothers, Gino and Mario Barbera, took off in a Liberator on the night of 20 March with the intention of making a blind drop midway between Carpi and the River Secchio. According to Major Charles Macintosh, officer commanding Tac HQ in Florence, Barton was in no fit state to drop as his back was a mass of boils in various stages of maturity. He rushed him to hospital for attention and two days later he was pronounced fit to drop. The drop itself went smoothly but on landing, the container with their arms and equipment was nowhere to be found and furthermore they were thirty kilometres north of their DZ. As Barton noted, 'a few more flying seconds, we would have been north of the River Po [in the middle of the

German army!] instead of south'. The next day a Fascist patrol found the missing container and thus the mission was effectively compromised. Having persuaded a friendly farmer to move them in his cart under a pile of straw, they made their way to Bondanello village and from there to a hamlet north of Concordia where they were hidden by a farmer in a small hole built under the stable while a German 88mm gun was being 'dug in' in the garden by its German crew. The next night, having made contact with the Partisans, they were taken to a hide-out in the middle of a ploughed field where they spent the next ten days. In the evening a local farmer would come and dig open the entrance and at dawn he would fill it in.

The future for Barton looked dismal. The Partisans were unarmed, dispirited, afraid and in the process of disbanding and heading for the mountains. Sergeant Barratt was having great difficulty getting through on the W/T set and the locals were increasingly anxious when he used their

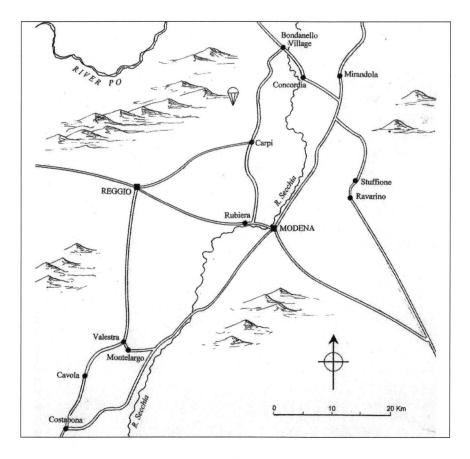

houses to transmit from. It was at this stage that Barton realized that his original plan had been over-optimistic and so he signalled Bari to stand down Captain MacDermot and to redeploy Captain Oughtred to another mission. It was a disappointing start. On 1 April, Barton contacted the Remo Brigata at Mirandola and moved off to rendezvous with them the next night. About 800 strong, about half the brigade lived in underground holes and the other half quite openly among the Germans and in many cases were employed by them. Barton quickly set to work, making an inventory of stores required and after a few poor drops, the Brigata received ten Liberator loads of arms and ammunition. On 14 April, Barton and the mission had a narrow escape. They were in a safe house when a Brigata Nere patrol surrounded the house and an officer entered, demanding to see Barton's papers. Realizing he had left his pistol in the next room, Barton flung himself at the enemy officer and killed him with his bare hands but not before he had alerted the rest of the Fascist patrol. Fortunately some Partisans hiding out nearby came to the mission's rescue with their newly acquired Sten and Bren guns and after a spirited battle, chased the Brigata away, killing five officers and one German RSM.

On 20 April, Barton received orders for an all-out Partisan effort and although he managed to orchestrate a general attack on the retreating German columns, the situation became confused when Italian paratroopers of Operation Herring dropped without having made any plans to liaise with the Partisans. On the night of 19-20 April, the 114-strong Italian 'F' Recce Squadron under Captain Carlo Gay, and four platoons led by Lieutenant Guerrino Ceiner from the Italian Nembo Parachute Regiment jumped from fourteen C47 aircraft of the U.S. 64th Troop Carrier Group onto their drop zones. Scattering was considerable and a few were captured on landing. Despite an early setback when sixteen paratroopers were surrounded by German forces and after barricading themselves in a farmhouse, all but two died fighting to the last round, other groups were more successful, with two F Squadron squads seizing Ravarino and Stuffione, and in the process capturing 451 Germans. Operation Herring lasted over seventy-two hours instead of the thirty-six initially foreseen, but it turned out to be a success. With some help on the part of the local Partisan groups, according to some sources 481 German soldiers were killed, 1,083 surrendered, forty-four vehicles were destroyed and many 'liberated'. The price the Italian paratroopers paid was thirty-one dead and twelve wounded.

Despite the confusion, Barton and his Brigata continued their harassing operations and slowly became to take control of the evacuated towns. By

2300 hours on 21 April, Mirandola was cleared and two battalions of Partisans set up roadblocks and started patrolling. At 0100 hours the next morning, unaware of its change of ownership, the Americans shelled and mortared the town for three hours, so Barton, Barratt and two Partisans set off to try and find the American HQ to stop 'the wanton destruction'. Mistaking a German roadblock for an American one, Barton soon found himself under guard and spent the night in a small room disposing of his signals plans and other incriminating documents. His German captors, well disciplined infantry troops, thought he was from an advanced patrol of the US Fifth Army and did not pass him back down the line to the Gestapo. When an American attack came in at midday, Barton and his Partisan colleagues successfully made their escape. When he put his final report in, Barton concluded that 'the Partisans on the plains deserved all the support we gave them and fully justified themselves as brave patriots.'

When he returned from the field, Barton wrote a personal letter to Brigadier Tom Churchill who had been his commander on Vis, asking to rejoin the Commandos. Before he had time to answer it, the war had come to an end.

Major John Barton: 22 June 1945: recommendation for bar to DSO

Major Barton was dropped by parachute in November 1944 to the Apennines with the task of killing or capturing the German General Von Vietinghoff whose HQ was reported to be at Ferrara. Major Barton was deserted at a very early date by his guide and interpreter, but despite this and although handicapped by his inability to speak the Italian language, he remained in this area and continued alone to search for his objective. He was forced to leave the hills and to penetrate the plains in search of his quarry and his journey took him into the main towns of Reggio and Modena where German patrols, Fascist checks and house to house searches were made at every stage of the journey. Major Barton spent over a month in this area moving short distances at night and living by day in barns, stables and holes in the ground. Intense enemy activity was encountered and for a period of ten days he was confined to a hole in the ground relying on an occasional meal brought by some friendly contact.

For over two months he persisted in his task of searching for the German general and only gave up when he received definite evidence to prove that General Von Vietinghoff and his HQ had moved from the area.

After a few weeks rest Major Barton volunteered for a new and more hazardous task. With the approach of the spring offensive in Italy it was necessary to contact and organize the Partisans in the Po valley and with this in view,

Major Barton parachuted blind in the Carpi area on 21 March 1945. In spite of the presence of numerous enemy garrisons, the party landed safely and after some days of extreme hardship and danger made contact with local Partisans. These proved to be few in number and the task of Major Barton more hazardous and difficult than had been expected. In spite of this he succeeded in arranging eleven air supply sorties and in a short time he was able to build up an efficient Partisan fighting force in the area.

During this time major Barton and his W/T operator were surprised on one occasion in a house by a Fascist officer, who catching them unarmed, held them up at the point of an automatic. Major Barton regardless of his own safety leaped on the officer and succeeded in killing him. Whilst retrieving his automatic from an adjacent room he found the house to be surrounded by Fascists, but with the aid of his wireless operator he succeeded in shooting his way out of the building.

When in April 1945 a call was made for all out action by the Partisans, Major Barton mobilized and led his force to the assault. They captured the important bridge at Mirandola, holding it against enemy counter-attacks; but eventually it was shelled by forward Allied troops. In order to prevent damage being done to the bridge, Major Barton attempted to make his way alone through the enemy lines to warn the Allied troops, but he was captured and only with great difficulty succeeded in destroying compromising document which he was carrying. After being held for twelve hours this officer made good his escape.

Major Barton has shown outstanding courage and devotion to duty, carrying out the most hazardous tasks in the middle of the enemy who, had they caught and identified him, would undoubtedly have killed him. He is strongly recommended for the immediate award of a bar to the DSO.

Awarded

Lieutenant John Barton: 17 May 1944: recommendation for immediate DSO

This officer landed on the German-held island of Brac, Dalmatia on 13 February 1944 with the intention of finding the German commander of the troops there and killing him. He spent several days on the island living in cave in the hills with the Partisans. During this time he carried out many useful reconnaissances and when he later returned he brought back much useful information about the enemy garrisons. He also completed his preparations for liquidating the commander. As the road to Nerezisce, a town in which the German HQ was located, was guarded by sentries, Lieutenant Barton took his Sten gun to pieces and sent it forward hidden in a bundle of sticks on the back of a donkey. He himself ran the gauntlet among a number of shepherds who entered the town as dusk was approaching.

Guided by a Partisan, he entered the house of the German commander at 2100 hours on 20 February 1944. He quickly examined a kitchen and bedroom which were full of local inhabitants, before entering the dining room where he saw a German officer. He at once opened fire and killed him with two bursts from his silenced Sten gun. Confirmation has since been obtained of the rank and name, death and burial of this officer, who was in fact the German garrison commander and held the rank of Hauptman. Lieutenant Barton then withdrew rapidly from the house and escaped from the town under cover of night, although the alarm was raised. He had to hide in caves for a further two days before arrangements could be made to take him off the island.

On 2 March 1944 this officer again visited the Island of Brac with a small party of Commando soldiers. He located an enemy post at Pusisca and attacked it at night. Two Germans were killed and eight captured some of whom were wounded. Lieutenant Barton was again compelled to lie up for several days before he could leave the island but he kept the eight prisoners and brought them back with him when he returned.

The careful reconnaissance and planning of Lieutenant Barton and his resourceful and resolute leadership ensured the success of this small but highly important raid.

No publicity to be given to this citation.

Awarded

Lieutenant John Barton: 7 June 1943: recommendation for an immediate MC

On the coastal sector north of Enfidaville on the night of 9 May 1943, Lieutenant Barton was in command of a night reconnaissance patrol consisting of himself, a RE corporal and seven other ranks.

In the course of the patrol it was necessary to negotiate an enemy minefield which was known to be sown with anti-tank and anti-personnel mines. Half way through the minefield an "S" mine exploded, wounding the corporal and five other ranks. After arranging for their evacuation to the rear, Lieutenant Barton continued the patrol accompanied by the one remaining Sapper, and having crossed the remainder of the minefield, located two enemy posts which were known to be occupied by day, but were found by him to be unoccupied at night. Lieutenant Barton was successful in retracing his steps through the minefield. He brought back valuable information and throughout the whole operation showed great determination and courage of a high order.

Awarded

7

Major Charles Holland MC, MBE, Bronze Star [US]

Brought up in The Argentine, fluent in Spanish, Charles Holland had studied electrical engineering with GEC, so after enlisting in the Signals Corps in 1940, it came as no surprise when he was recruited by SOE in May 1942 at the relatively young age of twenty-three. Worried that Spain could still come down on the side of Germany and Italy, Section H sent him that July to recruit and train W/T operators in the north of the country as part of a sort of 'Carlista' resistance. During this mission, Holland wore plain clothes which put him at an increased risk, albeit in a neutral country; fortunately his efforts bore fruit, including the recruitment of a local priest. In July 1943, he was moved to MO4 and infiltrated into the Peloponnese with Force 133's Operation Staverton on 18 September where as signals officer to Lieutenant Colonel John Stevens' mission, he had the demanding task of managing the mission's six stations which all operated over a particularly tricky radio span, given that their close proximity to Cairo made the use of high frequencies extremely difficult. Exfiltrated by sea on 20 June 1944, he was then attached to No.1 Special Force in Monopoli where he joined the Envelope Blue Mission, at the time earmarked as the Allied Advisory and Liaison Section to the Italian Army's Nembo Divisional HQ.

On 28 July 1944, Holland dropped with Major Jim Davies, who knew him well as he had been Stevens' Sapper officer in Greece, and Captain Wilky Wilcockson at the Barr DZ near Frassinoro run by Major Vivian Johnston* of the Envelope Mission. As signals officer for the advance party, Holland was responsible for all radio traffic back to base and for intercom links between the companies of the Nembo† 185th Parachute Battalion, which were due to drop on Operation Batepits, a diversionary ploy timed to coincide with the US Fifth Army's advance on Lucca to breach the newly established Gothic Line. On 31 July, a massive *rastrellamento* was

---

*   See Chapter 13.

†   After the September 1943 armistice, Italian troops loyal to the King and the Allies formed the Italian Non-Belligerent Army. In April 1944 it assumed the new name of Italian Liberation Corps organised into two Divisions, the Nembo and the Utili.

launched by the German Hermann Goering Division and the Decima MAS and an ill-judged order to his men by the Partisan leader in the area to disband resulted in individual Partisans throwing away their arms and bolting*. As the German attacks gained momentum, it was clear that the main Nembo drop would have to be cancelled and secondly that the advance party needed to disperse as quickly as possible. To this end, Davies managed to send a message to base which was decoded just in time to abort the operation.

Having destroyed all secret equipment and codes, parties of five were formed to head west and Holland left with Sergeant Barratt, twenty-year-old Corporal Hayhurst and two Italians to link up with Major Gordon Lett and his Partisans in the Pontremoli area. En route they learnt that Lett had also been hard hit by a *rastrellamento* so they turned around and marched to Comano near Monte Acuto where they found Jim Davies. Word then reached them that the situation at Frassinoro had calmed down, so Holland returned to retrieve his signals equipment and leaving Barratt who was no longer required by the advance party with Johnston, he returned to Monte Acuto where by 20 August Hayhurst had established the Envelope Blue radio link to base. The three officers were ordered by 1 Special Force to remain where they were and to convert to the role of BLOs. These had been dangerous and testing days; when Major Johnston returned after three weeks on the run with virtually no food, he was described as 'thin as a chorus girl'. As a gifted linguist, Holland was well on his way to mastering Italian with the same alacrity as that which he became fluent in Greek a year earlier.

The background to the Partisans in Holland's area was provided by Fritz Snapper, an officer of the Royal Dutch Army and escaped POW, who had joined Giovanni Rossi and his band of forty Partisans early in 1944 at Valorsara in the mountains of Modena on the borders of Reggio Emilia. On 20 February they had attacked Frassinoro but withdrew after Milizia counterattacks. Rossi fled and was replaced by a new Partisan commander, Barbolini, who decided to move to Gazzano in Emilia and the Partisans duly arrived there, including their Political Commissar, Dodimi Ferrari [Eros], a former farmhand who had taught himself politics and the theory of warfare when imprisoned for twelve years by the fascists. Numbers quickly increased so the band was split into three detachments and by 14 March, they numbered about 220 men of whom 100 were armed.

---

* Major JTM Davies report

An attack on Ligonchio on 15 March went seriously amiss; the Partisans were in the wrong place and their sentries gave no warning of an advancing German column. A week later, they decided to disband in the face of determined German and Republican counter-attacks, a decision which prompted Eros to form his own eight man squad and to revise the Partisans' tactical doctrine which was clearly unworkable. In order to prevent the continuous disbanding and reorganisation of Partisan forces, Eros formed a Brigata consisting of several self-contained squads of about ten men armed with LMGs and grenades and a number of special sabotage teams to take on major infrastructure targets. By May, there were five such squads and after several successful supply drops, the brigade cut Route 63 which led to a three day battle against over 1,000 fascist troops. This time there was no need to disband as the small teams just vanished into the hills.

On 14 July, Snapper met Major Johnston to discuss a plan to arm about 15,000 men in the mountains of Reggio Emilia and Modena with a view to permanently excluding German and Fascist troops from the area. It was an ambitious and controversial idea since it was contrary to the basic 'hit and run' tenet of guerrilla warfare and Snapper set off to cross the lines to explain their thinking to SOE HQ Italy. He was unable to make his way through and returned on 25 July in time to witness the major German drive which had engulfed Holland's party. Snapper was horrified by the virulent politics which had begun to undermine the Partisan movement; an Italian officer, Umberto Nari-Ferrari, had delivered the German plan of attack to the Partisans in Montefiorino at the end of July but when the Commissars discovered he was not a communist, they imprisoned him and his valuable intelligence went no further.

Holland and Davies were now fully equipped as a mission and moved north to the Alpe di Succiso in Parma province to contact a 200 strong *Giustizia e Liberta* band of Partisans under Ambanelli, described by Holland as "unprincipled and of strong passions". In early September the 47th *Garibaldi* and 12th *Garibaldi* bands were formed in the Ranzano and Calestano areas respectively. Politics tended to predominate until on 17 September the Germans ambushed the Comando Unico for Parma Province at Bosco, killing its commander and four officers and capturing all its documents. This was a severe blow and after Davies crossed the lines on 7 November to have a face to face discussion with Tac HQ No.1 Special Force in Florence regarding an uplift in Partisan supplies, Holland's mission experienced a disastrous day drop over the Monchio DZ when seven Halifax bombers overflew the area for four hours looking for the ground signal. 'There must have been at least six fighters escorting the dropping plane, and they kept circling round and round the area. Our position had clearly been pinpointed, and we could expect reprisals' [Hayhurst]. Most of the stores fell into the hands of the Fallschirm Jäger Mountain Battalion as Holland personally discovered when he went in search of them and almost bumped into five Austrian soldiers setting up a MG post a mere fifteen yards away from him. Once more the mission now consisting of Holland, Hayhurst, Hill and Tyler had to cache their stores and run for it. Holland and Hayhurst together with a mule were almost immediately separated from the others but later found them and the party spent the next five days in a deep cave, subsisting on bread and a large ball of butter the villagers had given them.

Frank Hayhurst remembered the scene well: 'There were many caves in the vicinity, with concealed entrances, and the Germans, who I am sure had a suspicion we were there, spent some time throwing hand-grenades into the

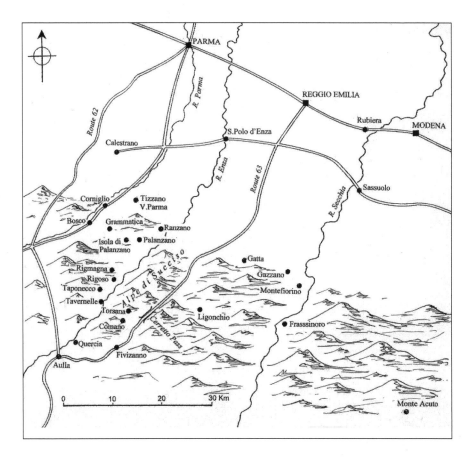

mouths of the more likely-looking ones. It was a sort of unwilling participation in a game of Russian roulette. When eventually we emerged, I was able to see a German column marching back down the road from Grammatica towards Corniglio. The *rastrellamento* was evidently over, but although the villagers gave us food we obviously could not stay there, and so we went back up towards Pianadetto and Valditacca where at least there were no roads. Winter had now set in, and we sent on our Partisans with the mules to make their own way upwards, while Charles and I plodded up through Rimagna to Rigoso in thick snow. The only real option we had was to get through the Passo di Lagastrello, over Monti Giogo and down into Tuscany. It was not a pleasant journey — 'Il Giogo' had a fearsome reputation for killing a few unwary travellers each year, and this was a particularly bad winter. Fortunately we had an excellent guide, and finally made it to Taponecco and Tavernelle. I took up residence in the loft of one of the village houses (not that it would have done much good if any Germans had arrived) and resigned myself to a diet of chestnuts, which was the only food available. We had them boiled, roasted, made into soup and, of course, as *polenta di castagne*. From now on things could only improve, and we moved back up to Rigoso. I set up my aerial, and we organised a small daylight drop for just before Christmas. Rigoso looked like a picture postcard — the sun was shining, the snow sparkling, and the coloured parachutes were dropping perfectly on target all round us. Besides arms, ammunition, boots and clothing for the Partisans, we received some welcome tinned food and a few bottles of whisky'.

The most pressing dilemma faced by the Partisans was how to best organize themselves before the rapidly approaching winter set in. They had survived the winter of 1943-44 in the mountains but in much smaller numbers than their current strength. Captain Mario Nardi, the Modena Chief of Staff, argued that it was impractical to keep his 1,200 strong formation of Partisans together in the mountains during the winter months and it was more sensible for 900 to cross the line into liberated Italy, leaving 300 well-equipped men behind to continue the fight; so in October, Armando, the Commander General of the Modena Partisans, duly crossed the lines with 700 men. The Reggio Partisans remained undecided until in early November a German drive brought the issue to a head. The BLO, Johnston, initially endorsed the idea of them crossing the lines, indeed he suggested raising the amount to two thirds. However, Commissar Eros forcefully objected, pointing out that as they had all survived the winter of 1943-1944, they should stay put, providing the British arranged adequate supply drops. If these failed to materialize, then Eros agreed to the Partisans crossing on the proviso that Johnston would take personal responsibility for relieving the pressure on a large number of Germans. He reluctantly agreed.

Throughout that winter, resentment smouldered away between the different Partisan political factions, particularly over the allocation of precious supplies, with the BLOs often finding themselves caught in the middle. Only fifty per cent of the Partisans had a coat or a blanket and fifty per cent were without boots. When a drop was due on a DZ controlled by the Green Flames, Vincenzo Corti, the commander of 4th *Garibaldi* battalion of 26 Brigata, ordered his men to go to the Drop Ground to steal the stores as soon as they touched the ground before they were all appropriated by the competition. The Green Flames promptly arrested two of his men which sparked off a furious reaction; Corti concentrated his entire battalion on the heights overlooking Gova and threatened to destroy the whole Green Flame Brigata of 270 men, including Major Wilcockson who happened to be there at the time. The Partisan leaders descended on the scene to adjudicate but it was Wilcockson who defused the situation by saying there was no proof against the two *Garibaldini* who had been arrested and adroitly ordered their release.

On 7 January 1945, the Germans started another drive in Modena and eastern Reggio and the Comando Unico quickly left with the British Mission and only came to a halt when finally calmed down by Holland. Five out of nine Green Flame detachments had disbanded, leaving the 26th Brigata at Ligonchio and Gatta weakened and forced to withdraw after three days. The drive stopped on 20 January, leading to bitter recriminations between the Partisan bands except for their shared loathing of the commanding general, General Monti, who all agreed had to go. It was only now that the Partisans re-emerged into the open and started to fight off incursions into their area. Snow was still on the ground but by the end of February the zone was fortified and ready. Colonel Paul Ceschi, the new Comando Unico commander, had done an excellent job of reorganizing the various bands* and in the process executing thirty Partisans for theft and sentencing the disreputable Ambanelli to ten years. On 24 January, Snapper brokered a meeting between the Partisan commanders under the auspices of the new Reggio Emilia BLO Captain Michael Lees. In February, Jim Davies returned bringing with him Captain John Stott of the Intelligence Corps who was an expert in the interrogation of captured Germans. Resources in men and material were finally arriving.

Envelope Blue had been reorganized in January as Toffee, with communications switched from Bari to Tac HQ in Florence, a change greatly welcomed

---

* By March 1945, the Toffee area had 3,300 armed and organised men in the field.

by SOE officers in the field since it speeded up answers to their queries and also formed a closer bond between field and base. When Holland had arrived in Torsana, he met an escaped POW called Captain T.G. Philipsz and allocated him the task of organizing an intelligence service covering Routes 62 and 63 up to the Garfagnana front. Holland also told him to reorganise and rearm the 4th Apuania Brigata and the Borrini Brigata which occupied to area on either side of Route 63. Holland's assessment of these two brigades was that they were 'very badly armed, ill clothed and led by extreme communist elements" with 'stupid criminally inefficient commanders*'; furthermore the food shortages in the area were appalling. Philipsz found the commander of the Apuania Brigata "incompetent, pleasure-loving and lazy individual" who left the day to day running of the brigade to his political commissar, Benassi. He engineered the replacement of both of them by Lieutenant Gianni, a former tank officer, who immediately reorganised the brigade on military lines and started a series of actions on Route 63. The Borrini Brigata was also taken to task and 'when finally organized with the correct chain of command these brigades fought so well that they killed or wounded over 250 of the enemy, captured 900 in combat and rounded up a further 1,000 during the final stages of the offensive'[†].

The mission now primarily operated as a military intelligence organization – Philipz had built it up from its original staff of seven to forty-nine – and three intelligence collecting centres were established at Rogoso, Palanzano and Corniglio, run by Philipsz, Hill and Tyler, who as the manager of the Hotel Adlon in Berlin before the war, turned out to be a natural intelligence officer. Twelve female agents, *'staffette'*, were recruited and trained to go down on the plain to check targets and verify information; one of them, a mature lady known as Maddalena, would go down into Parma, pick up a German officer and, while he was asleep, make off with his pistol and papers. This was dangerous work and one of the girls caught by the SD in Parma was interrogated twenty-six times in fourteen days. Subjected to electric shocks and badly bruised, she was finally released but not before giving away everything she knew.

During this period Holland moved with Hayhurst and the W/T set to the Castiglioni farm overlooking the hydro-electric station at Isola di Palanzano where they stayed until the final move to Parma took place. Captain Neil

---

*   Holland letter to Officer commanding Tac HQ dated 10 May 1945
†   Holland letter to Macintosh 9 March 1945
‡   Report by Captain T.G.Philipsz page 5.

Dakota dropping stores

Oughtred joined the mission in April as LO to the Comando Unico. In March and April, eighty plane loads of stores were dropped which compensated for the abysmal experience of February when three sorties failed to find the ground signals. Runways were limited to strips for Fieschler Storch's and Holland supervised three extractions, including Lieutenant James of the USAF whose injured leg was of concern* since 'all the various quacks who have seen him here not one had so much as one centimetre of elastoplasts and very little more sense' and that of Captain Michael Lees after he had been wounded in the SAS attack on the German HQ at Albinea.

A constant thorn in the side of Holland and his fellow BLOs was the activities of the American OSS. In a letter to Major Macintosh on 19 April, Major Jim Davies at Modena Partisan HQ did not pull his punches: 'Activities of OSS here stink to high heaven...there are too many missions here and with unknown responsibilities'. Holland was more tactful, enquiring 'Why should all Partisans west of here be well dressed, booted, armed [to the extent of eight bazookas per brigade etc.] whilst these here are clothed to about seventy per cent and booted to about fifty per cent? It is very hard to find an answer to this and a certain amount of bad feeling has thus originated'.

---

*   Holland letter to Macintosh 9 March 1945

On 5 April 1945, orders came from AFHQ for an all-out assault and soon all eight Partisan brigades* were engaged in attacking enemy garrisons in the foothills and hampering road movement on Route 62. On 20 April, 143 and 144 Brigate blew down a thirty-five metre section of cliff in the Cerretto pass area, effectively blocking Route 63. After Aulla, Quercia and Fivizanno were occupied by Partisans, Parma was invested from 22 to 25 April with Captains Stewart and Oughtred directing Partisan assault brigades. On 26 April, Captain Beatt arrived from Tac HQ and he and Holland drove into Parma together the next day.

In Holland's Officer's Report dated 14 May 1945, the Army wrote 'this officer has given every satisfaction in the field and is recommended for further operational work in the Far East'. Praise indeed. As it happened, Holland ended the war as Allied Communications Officer of Civil Posts and Telecommunications North Italy, a position that perfectly reflected his aptitude and love of signals and his flair for organization and leadership. There was nothing of the *prima donna* in Holland; he was both a team leader and a team player. Through skillful and patient negotiation, both with the Partisans and his own SOE colleagues, he managed to establish a highly effective *modus operandi* of how to best conduct operations in the Reggio Emilia region.

Major Charles Holland: 20 April 1945: recommendation for immediate MC

Major Holland was infiltrated by parachute into the Apennines in July 1944. His object was to unite the various formations of Partisans into a disciplined force under a joint command. Despite many difficulties and political differences, and although constantly attacked by enemy troops, he succeeded in building up a formidable Partisan force in his area.

During the exceptionally hard winter, attacks by the enemy increased in violence and the Partisan formations were threatened with total destruction, but, by his personal efforts, Major Holland not only kept his men under control but maintained their morale at a high level and was also able to organize and execute frequent sabotage attacks and ambushes on enemy lines of communication. Under his personal guidance and leadership, the

---

* 12 *Garibaldi* Bde, Pablo Bde, 3rd Julia Bde, 143rd *Garibaldi* Bde, Mountain bn 3rd Julia Bde, 4th Apuania Bde, Borrini Bde, 7th Julia Bde. In all about 2,600 armed men.

W/T Operator Frank Hayhurst

Partisans have accounted for over seventy enemy vehicles, 200 men killed and more than 300 wounded and captured.

He operated in enemy occupied territory for over eight months, during the whole of which time he had to live under conditions of great discomfort, constantly on the move to avoid capture, often without food and subjected to constant attacks by the enemy. Despite this, he maintained constant contact with base and has shown outstanding qualities of leadership and courage which had a great influence on the morale of the Partisan forces in his area.

Awarded

Captain Charles Holland: 19 August 1944: recommendation for MC

Captain Holland was dropped into the Peloponnese as Signals officer in September 1943. On 7 October he went down to Aiyion where he remained for several days to arrange the tapping of the German telephone wires. He carried out his work successfully, working in a building on which there was a German guard.

Captain Holland has made extensive tours of the Peloponnese to ensure the correct working of the wireless links. These journeys have always been made without *Andartes* protection and often when German drives were taking place in the area. At all time Captain Holland has shown compete disregards for danger and a great technical efficiency, as a result of which the Peloponnesian communications net has been kept going despite very difficult working conditions. I therefore recommend him for the award of the MC

Revised to MBE

8

Colonel John Stevens[*], DSO, OBE, TD
Major Derek Dodson, MC
Captain Pat O'Regan, MC and bar

On VE day 1945, John Stevens emerged from the shadows of clandestine warfare with one of the most distinguished and courageous SOE service records, initially as a Staff Officer and then as a senior field operative. He had served in four separate countries, all with their own complex political and military problems, innate dangers and often Herculean challenges, and on each occasion, with his superb powers of critical analysis, inexhaustible energy and relentless determination to overcome what appeared to many at the time to be insurmountable difficulties, succeeded in carrying out the aims and objectives entrusted to him.

John Stevens was born on 7 November 1913 and after attending Winchester was admitted a solicitor in 1937. In the same year he joined the Territorial Army's The Princess Louise's Kensington Regiment. Mobilized in the summer of 1939, he was attached to the Middlesex Regiment [Duke of Cambridge's Own] as Intelligence Officer and in September went to France with the 4th Division. Rescued at Dunkirk, he was ordered to return to France in the hectic first two weeks of June 1940 but the train taking troops to the defence of Paris was halted and the expedition withdrawn. As an officer with obvious potential for the General Staff, in January 1941 he was sent on a short wartime course at the Staff College at Camberley and then after a tour as Machine Gun Officer in Sussex flew to Cairo to join the Spears' Mission then confronting the Vichy French in the Levant. The Syria-Lebanon campaign reached its successful conclusion in mid-July while he was in transit and so shortly after arriving in Cairo, he joined SOE, having been recruited by fellow Wykhamist, Major J.S.A.Pearson, who ran the Balkan Desk.

At first he worked with the fledgling Yugoslav resistance for which he was awarded the OBE in recognition of his outstanding contribution: then at the beginning of 1943, he was put in charge of the Greek desk at SOE Cairo. Because of the confused situation there in regard to the activities and

---

[*]   Later Sir John Stevens KCMG

motivations of EAM and ELAS [the Greek Communist controlled National Liberation Front and its military wing], it was decided to send Stevens on a tour of the mountains to make an independent assessment. He was dropped in late March 1943 near Avlaki in the Pindus, code name Lieutenant Colonel Brown. He left Greece by *caique* in June and was interned when he disembarked near Smyrna in Turkey for wearing British uniform. He was eventually released but arrived back too late in Cairo to take part in the stormy meeting between Brigadier Eddie Myers* and the six Greek guerrilla leaders, who had been flown there on 10 August to discuss future resistance plans. Perhaps he was fortunate since 'the affair of the Cairo delegation' as it became known ended in a shambles with ELAS adopting a strident anti-monarchist stance which unsettled both Churchill and the Foreign Office. Heads rolled including those of Lord Glenconner, political head of SOE in Cairo, and Brigadier Mervyn Keble, his Chief of Staff; Brigadier Myers was never allowed back into Greece on the orders of the King of Greece himself.

Steven's report on *Present Conditions in Central Greece* ran to 162 paragraphs. He did not pull any punches as to what he found. For instance, when reaching his conclusions, he wrote that 'left-wing dictatorships, judged by British standards, are drab affairs where the power is held by uncouth half-educated types who have no feeling for tradition. As dictatorships go, the EAM is no different from the usual run. Upstart leaders eat the best food and drink the best wine. Private vendettas are settled. Truth is twisted and suppressed in private interests. But the worst feature is the foundation of gross deceit on which this structure is built, for I am absolutely convinced that it is not genuine. What the rank and file of EAM believe they are furthering is the cause for democracy as laid down in the Atlantic Charter. What, in fact, they are furthering are the political careers of a small clique of Left-wing politicians.' However, he was in no doubt that the EAM/ELAS *andartes* were by far 'the most efficient organization for fighting the Axis in Greece...' and the only ones who could inflict serious damage on the German occupying forces and their lines of communication. The stark problem was that their Communist affiliations directly conflicted with British government support of the King of Greece: SOE BLOs sat uncomfortably in the middle of this strange strategic contradiction.

---

* In November 1942, Brigadier Myers had led Operation Harling which had resulted in the destruction of the Gorgopotamus bridge on the critical Germany-Piraeus-Tobruk supply route. However, it was too late to influence Montgomery's planning for battle of El Alamein and the FM thus had little time for SOE during the rest of the war.

John Stevens by Peter McMullen, Greece 1943

In his final paragraph, Stevens rather balefully concluded that 'I have tried faithfully to portray Free Greece as I saw it during the course of my three month tour. If the tone of my report is somewhat depressing, it is because it is a sorry sight to see great patriotism, courage and self-sacrifice stunted and rendered sterile by political chicanery and above all lack of leadership.' In September 1943, Stevens again jumped into Greece, this time to take command of the fifteen strong BMM in the Peloponnese which was in the process of separating from the Central Greece BMM since there were few political or military synergies between the 'mainland' and the Morea. On his arrival, he observed the grim spectacle of a civil war in which ELAS systematically set about destroying all non-communist resistance fighters. From then on, this was to mar relations between the BMM and EAM/ELAS since Stevens, acting on orders from Cairo, refused to supply them with arms and equipment until they had rehabilitated the other nationalist bands. Since they had killed most of them, this was a tall order.

On a daily basis life was frustrating and dangerous. Stevens personally conducted a surprise raid on an ELAS HQ company to check the accuracy of their nominal role, which 'disclosed, not unexpectedly, that a number of people figuring on the roll had not been born yet.' On another occasion, after a German drive, he returned to his base in Mikaleika to find that his stores had been stolen by the *andartes*. He followed the footprints of one of them bold enough to wear his own rubber waders into a house where he demanded their return and that of his personal clothing. One *andarte* drew his knife and the others cocked their rifles and threatened to shoot him. It was only the fortuitous arrival of an *andartes* officer that saved his life. In December 1943, along with the rest of the mission, Stevens became embroiled in the aftermath of the German sweep against Kalavryta, triggered by the murder of eighty German soldiers by ELAS fighters. Rather than flee from the area, Stevens ordered his men to stay put and hide up in the mountains, an action that greatly enhanced their prestige with the villagers.

Life for the BMM became increasingly difficult and Stevens left the Peloponnese with most of his mission in June 1944. In the prefix to his *Second Report on Conditions in the Peloponnese* [21 September 1943 – 21 May 1944], he volunteered that 'it is my duty to point out to all who read this report that my experiences, particularly in the Peloponnese, have embittered me greatly'. Stevens had witnessed at first-hand how the Germans had exploited the senseless situation of Greek fighting Greek, how the real 'losers' were the villagers and farmers who lost their livestock, foodstuffs, homes and often entire villages. He warned of the grave dangers that lay ahead for Greece if EAM and ELAS were not brought to heel. On returning to England, he was almost immediately dropped into France, first into Brittany and then near the Belfort Gap.

The first British mission into Piedmont in the summer of 1944, codenamed Flap, had been led by Major Neville Darewski, son of the famous band leader Herman Darewski. Darewski, who had completed a punishing six month tour with SOE in Slovenia the previous year, managed to achieve a great deal before his death in a road accident on 15 November 1944. He had organised the two principal Partisan bands of *Garibaldini* and *Autonomi*, supplied them with air drops and built a landing strip for Lysander aircraft at Vesime. It was to this make-shift facility that Stevens flew by B25 Mitchell on 18 November with Captain Hugh Ballard and a W/T operator; knowing that a *rastrellamento* was in full swing, it came as no surprise to them when the defensive perimeter of the airstrip came under fire as they landed.

Stevens' general terms of reference were to report on military and political conditions in Piedmont but more urgent was the need to rally the Partisans who were fading away in the face of sustained German attacks. However, right from the start, the mission's signals plan was unsatisfactory. Lieutenant

Lysander at the Landing Ground at Vesime

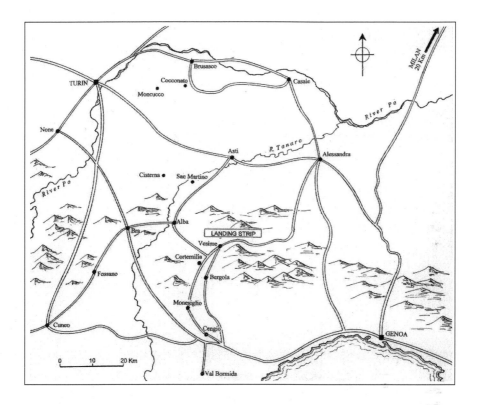

Colonel Selby Cope who had come out by Lysander, leaving both his own and Major Darewski's W/T Operators behind, had informed Stevens that the Italian Pluma mission which was in situ could be relied on for an extra link to base. Unknown to Stevens, Darewski's W/T Operator had left on the same B25 Mitchell that brought Stevens in, having first buried his set which was never found again. Furthermore, the Pluma mission, having cached their set, was on the run from the Germans. The battery to Steven's own set was stolen on the first day and it was not surprising that beset by these difficulties, it took some three weeks before reliable communications were established.

Stevens's team soon discovered that the Partisans had little or no intelligence service and consequently had only a vague idea about what was going on in the adjoining areas. What was patently apparent was that there was no sign of a let-up by the Germans and the mission had to abandon all its personal kit and go on the run, never more than two to three hours ahead of enemy patrols, forced to live in the woods by day and travel by night. They tried moving West in an attempt to find less dangerous ground but the plan was thwarted by unexpected enemy troop movements and by 1 December they were more or less back where they started except at least the onset of winter had had the mitigating effect of reducing enemy vehicle and foot patrols. However, the bad weather also meant that it was impractical to expect any airdrops from Bari. At this point, Stevens left Ballard and set off on his own to try and contact the regional CLN and it was not until just before Christmas that they joined up again, only to be caught up in a new enemy drive that opened on 23 December. Stevens was itching to return to Bari and file his report but the heavy snows which fell at the end of December and the beginning of January ruled out Lysander exfiltration operations.

The situation which Stevens had found in Piedmont and West Liguria was somewhat surprising. The German forces of 5th Mountain and 34th Divisions were winding down their anti-Partisan operations and preparing for the evacuation of Turin though there appeared to be no set timetable. The slack was being taken up by an estimated 45,000 Republican fascist troops who assisted the Germans in internal security. Stevens was scathing about their performance as fighting troops, finding them 'without exception poor...their discipline and morale is low, their equipment poor and turn-out Central American'. As far as the estimated 11,000 strong Partisan forces went, Stevens identified five 'brands' – *Autonomo* [25%], *Garibaldi* [40%], *Giellisti* [30%], *Matteotti* and Christian Democrats [5%]. Despite their party colours, 'the Partisans seem to have much in common, both virtues and vices...they are not brave and have a flare for muddle. On the other hand, they are well-meaning and co-operative. Like all Italians, they are moody and unreliable. They are extremely good saboteurs.' Engagements with Republican forces seemed to be limited to long range MG duels and although there was supposedly a unified CLN military command vested in General Trabucchi, the five parties tended to interpret his orders as they saw fit. Not surprisingly, his relationship with the SOE Italian Pluma mission was lukewarm, given his observations that 'Antonelli plays cards, Mario drinks and Georgi is too grand to work: all are extremely windy and spendthrifts.' Stevens consequently noted that 'it is a cardinal rule that one should never rely on the Partisans for one's personal safety, still less for the safety of one's kit'.

The everyday life which Stevens observed in Piedmont was far from easy. Based for a time in hiding with the Donadei family in Cuneo where he mastered both the Tarocchi card game and the knack of hiding down a well, he noted that meat, salt and sugar were scarce and a grain shortage was forecasted for the coming May, although he was surprised by how much could still be bought in the shops. Medical supplies were also scant. Most industries were closed down due to lack of coal, removal of plant and equipment by the Germans to the Reich and deportation of labour, especially young men, to Germany to work for the Todt Organization. Few trains ran, most horses had been requisitioned by the army and the unwary cyclist likely to be stopped by troops and have his machine stolen. All military movement took place at night due to Allied air superiority during daylight hours. With the Germans in charge of printing money, prices had doubled in the last three months and a rise in inflation looked set.

As far as the Allies' efforts to organize the Italian resistance were concerned, Stevens reiterated what many BLOs had privately expressed, namely that 'a disturbing feature of the present situation in Piedmont is the fact that there are British, American and French Allied missions all operating independently. This gives the Italians a wonderful chance of playing one off against the other, and weakens the missions' effectiveness. Whereas differences between the British and Americans can be smoothed out by 15th Army Group, the French report to SHAFE which presents greater difficulties particularly in their support for separatist movements in Val d'Aosta.'

In his report of 3 March 1945, written in the field before he returned to Bari, Stevens warned of the difficulties which lay ahead. To avoid replicating the 1944 situation in Greece where two groups of political opponents armed by the Allies had started to fight each other, Stevens advocated stressing the intelligence gathering function of the Allied missions. If it proved necessary to stop arming the Partisans in order to head off the possibility of a civil war, then at least there would be a justification for continuing their presence. Another concern was the potential lengthy interval between liberation and the arrival of Allied troops, with a free-for-all between Partisans, fascists and German stragglers almost inevitable. Finally, there was evidence of growing French interest in Piedmont which begged the question as to whether a French occupation might not be a good idea to preserve the peace after German withdrawal.

Stevens concluded his report by predicting that the Partisan movement would dramatically expand over the next three months and a parallel weakening of the Republican fascist forces would take place as Germany continued to lose the war. He also saw a sharpening of political differences between the various Italian political parties including the possibility of clashes between their military brigades unless French expansionist actions aroused Italian nationalism, which would in turn have a unifying effect. The major impending problem as he saw it would be how to restore order in an area where presently the Germans were the only stable factor. The all important question of whether the CLN would be able to establish its authority

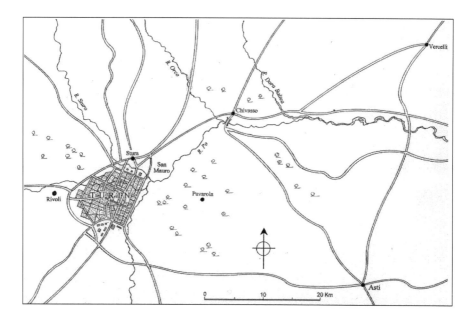

and maintain an all-party coalition would remain in doubt right up to the moment of liberation.

Bringing with him twenty-five year old Major Derek Dodson as his second-in-command, Stevens returned to Piedmont on 2 April. A seasoned Greek hand like Stevens, Dodson had started his career as a professional soldier, commissioned in 1939 as Second Lieutenant in the Royal Scots Fusiliers and posted to India with the 1st Battalion. In 1941 he joined SOE, arriving the following year in Cairo, where he helped to supply agents in occupied countries such as Greece and Yugoslavia. In September 1943 as Italy was in the process of leaving the war, he flew into Greece, landing on an isolated strip near Kardhitsa in Thessaly, where he was fortunate to meet the Italian General

Turin, the industrial capital of Italy

Adolfo Infante, commander of the Pinerolo [24] Division, and thus was able to obtain from him the complete order-of-battle of the Axis forces in the Balkans. In January 1944 he made his second trip to Greece, parachuting into Epirus to meet General Napoleon Zervas, the anti-Communist EDES resistance leader. Dodson returned to Cairo in March, travelling by *caique* to Turkey, where he was narrowly escaped arrest as he crossed the main square of Izmir in full military uniform. In August 1944 he again parachuted into Greece, dropping into Skaramagas in Thessaly from where he hitched a ride on a fire engine to the centre of Athens and found himself carried shoulder-high by cheering crowds. A few weeks later, he headed north to Thessaloniki and was the first BLO to enter the city on 30 October.

The plan was for Stevens to enter Turin in civilian clothes and control any Partisan uprising from within by direct contact with the CLN and also attempt to control political developments*. Dodson was to remain outside but as near to Turin as possible and control the Partisan attack. He was also to provide Stevens with his W/T link to HQ and to bring his HQ into the city when it had been liberated. Delayed by an impending enemy drive, Stevens set off on 9 April and bicycled to Fossano where he stayed in the local hotel, somewhat unnerved by an impromptu celebration held there by local German commanders. The following day, he was driven in a van to Turin through no less than seven roadblocks and successfully reached his safe house. On 14 April, he met with the Regional Military Committee [CMRP] and five days later met with the whole of the CLN. He was not impressed with the former: General Trabucchi, who he had previously met, had been arrested and replaced by General Drago, who "though charming, I found incompetent and I ordered him to be replaced."

He was confronted by three problems. First, the Partisan military command had issued an order to all Partisans to march on Turin at a given signal. This was directly contrary to 15th Army Group instructions, so Stevens rescinded it.

---

* Appendix 1 to 15 Army Group Operations Instruction No 5, 12 April 1945. Treatment of Partisans in Northern Italy. *"On their entry into Northern Italy Allied troops will make contact with Partisans in numbers considerably larger than any hitherto encountered. These partisans have in large measure loyally obeyed the orders of the Allies and have caused very concrete losses and embarrassment to the enemy; they have thus earned as good treatment as can reasonably be afforded them. In addition, in the absence of fair and yet firm treatment and, in the absence of positive and constructive employment, they might form a disillusioned and dangerous element under the disorganised conditions likely to exist during the period immediately following the withdrawal of the Germans and the arrival of the Allies . . ."*

Furthermore, he stated that no Partisan was to leave his own operational zone. Later, he was to be roundly criticized for this by Marxist historians, accused of being anti-Communist and a proxy of the Agnelli family who owned Fiat. Indeed, Vittorio Valleta, the Managing Director of Fiat, had been rescued by Stevens who refused to hand him over to CLN to be tried as a collaborator. Secondly, the fusion of the various Partisan bands into a single force was proceeding very slowly, though there was little that he could do about this. Thirdly, the *Garibaldini* and communist politicians were adamant that policing should be left to them and not the Carabinieri. Stevens solved this last problem by forcing the CLN to accept a percentage of Carabinieri into the Partisan police to give them 'technical backing'. To flex their muscles, the CLN ordered a one-day strike on 18 April which was a resounding success; tellingly, the Germans and Fascists took no countermeasures.

Around this time, Stevens met up with Captain Pat O'Regan who was commanding a mission at None and arranged a regular courier service to him. Pat O'Regan was one of SOE's most colourful and successful operatives in Italy. A Classics scholar and son of a Marlborough schoolmaster, he had originally joined the RAMC as a private in 1940 before transferring to the Intelligence Corps and then been seconded to SOE for operations in Greece. His first mission, Hedge, was sent to the French-Italian border region on 1 August 1944 where they set up base at Guillestre in the Hautes Alpes. Despite vigorous cross-border activity – he crossed into Italy at great risk no less than three times* – the mission never really got off the ground due to intense German patrolling and so he was reinserted into the Turin area where he lived as a civilian, on one occasion having to replace his 'double-breasted purple concoction' for Italian tweed. His British Army uniform had been discovered by a villager and cut up to make winter clothing for a baby.

Establishing his HQ in Pinerolo in a draughty Palazzo belonging to two old ladies, the Comtessas Cumiana, who were famous for their loathing of the Fascisti, O'Regan set up a sabotage network to hinder the German withdrawal North. Although well versed in classical Latin, his Italian was rudimentary to start with which meant that he always travelled on public transport with a Partisan escort. On one occasion as he prepared to leave the Palazzo, a German General arrived in his staff car and announced that he had requisitioned it as his HQ. Quick witted as ever, the Comtessas ordered their staff to pull up the floorboards of the drawing room and prepare a hiding place for O'Regan. As the last carpet was relaid, the General walked in and set up his

---

* 10 August 1944, 20 September 1944, 19 November 1944

office. Fortunately his tenure was short lived and O'Regan re-emerged from his 'hole' a day later, extremely cold and stiff but still a free man.

O'Regan was running two Austrian signallers, Gefreiters Biegelmeier and Stachl, at General Schlemmer's LXXV Corps HQ, who supplied him with copies of all enemy operational signals and orders of battle. He also had contacts at the SS HQ in Turin where he used to stay at the apartment of Giovanni Hertel, the interpreter of Captain Schmidt of the SD, and was thus able to establish that they knew nothing of Stevens's alias or the address where he was staying. Stevens remembered him later as '...extraordinary brave and always cheerful....even disguised as a pig dealer [according to his papers] he was an obvious Irishman and one of the most charming I have ever known."Under the cloak of anonymity, Stevens was therefore able to move freely about the city by tram and all messages were delivered to him by cut-outs, usually at tram stops. Telephoning was always done from nearby shops by the family who hid him. He had German and Italian papers and when he moved about he generally spoke German. He was never stopped.

Dodson had come in on the same plane as Stevens and within a week had set up HQ Piedmont in a farm house at Pavarolo, just east of Moncucco in the Monferrato. With him were Captain Sayers, his signals officer, and Major Hope, the area BLO. Two-way contact by courier was established with Stevens in Turin by 13 April. A series of meetings with the military command of the CLN followed and Dodson himself moved to Cocconato from where he found it easier to keep in touch with events in Turin. On 18 April, Dodson learnt of Major Hope's death [as a result of an accidental discharge] at Cisterna; he took control himself of all political liaison in Hope's area and split the military liaison duties in two, with Captain Powell in charge of the area south of the main road. At 2200 hours on 23 April, Dodson received an unconfirmed report that German forces were preparing to leave Turin that night.

The battle for Turin had begun but with a whimper for no move took place and it was at the same time the following evening that Dodson received news that the whole of Zone VIII Partisans under Barbato was moving on Turin, exactly what Stevens had made clear he did not want, for 15th Army Group were not ready. Couriers flew back and forth between the various parties and Dodson met Barbato at six the next morning, who told him he proposed to attack Turin at 2300 hours that night. Meanwhile Captain O'Regan had sent Stevens the entire German LXXV Corps withdrawal plan including the three choices of escape routes for the 34th Division.

---

*   KCLHL: Letter Stevens to Mrs O'Regan

Summoning a meeting of the CMRP*, Stevens ordered a general strike and laid down that no Partisans were to leave their zones except for III, IV and VIII who were to attack the city but only on his orders. The unsuitable General Drago was sacked at this meeting and replaced by Colonel Contini.

Now back in the loop, Dodson ordered Barbato to stand fast and to prepare for all round defence. On the afternoon of 26 April, Stevens held his last meeting with the CMRP when he was roundly criticised by the *Garibaldini* for halting the VIII zone attack. Refusing to budge, he ordered 2,000 Partisans to be infiltrated into the city to defend the Fiat and Lancia factories and the Stura electricity substation. Realizing that he needed to meet up with Dodson, he sent a courier asking him to come into the city, which, after quickly changing into civilian clothes, Dodson duly did, only to find he couldn't contact Stevens as the telephone exchange was down. He returned to Pavarolo where he found General Clark's order for an all-out Partisan attack waiting for him. He immediately ordered Barbato to attack Turin with all available forces and then moved to San Mauro where he established the Mission command post. Stevens only finished the meeting with the CMRP at 1730 hrs and just managed to get back to his safe house before curfew in the midst of fierce street fighting.

The Partisan attack on 27 April went in successfully though for the whole day Stevens was confined to the area around his house by heavy street fighting. The centre of the city was still held by a strong German force of about 3,000 troops supported by tanks and backed up by 5,000 Fascist troops. That afternoon, Dodson met General Trabucchi in San Mauro to whom he passed on General Clark's order; in response, Trabucchi promised to mount a further attack as soon as he got into the city. Stevens meanwhile, realizing that he could no longer control the CMRP from within the city, sent a courier to Dodson handing over command. As Dodson headed back to the city to inspect preparations for the final attack, Trabucchi informed him that it would go in at 0500 hours the next morning. During the night of 27/28 April, the Germans withdrew in good order, leaving only the Republican garrison for the Partisans to contend with and by 0915 hours, Dodson was able to join Stevens in his house. Apart from heavy sniping, Turin was entirely in Partisan hands by 1200 hours on 28 April.

However the situation was far from secure as there were still about 50,000 German and Republican troops in the area surrounding Turin. So when news came that General Stets, commanding the German 5th Moun-

---

* Piedmontese Regional Military Command created in 1943.

tain Division, wished to discuss terms of surrender, Dodson and one of the Partisan commanders dashed off to meet him on the Rivoli road. The attempt proved abortive. A Partisan attack on the night of 28 April resulted in the Germans retreating north of the Po and, in the process, blowing the Chivasso bridge which meant Axis troops could no longer use the east bank of the River Po. Two further flanking attacks on 34th Division on 29 April were partially successful and by the evening of 30 April all threats to Turin had effectively ceased. General Schlemmer finally surrendered his forces to SOE's Major Redhead, who had swum the River Po at Chivasso on 29 April after the bridge had been blown. Taken blindfolded to Schlemmer's HQ at two in the morning, after lengthy discussions, he persuaded the General to sign a provisional article of surrender at the mission HQ in Biella on 2 May.

One of Stevens's principal preoccupations was the possibility of a French advance into the Piedmont and the likely catastrophic consequences of a French occupation of Turin for such an outcome would inflame Italian nationalism, ever mindful of French annexation in 1801. When he received news of the arrival of French patrols in Rivoli fourteen kilometres to the west of the city on 30 April, Stevens knew he had to organise an immediate occupation of Turin by American troops and so despatched Dodson to find the forward elements of the US Fifth Army. He duly found them near Alessandria ninety kilometres to the southeast and urged them to bring forward their arrival. The following morning the American advanced guard swept into the city, thereby averting what could have been a most testing Franco-Italian political fracas.

With the fighting over, Stevens, Dodson and O'Regan played a leading role in resuscitating and directing the civil administration of Turin, including the housing and feeding of 10,000 armed workmen and 7,000 Partisans. Banks and shops reopened on 28 April and the trams restarted despite intermittent sniping. Stevens broadcast to the population appealing to them to return to work and urging the Partisans to continue to fight the Germans for the war was by no means over. A food crisis was narrowly averted by escorting a supply convoy from Vercelli into the city and the much vaunted political crisis never materialized thanks to the good collaboration between the parties and the Regional CLN. However, nothing could be done about the instant re-establishment of law and order and over 1,000 fascists were executed by the Partisans in the first week. Disarming the Partisans proved tricky and it was not until the arrival of the AMG Patriot Officer that the process got underway. Stevens and Dodson handed over their responsibilities to the AMG on 5 May.

Colonel John Stevens: 27 May 1945: recommendation for immediate DSO

In October 1944, it was decided to send a senior British Liaison officer to the enemy occupied province of Piedmont to coordinate and direct the work of the several British missions already in the area. Lieutenant Colonel Stevens was appointed for this task and in November was landed to an airstrip south of Turin. The circumstances of his entry were particularly gallant in that he choose to be infiltrated in a plane sent most urgently to exfiltrate personnel who were on the run and gathered together on the landing strip already being attacked and under enemy fire.

In order to complete his task Lieutenant Colonel Stevens spent over three months continuously on the move from one mission to another through areas infested with German and Fascist troops, SS and spies, encouraging, advising and coordinating the various Partisan and underground forces into a unified and powerful fighting force.

In March 1945 Lieutenant Colonel Stevens was exfiltrated by Lysander and returned to his base to report and receive detailed instructions from 15th Army Group for the final stages of the attack. He returned to the field on 2 April 1945 and after visiting all his missions and giving them detailed instructions he entered Turin in civilian clothes in order to effect the closest possible liaison with the CLN during the vital stages of the Allied assault. For over four weeks, speaking little Italian and with inadequate identity papers, Lieutenant Colonel Stevens lived in Turin in civilian clothes maintaining close and constant liaison with the CLN and directing, in agreement with them, the whole Partisan effort in Piedmont. On several occasions, walking or driving through the streets of Turin, he was stopped and questioned by Fascist officers and only managed to bluff his way out of his difficulties by speaking German. Throughout this period, in spite of the almost insuperable difficulties, he remained in constant W/T contact with base and with his mission and was able to control and direct the insurrection within Turin and the Partisan assaults on enemy forces from without, in accordance with directives issued by 15th Army Group.

By his great courage, superb leadership and devotion to duty, both as a clandestine worker and as a soldier at the head of his troops, Lieutenant Colonel Stevens was without doubt largely responsible for the successful liberation of Turin and for the routing of enemy forces in this area. He is most strongly recommended for the immediate award of a DSO.

Awarded

Colonel John Stevens: 19 November 1944: recommendation for DSO

Recommended for the award of the DSO in recognition of outstanding qualities of leadership in action. This officer volunteered to be parachuted behind the enemy lines in Brittany as the chief British Staff Officer to an inter-Allied Mission to the French Forces of the Interior, a mission in the organization of which he played a leading part.

After working night and day to enable the departure to be made in time to link up with the rapid movements in Normandy, Lieutenant Colonel Stevens with the mission was successfully parachuted to the field on the night of 5/6 August 1944. On the afternoon of 6 August a force of about 150 Germans of 2 Parachute Division attacked the HQ of the mission at the village of Kerrien*. The headquarters' staff of fifteen [including Lieutenant Colonel Stevens] aided by twenty men of the Maquis successfully defended the village until after nightfall when the Germans retired, leaving three dead, four prisoners and eighteen car-loads of equipment. The Allied losses were three civilian killed and one French officer [Lieutenant Martin] wounded.

This successful action, which took place very soon after the arrival of the mission and in which Lieutenant Colonel Stevens showed qualities of leadership of a very high order, acted as a stimulus and inspiration to the important resistance movement in Brittany. For his part in this operation it is recommended that Lieutenant Colonel Stevens be awarded the DSO.

Downgraded to Mention in Dispatched

Colonel John Stevens: June 1944: recommendation for immediate OBE

Colonel Stevens joined G[R] in November 1941 and for seven months did invaluable work as GSO2 Ops Yugoslavia and subsequently GSO2 Plans.

It was largely due to his initiative and foresight that Yugoslavia was developed as an SOE country and the foundations laid for the expansion of the Mission to its present large proportions.

In June 1942, Colonel Stevens was appointed Field Commander Egypt and put in charge of the post-occupational organization should Rommel's expected drive into Egypt materialize.

In September 1942, the threat to Egypt having lessened, Colonel Stevens became head of the Greek Section as GSO2 and was responsible for the infil-

---

* The Report of Jedburgh team Giles describes the situation in the vicinity in greater detail.

tration and maintenance of the Mission from the time of the original 'Harling' party under Brigadier Myers was infiltrated and successfully demolished the Gorgopotamos Bridge.

On 13 April 1943, Colonel Stevens parachuted into Greece to join the Mission and to bring back to Cairo the first hand information which was required for the development of the guerrilla army. The boat sent to collect Colonel Stevens in July failed to make the RV and it was left to his own initiative to get himself back to Cairo.

During his stay on the mainland and while searching for a boat to bring him out, Colonel Stevens on three occasions narrowly escaped capture by the Germans. He arrived in the Middle East after a period under arrest in Turkey, on 13 August 1943.

Stevens was then promoted to his present rank and sent into the Peloponnese on 21 September 1943 to take charge of the Allied Mission there. From then until his evacuation in June 1944, he was in control of the Mission and although subjected to great discourtesy and personal attacks by ELAS, he kept his officers and men up to their jobs and managed to establish a most valuable intelligence network throughout the country. It was entirely due to his personal courage in the face of great opposition from the *andartes* and the Germans that the Mission was enabled to remain in the country at all.

During these nine months Colonel Steven's HQ was subjected to direct attacks by the Germans on three separate occasions [8 December 1943, 26 February 1944 and 13 April 1944] and in each case although accurate shelling and mortar fire was brought to bear, he withdrew his W/T station intact and without casualties.

For displaying exceptional fortitude under very trying circumstances and for his display of personal bravery in the interests of the Mission in Greece, Colonel Stevens is recommended for the immediate award of the OBE.

Awarded

Major Derek Dodson: 25 May 1945: recommendation for immediate MC

Major Dodson landed by plane in enemy occupied territory at Vesime on 2 April 1945. He was given the task of organizing as quickly as possible a HQ as close to Turin as possible for the BMM in Piedmont attached to the Piedmont Regional Liberation Committee and the Piedmont Partisan Command. On 3 April Major Dodson travelled by car to the area Albugnano about fifteen miles east of Turin. This journey involved the crossing of two main roads and a railway constantly used by the enemy and passing three areas which the enemy actively patrolled.

On 6 April he established his HQ near Cocconato approximately twelve miles from Turin and summoned the local Partisan commands to make plans for eventual operations against Turin. He then made contact with the Partisan Command and with Lieutenant Colonel Stevens in Turin, organizing courier services to Turin, and passing all their wireless traffic.

On 19 April, Major Dodson was informed of the death of Major Hope, BLO for Asti Province. Major Dodson immediately went to Cisterna, Major Hope's HQ, and took over his duties until the arrival of a substitute. On 24 April he supervised the general mobilization of Partisan forces in his area and on 25 April he entered Turin in civilian clothes to confer with Lieutenant Colonel Stevens but owing to heavy street fighting, Lieutenant Colonel Stevens was unable to reach the RV.

On 26 April, Major Dodson organized and directed the Partisans in their attack on Turin and personally led the street fighting of the group of Partisans who entered the town from the East, remaining the whole day under enemy fire. He made a second attempt to get through to Lieutenant Colonel Stevens but after getting within 400 yards of his HQ was forced by enemy fire to abandon the attempt. During the afternoon the enemy counterattacked and forced the Partisans to give ground. Major Dodson immediately ordered up reinforcements and the situation turned in the Partisans' favour. By the morning of 27 April Turin had been cleared except for isolated points.

On the same day Major Dodson organized the Partisan operations against Chivasso and Carmagnola which resulted in ending the enemy threat to cut off Turin from the East and thereby isolate Turin.

Throughout this time Major Dodson had shown outstanding qualities of leadership and courage as well as great initiative. In addition, by great tact, he gained the complete confidence of the Partisans and was thereby able to exert a control over them without which the highly successful operation in and around Turin would not have been possible.

Awarded

Captain Pat O'Regan: 17 August 1945: recommendation for immediate bar to MC

Captain O'Regan entered Piedmont for the third time in November 1944 as BLO to the Italian Partisan forces in the area South West of Turin. He passed the winter months in this area organizing, equipping and training the Partisan Forces in preparation for a Spring offensive.

On 1 April 1945, the final phase of the Partisan campaign in the Piedmont began. Forces under Captain O'Regan, on 5 April, attacked and blew up the points on the railway station at Candiolo, thus causing a serious break in the enemy's lines of communication at a most vital time. Steps were also taken by him to ensure coordination of the Partisan forces in the protection of certain vital anti-scorch targets in the Saluzzo area.

Throughout this period, Captain O'Regan was in touch with two Austrian signallers and obtained from them all important messages coming into the German LXXV Corps HQ at Cumiana where he used to visit them. These messages gave all the movements of the German forces in the area and were immediately passed by Captain O'Regan to Lieutenant Colonel Stevens, the senior BLO in the Piedmont area, in Turin, to whom they were invaluable in controlling the Partisan operations against Turin in the last days of the offensive.

During the second half of April, Captain O'Regan was largely occupied with preventing a too precipitated Partisan attack on Turin and he also succeeded in obtaining the appointment of two Partisan Liaison officers with the French forces in Val Chiasone and Val Susa. These officers proved of great use and were able to maintain good relations between the French forces and the Partisans.

On the night of 25 April, Captain O'Regan went to Lingotto to see the Partisan troops of the IV Zone, and while returning by car, in uniform, encountered a German tank at Stapinizi which fired at and hit the car in which he was travelling. Captain O'Regan succeeded in escaping across the fields and returned to his HQ. During the following days Captain O'Regan made frequent further visits to the Partisan HQ in Lingotto, travelling in civilian clothes and crossing the line of retreat of the German 34th Division.

Throughout the entire period Captain O'Regan showed great qualities of daring and leadership and he is strongly recommended for the immediate award of a bar to the MC.

Awarded

Captain Pat O'Regan: November 1944: recommendation for immediate MC

This officer was parachuted into France on 1 August 1944 to work across the Italian frontier, co-ordinating the activities of the French Forces of the Interior with those of the Italian Partisans in denying the passes to the enemy.

His example to the Italians in the face of German attacks did much to restore their uncertain morale.

On 8 September 1944, Captain O'Regan was on the Col de Mayt with a small group of Italian Partisans when they were attacked by a strong German detachment, with mortars. They resisted for more than twenty-four hours, inflicting losses on the enemy, and when forced to withdraw, Captain O'Regan remained behind to the last to give covering fire.

It is recommended that, in recognition of this officer's courage and example which were of a high order, he be awarded the MC.

Awarded

9

Major Hugh Ballard MC
Captain Buck MacDonald MC, Special Air Service

The son of a small farmer in Worcester, at the age of seventeen to avoid further burdening his hard-pressed father, by then a widower with nine children to bring up, Hugh Ballard set off for London on his bicycle to seek his fortune. After a spell selling Old Moore's Almanacs on the street, he joined the Army in 1935 and was posted to a light tank company of the Royal Tank Regiment in India, where he saw active service in the Waziristan campaign on the North West Frontier. After reaching the rank of sergeant, he resigned and went to Southern Rhodesia where he joined the British South African Police, a paramilitary organization which combined the roles of police and army.

On the outbreak of war, determined to join the colours once more, Ballard managed to extricate himself from the police*, by now regarded as a reserve occupation, and after obtaining a temporary commission in December 1942, was posted to 'F' Reinforcement Squadron Southern Rhodesia Armoured Car Regiment, which had been raised in February the previous year. Wearing the sable badge with the motto *Asi Sabi Luto* ['We fear nothing'], Ballard sailed with the Regiment to Suez in January 1943 as part of the 6th South African Armoured Division. On arrival, he was sent on an Officers Radio Telephony course and then posted to the South African Special Service Battalion Armoured Regiment in early May. By the end of that month, Ballard had been seconded to UK Forces and posted to MO4 GHQ MEF, in other words to SOE. Passing his paramilitary courses in July 1943, when he was assessed as 'an ideal commando type... invaluable as a member of a sabotage party or as commander of guerillas... definitely a good bet' he remained in Cairo† with Force 133 until October when he became conducting officer for Yugoslav Partisan troops to the Dalmatian Islands, Liaison Officer 12 Partisan Brigade on Brac and then on Vis until joining No.1 Special Force in Bari as a temporary Captain in August 1944.

---

*   Purportedly by staging a brawl to get himself thrown out.
†   He married a Maltese beauty, Mary Said, in Cairo in 1943.

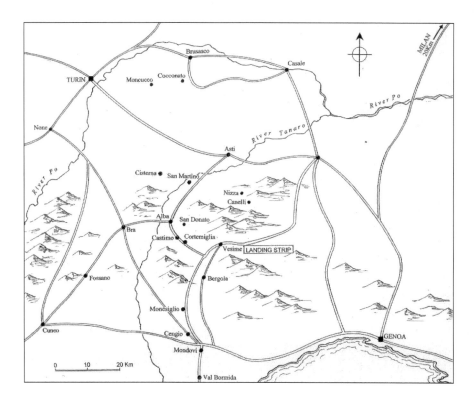

His first assignment was to take over from Major Neville Darewski DSO of the Flap Mission who had died on 15 November 1944 in the Val Ellero area as a result of being crushed by a Partisan truck while directing the evacuation of his mission under sustained enemy mortar fire. Darewski had been in the field since 7 August and was well known and liked by the Partisans. This was a considerable loss for SOE as Darewski was one of its most experienced officers having spent from August 1943 to March 1944 in the area of the Slovenian and Italian borderlands, a period in which he 'covered some one thousand miles on foot, carrying my kit and arms.'*Neville was the son of the famous Russian-born conductor and composer Herman Darewski whose Melody Band was so much part of the British seaside experience between the wars.

Hugh Ballard was infiltrated into the Langhe on 18 November, along with Lieutenant Colonel John Stevens, when a major German *rastrella-mento* was underway. Almost immediately they were on the run, abandoning all personal kit except what they could carry in a light ruck-

---

*   Livingstone II report

sack, never more than two to three hours ahead of enemy patrols. The Partisan forces were completely demoralized and disbanded in the face of this German onslaught and Stevens ordered Ballard to 'stay on the ground' in Val Bormida di Millesmeo, build up an intelligence service and take stock of the Partisan forces in the area, all the time maintaining radio contact with base. The weather was too bad to expect any drops from base and, in any case, the complete absence of Partisans made their reception impractical as well.

Over the next three weeks, by moving every second day, Ballard succeeded in building up a good picture of the Partisan movement in the area and held a conference on 17 December at San Martino with the various different parties, predominantly *Garibaldini* and *Autonomi*. The outcome of this meeting was the implementation of a courier network and outline plan to revive and reinvigorate the Partisan forces. Although the heavy snow which fell at the end of December and the beginning of January ruled out Lysander operations, the mission received its first drop of stores on 12 January which enabled Ballard to concentrate on reforming the Partisan bands and begin sabotage operations against enemy lines of communication.

In February another conference was held in Cortemiglia with the aim of fusing the Partisan formations into a single entity[*]. Not surprisingly given the political profiles of those taking part, deadlock resulted but Ballard was able to extract a promise of a bi-weekly intelligence report from the various parties in return for him acting as an impartial distribution centre. Furthermore they undertook to provide him with liaison officers and by the middle of March he had at his HQ an officer representing every Partisan formation in the area, which by now had grown to four *Garibaldi* divisions, two divisions of *Giustizia e Liberta* and five divisions of *Autonomi*.

The necessity of moving his HQ on a regular basis was brought home to Ballard at the end of March by a surprise night attack on it by Republican units. Fortunately it failed. Visible results now began to show through as the Partisans became more confident and more effective. Enemy attempts to capture the airstrip at Vesime were beaten off. An exceptionally audacious Republican attack in the area on Monesiglio which began of the night of 7/8 April came within a whisker of discovering Ballard's HQ but due to the stalwart efforts of the Partisans, whose morale was now high, all attacks were repulsed.

John Stevens, who had gone back to Bari to report on the situation in the Langhe, now returned to Vesime and brought with him Captain 'Buck'

---

[*]   His record of service states he was wounded on 18 February 1945

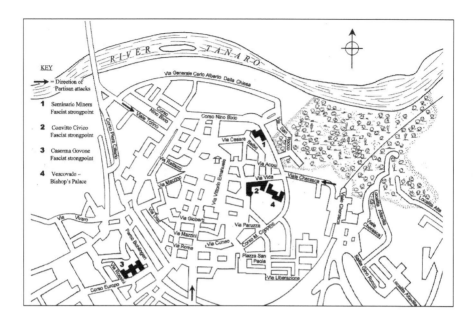

McDonald of the SAS who he attached to Ballard, now an acting Major. Robert MacDonald, a Canadian from New Glasgow, Nova Scotia, had been a fine athlete before the war and after attending the Royal Military College in Kingston in 1939, had arrived in England in 1941 with the Royal Canadian Dragoons. On 11 April, the main SAS party dropped onto the landing strip at Vesime. Ballard recalled that 'the first party consisted of one officer and twenty men, and due to bad weather conditions or bad pilots their arms were not dropped. I then found myself in the middle of what was then a large drive with twenty SAS armed only with carbines and one broken mortar and a Polish Mission who happened to have no kit and very little idea of what they were supposed to do or how they were going to do it.' Fortunately more stores, including heavy weapons, arrived soon after.

The first attack on Alba was organized as part of the SAS activities designed to stir the Partisans into action. Both Roy Farran and Bob Walker-Brown had by now developed the tactical concept of the SAS using heavy weapons behind enemy lines in Italy: as Farran later wrote in his Tombola report 'the overall effect of shelling an enemy-occupied town, I am quite certain, is much greater than killing a few Germans with small arms fire on a road, even if the shell fire produces no casualties whatsoever'. The operation was planned by MacDonald, Ballard and Major Enrico Mauri, the leader of the local *Autonomo* Partisans nicknamed 'the bandits of Cisterna Castle'. The object of the plan was to destroy the enemy garrison in Alba; to capture material for use in other operations, in particular motor vehicles of which it was known that the Republican forces had quite a number; and to try out a communications system with the Partisans in conjunction with the SAS. There was no intention of holding the city of Alba as this was not considered feasible at that time.

The operation started at 0630 hours on 15 April with concentrated fire by heavy weapons under the command of Captain MacDonald. During this barrage, three Partisan columns attacked the city, all being in communication by radio and by 0830 hours they had driven the enemy into three main strong points. Communication with one column was lost due to the wireless operator being wounded and his radio set falling into the river. Attempts were then made by Major Mauri to negotiate the surrender of the city. These negotiations delayed any further offensive action until well towards midday.

The junior Partisan commanders were in favour of assaulting the three main strong points but at 1600 hours, on account of an erroneous report that heavy enemy reinforcements were arriving from the direction of Bra, Major Mauri ordered the withdrawal of all Partisan forces. He was assisted in this by covering fire directed by Lieutenant Philip Fell of the SAS; the enemy, discovering that the Partisans were withdrawing, retook the initiative and opened fire with a 75mm gun, mortars and heavy MGs on the road along which vehicles would have to be driven to carry away the heavy weapons of the SAS.

Due to mistaken orders, the control radio station, Major Ballard and one mortar detachment of the SAS, together with the car belonging to Major Mauri, remained in position after the Partisans' covering screen had been withdrawn and it was only due to the gallant efforts of a Partisan officer called Biondo that they managed to extricate themselves without loss. The SAS separately withdrew on foot to their vehicle RV. Very little material was captured due to the fact that the enemy strong points commanded the only road out of the city, but losses were inflicted on the Republican forces and some damage was done to their barracks. The Partisan formations withdrew to their original positions and were not followed up by the enemy. On 16 April a further ten SAS soldiers dropped at Vesime and the detachment moved to Castimo and from there to San Donato where they received a major arms drop on 18 April followed by an interpreter on 23 April.

On the evening of 25 April, after Canelli and Nizza had both been occupied by the Partisans, Major Ballard received a report by radio which stated that preparations were being made in Alba for the evacuation of the city and that the enemy forces there intended a link-up with elements of the German 34th Division, at that time moving northwards from Cuneo and Mondovi.

At that time, the southern part of the Langhe was in the process of being occupied by four Partisan Brigate of 1st Division Langhe; Asti had been occupied by *Autonomi* and *Garibaldini* and certain areas to the south and southeast of Alba were also in the hands of Partisan forces. The latest report on the strength of the garrison at Alba showed a total of some 360 Republicans, with reasonably heavy armament and some light tanks.

A plan was made to capture Alba by encirclement, thereby forcing the garrison to surrender. It was not known whether the garrison was still in contact by radio, but it was certain that they were not in contact with their higher formation by telephone as the line had been cut. Accordingly, on the morning of 26 April, Partisan formations which included 1 Brigade of 2nd Langhe Division, 2 Brigade *Matteotti* and 3 Brigade 10th CL Division, moved into covering positions while the SAS, who were to provide the fire support with their heavy weapons, returned from the area of Nizza and Canelli where they had taken part in the liberation. Air activity and a lack of fuel delayed the arrival of the SAS until midday, by which time fighting had started and it was discernible early on that the enemy garrison was showing signs of throwing their hand in.

By midday some prisoners had been taken and the Partisans were anxious to attack the three main targets housing the enemy forces. Reports coming out of the town suggested that the enemy were prepared to stand and fight in these three strong-points, two of which lay in the centre of the residential quarter and were therefore difficult targets for the SAS mortars and heavy guns based in Altavilla to the East of the city. At 1415 hours a Republican officer, accompanied by a priest, presented himself to Major Ballard and stated that the commander of the garrison wished for terms, to which the SOE officer replied that only unconditional surrender would be accepted. However, Ballard did give an assurance that, as a British officer, he would personally guarantee their status as POWs under the Geneva Conventions and that they would not be handed over to the Partisans*.

He was then asked if he was prepared to go into town to talk to the enemy commander, to which he agreed, taking with him Lieutenant Ercole, a Partisan brigade commander, and one courier. The enemy commander, Major Gagliardi, was a noted war criminal and to insure against any trickery Ballard had arranged that should they be held as hostages, an attack would be launched at 1600 hours with the intention of taking the town. It was further arranged that a white flag on the bell tower of the cathedral would signify the surrender of the town. On arrival in the Seminario Minore, where Gagliardi

---

* Bruce Ballard

The bell tower at Alba

had his HQ, Ballard immediately explained to him the precautions he had taken and reiterated his terms which were unconditional surrender. Gagliardi replied by asking for twenty four hours in which to evacuate the city including safe passage to Bra, following up on each of Ballard's refusals with a shorter time limit until his last request for two hours in which to change into civilian clothes and disperse his forces. It was refused.

These discussions took some time and at 1525 hours Ballard again warned Gagliardi that the SAS artillery would open fire if the garrison had not surrendered by 1600 hours and repeated that the terms were unconditional surrender. Gagliardi then asked for more time to make contact with some of his officers who were in the Caserma Govone on the other side of town. Ballard agreed to send a courier to MacDonald delaying the opening of fire till 1630 hours, at the same time warning Gagliardi that he could not be responsible for the safe arrival of the message before 1600 hours. The Partisan commander Ercoli then warned Ballard that he had been told by an informer within the Republican garrison that Captain Rossi, the second in command of the enemy garrison, intended to hold them hostages with which to barter a safe passage to Bra.

Present during the negotiations was a Roman Catholic priest, Monsignor Vicario, who every now and then would leave the room and harangue the officers gathered outside, berating them for their stupidity in allowing a scoundrel like Gagliardi to represent them when the game was all but over. The message was not lost on them and they implored Vicario to ask Gagliani to address them. Acccepting the invitation of the Monsignor, Gagliani joined them and was left in no doubt as to their wish – unconditional surrender or they would resort to violence against the fascists. Yet although it was quite apparent that most of the officers and men wished to surrender unconditionally, Gagliardi and Rossi had no intention of doing so without a fight.

At 1550 hours, Ballard again asked Gagliardi whether he was willing to accept his terms and warned him that it would take him at least five minutes to put a white flag on the clock tower to prevent the opening of artillery fire. At one minute to four, Gagliardi commenced telling Ballard that he would not surrender without fighting and at that moment fire was opened by the SAS and the Partisans, everything being directed against the building in which they were negotiating. The third round fired by the SAS 75mm howitzer penetrated the roof of the Seminario, causing a complete collapse of the ceiling. Within minutes, Major Gagliardi presented himself to Ballard and surrendered the garrison without conditions. Ballard told him to hoist a white flag on the cathedral tower to announce the surrender. After some difficulty, a man was found brave enough to carry out this task. Meanwhile the SAS had received Ballard's message and ceased fire at 1604 hours. The enemy had not during this time replied in any way to the fire of the Partisans and SAS.

Public buildings were then occupied, all enemy forces collected in one building and arrangements made for guarding the prisoners. This last task was delegated to the steadfast Lieutenant Ercole who at 1650 hours reported to Ballard that he had arrested and placed in close confinement both Major Gagliardi and Captain Rossi as they had been caught attempting to set fire to the Convitto Civico, planning to escape during the resultant confusion. The prisoners were later handed over to Allied troops by the Partisans. A total of 325, including twenty-two officers were captured, with four heavy artillery pieces and several light ones, three tanks and six transport vehicles and large quantities of ammunition and small automatic weapons.

As the Bishop of Alba later wrote, 'Alba woke up from a nightmare, from which it seemed impossible to wake up, so long and so horrible it had been. The night, quiet and mild, descended on the city like a caress longed for a long time, a caress heralding peace and serenity after so much torment and so many trials'. On 17 June, Ballard was appointed SO2 at AMG and then returned to South Africa by sea on 22 December. His colourful military career finally ended on 6 January 1946 when he was demobbed.

Major Hugh Ballard: 12 June 1945: recommendation for MC

Major Ballard landed by plane at Vesime in enemy occupied territory on 18 November 1944 as BLO to the Partisans in the Cuneo district. A major enemy drive was in progress in the immediate vicinity of the aerodrome and Major Ballard had to move immediately. He continued to be chased by the enemy for three weeks, during which period he was, on more than one occasion, completely surrounded and in imminent danger of being captured.

Major Ballard eventually set up his HQ in the vicinity of Monesiglio where he remained throughout the winter months successfully reorganizing the Partisan bands which had been completely scatterd and reduced almost to nothing. During the months of December 1944 and January 1945, Major Ballard had to live without Partisan protection and escaped capture by constant moves. At the end of January 1945, Major Ballard was able to establish a Drop Ground, and from then onwards rearmed the Partisans in his area and formed them into an efficient fighting foce. This force carried out several minor attacks against the enemy during February to Aproil 1945, in some of which Major Ballard personally took part.

In the first week of April 1945, Major Ballard was reinforced by a detachment of SAS and with them organized two actions against Alba. The first on 15 April was only prevented from success by the sudden arrival of a large force of enemy reinforcements from Turin. The second action on 24 April ended in the surrender of the entire German and Republican garrison. In this Major Ballard showed great initiative entering the town while it was still under Partisan fire and calling on the enemy commander to surrender.

Major Ballard organized repeated sabotage operations against German lines of communication in the valley of Bormida de Spigno and successfully interrupted important German rail traffic during March 1945. He also organized a civilian anti-scorch action which resulted in the preservation intact of important electrical installations in Cairo Montenotte.

Throughout the period from November 1944 to 27 April 1945, when his area was finally evacuated by the Germans, Major Ballard showed outstanding initiative and resourcefulness. He was able to recreate scattered Partisan bands into an effective fighting force, organize their regular supply by air, and maintain contact with base by operating an aerodrome on which three planes landed during March and April 1945.

Major Ballard, during the entire period when he was in the field, showed a complete disregard for his own personal safety and by his energy, courage and initiative, inspired all patriot forces under his command. He is strongly recommended for the award of an immediate MC.

Awarded

10

Lieutenant Colonel Peter McMullen, DSO and bar, MBE, Bronze Star
Lieutenant Colonel Basil Davidson MC

The scion of Hertford brewers, McMullen and Sons, Peter McMullen was sent by his father when he left Rugby School to travel the world rather than go up to university, which his father vigorously opposed; experience gained in the real world was infinitely more character-forming and valuable in a business context rather than some mellifluous degree. So young McMullen set off on his travels and reached New Zealand which he enjoyed so much that he stayed put there for the next six months observing and occasionally hunting its wildlife until news reached him from England that his father had developed a duodenal ulcer and he was thus prematurely summoned home to join the family business management team.

When war broke out, the twenty-five year old McMullen, by now assistant managing director of the brewery after completing a six month stint with another brewery to gain work experience and a similar period studying accountancy, joined the Hertfordshire Regiment in which he had held a TA commission since 1932. After nine months with his regiment as a company commander, he was posted to II Corps as a GSO 3 Ops and then sent to the Staff College at Camberley for five months before being posted to MO [Military Operations] 12 at the War Office as a GSO 3 Ops on the Persian desk in May 1941. Unlike many of his SOE contemporaries, he had never been a great traveller and other than his New Zealand experience and one month honeymoon in Switzerland, he modestly wrote in his application form that he was only familiar with Hertfordshire and the west coast of Argyll. Furthermore he did not speak any foreign languages. This was about to change.

At the War Office, his name had been put forward to SOE who interviewed him on 14 September 1941. His apparent disadvantages of lack of travel experience and no languages were far outweighed by 'his intelligence, his common sense and his personality'. Transferred to SOE in January 1942, he spent the next six month on intensive training courses and was a star pupil, judging by his Finishing Report: 'A man of first class practical intelligence and with high organizing ability. He shows initiative and imagination and a very refreshing, lively interest in all he does. Has a most attractive personality and is a mature type for his actual years. He should do well in any capacity in which the organization wishes to use him.'

That capacity was as GSO 2 to Lord Glenconner at MO5 [Middle East HQ] based in Cairo and after travelling by sea to West Africa, and then overland via Libreville [Congo] and Khartoum [Sudan], McMullen arrived in Cairo and booked a room at the Continental Hotel. The next morning, he asked a taxi to take him to Rushton Buildings to which the driver replied: 'Secret House?' and promptly took him there. McMullen recalled 'I walked up the stairs and asked to see the BGS [Brigadier General Staff]. I received a very blank look at this request and it was not until I asked to see "the boss" that I was directed to a room from which a very harassed Brigadier ["Jenks" Jennings] shouted terribly "Come in". On entering and saying who I was, he said "My dear chap, I have heard of you and I am delighted to see you. I suppose you know that you have come to a madhouse and I expect you to sort it all out." I said that I had come for the purpose of a reorganization with a team of experts in whom I had confidence and that all I wanted was to be able to get down to work. He said "good – you've been Staff College trained, so get on with it. Quickly, please. I give you six weeks to produce the answer, which I will wish to approve. Let it be good." He also asked me if I knew "this chap Glenconner" who had come out to reorganize. I said yes and that I thought I could deal with him. He replied "Thank God for that".*

By basing the reorganization on country sections, McMullen quickly got to grips with the chaos he found around him and judging by his Confidential Report written by the new and already notoriously difficult SOE Chief of Staff, Brigadier 'Bolo' Keble, it was a dazzling success. 'McMullen is an officer of considerable personality and drive. Has proved an excellent organizer. Has plenty of initiative, is quick to appreciate a situation and make decisions. Always tactful and handles men well. Is a good judge of character and a good G Staff officer...' Many years later, his SOE colleague in Italy, Basil Davidson, wrote to him 'I do well recall how deeply impressed I was on meeting you around October 1942 and finding someone – for the first time in my experience with SOE – who actually did very clearly know how an organization should be organized and how it shouldn't. I don't think you may have realized it at the time but you were a real breath of good sense, straightforwardness and, yes, of hope in those days of muddle and general dottiness.' Now head of the Greek Country Section, McMullen designated himself for field operations, and on 24 August

---

* McMullen private papers

1943 dropped by parachute into the Peloponnese as commander of the Enoch mission in Area 5 [Skoupi] to the southeast of Patras.

The situation which McMullen found on the ground was tense, for 'there was still civil war in the Peloponnese during which ELAS eliminated all opposition.' What had happened was regardless of the agreement signed by all the different resistance groups which stated that an *andarte* could join the band of his choice, the Communist-controlled EAM and its military wing ELAS had systematically and brutally culled its competition in the Peloponnese. Consequently, SOE's stance as directed by Cairo was to keep at arm's length from ELAS and not to arm them until they had honoured the Myers agreement. Consequently, the BMMs swung into action themselves and on 30 September, along with Major 'Huffy' Campbell, Captain Gray and Sergeant Henderson, McMullen launched a daring night raid on the German airfield at Argos, personally destroying one fighter aircraft and for good measure a large steam roller used for runway maintenance which had been emitting a mysterious and terrifying hissing noise in the darkness.

Late that year, McMullen and his mission were caught up in the maelstrom which followed the capture by ELAS Partisans on 17 October of eighty one German soldiers from 749 Jaeger Regiment near Kalavryta. Four German prisoners were killed on the spot and the remainder detained at Mazeika south of Kalavryta and treated as POWs until, after protracted negotiations conducted in bad faith by both sides, the decision was taken to execute them; most were shot, others thrown off the cliff near Mazi. The Germans reacted by deploying 3,000 troops in four columns which all converged on Kalavryta, with the objective of engaging with the *andartes* and locating the German prisoners. The German drive from Patras bore down on the Enoch mission, forcing it to retreat to Mount Helmos, where it laid low for the next twenty days, completely surrounded and with little food or water. When the Germans discovered on 8 December what had happened to their men, they reacted with fury, rounding up all males aged thirteen and over and machine-gunning them – at least 463 men and boys were murdered. Having herded the women and younger children into the school building, the Germans then set fire to Kalavryta and destroyed most of it and several of the nearby villages.

Picked up by sea the following January, McMullen spend two months in Cairo and Italy preparing, in conjunction with Major John Harrington, a comprehensive report on *'Present Conditions in the Peloponnese'*, a model of clarity which was 'entirely endorsed in all its aspects' by Lieutenant Colonel John Stevens, who had been his senior officer in the Peloponnese. He returned to his mission in Greece in late March until finally coming out at

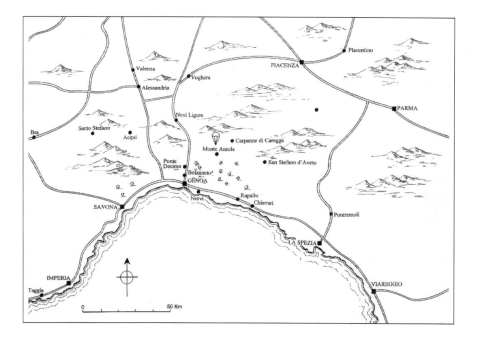

the end of June, again by sea. A visit to London followed and in September 1944, he was attached to No.1 Special Force to await instructions for Italy.

The Allies had by now taken the decision to concentrate their forces on the Eastern Italian seaboard with a view to breaking through into Austria once the Gothic Line had been breached. Western Italy was thus marginalized as a strategic objective and so both SOE and OSS were tasked to organize resistance there to tie down German and Republican forces and at the same time to keep the lid on the pressure cooker of Italian politics. SOE's plan was simple, based on the three major conurbations; Stevens was sent to Turin [Piedmont], Max Salvadori to Milan [Lombardy] and Peter McMullen to Genoa [Liguria]

On 18 January 1945, McMullen dropped with the Clover Mission on the south eastern slopes of Monte Antola, the mountain which dominates the country to the northeast of Genoa. With him were Major Basil Davidson*, Lieutenant Wochiecevich [an Italian Partisan known as 'Elio'] and W/T Operator Sergeant Armstrong. Davidson and McMullen had known each other in Cairo during the Keble era and then gone their separate ways, Davidson to Yugoslavia and McMullen to Greece. Davidson's deputy and

---

* The two had become good friends in Cairo; McMullen was Davidson's best man when he married Marion Young, also of SOE, in 1943.

Drop Ground at San Stefano

political fellow-traveller in Cairo was the controversial Major James Klug-mann, an active Communist since his undergraduate days at Cambridge in 1933 and later editor of *Marxism Today*.

Stephen Hastings', one of McMullen's sub-mission commanders, wrote of this unusual duo: 'Peter came of a conventional, conservative, county family and his political views were entirely consistent. Basil was an intellectual and a Marxist – albeit a romantic one. This would not have mattered except for the fact that all Partisan life is governed by politics and the mountains were full of well organised communist bands. It was much to the credit of Peter and Basil that their political disagreements were never bitter and their mission an unqualified success.'

The mission's task in Davidson's shorthand was 'to join the Ligurian Partisans as soon as possible, carry out the usual tasks of liaison and supply and gather information on the rear dispositions of enemy units. This information would be for the benefit, or so it was hoped, of US Fifth Army...' It was in fact somewhat more challenging since in addition to its normal liaison function between 15th Army Group and the Partisans, the mission was expected to play a major role in coordinating the interface between whatever ad-hoc civil

---

* Later Sir Stephen Hastings MP

administration emerged after the German withdrawal and the incoming AMG. It was presumed that this could be for as long as four weeks. Lastly, it had responsibility for supervising all anti-scorch measures, particularly in respect of the key facilities of the strategic port of Genoa.

The area to be covered by the Clover Mission was daunting in size; it included the Ligurian provinces of La Spezia, Genoa, Savona and Imperia, in effect the entire coastline between La Spezia and the French frontier, and inland, the Emilian Province of Piacenza and that part of the Lombardian province of Pavia which lay south of the River Po. In support, McMullen had four sub-missions: Captain Robert Bentley in Imperia, Major Vivian Johnston in Savona [who arrived on 23 March to take over from Captain Irwin-Bell who had been captured] together with Captain Brown [Val d'Arda] and Flight Lieutenant Rippingdale, Captain Basil Irwin in Voghera and Captain Stephen Hastings in Piacenza [who dropped on 2 February]. Major Charles Gordon later joined the mission and was based at Chiavari. A corollary mission under escaped POW Major Gordon Lett was operating to the east of La Spezia but reported directly to Major Charles Macintosh at Tac HQ Florence.

During November and December, many Partisan formations in the VI [Genoa, Pavia and Alessandria] and X [Piacenza and Parma] Zones had suffered badly from the *rastrellamenti* of the German 162nd [Turkestan] Division* and Italian Fascist forces. On arrival, McMullen's mission immediately met up with Miro, the commander of the VI Zone, and his staff at the hamlet of Capanne di Carrega but their conference was soon disrupted by enemy patrols and after one or two hurried withdrawals, they had to keep moving on an almost daily basis in thick snow for the next three weeks. The VI Zone comprised four main units, the Chichero, Americano and Mingo Divisions and the mobile Caio brigade. All had been badly mauled by the *rastrellamenti* and now totalled between 2,000 to 2,500 men, many without equipment and all tired and dispirited. Miro had previously decided to wind down operations over the winter months as there was no sign of an Allied advance and most importantly no Allied Mission attached to him to orchestrate supply drops. He had wisely taken the opportunity to cull his forces of grumblers and the weak-kneed, most of whom came from the cities and had no knowledge or interest in the peasant way of life that was so key to their survival in the mountains during winter. The sudden appearance of the British mission acted as a tonic and with the capture of a thirty-two strong German column in the upper Val Borbera on 30 January, the VI Zone was back in business.

---

* Ethnic minority POWs captured by the Germans in Russia.

The story of the X Zone, which had meanwhile been redesignated XII Zone, was different. A section of the Clover report floridly written by former journalist Davidson reads: 'This Zone...had had a brilliant summer season with a huge booty of enemy MT taken from the Via Emilia. The formations had waxed fat on a land which, compared to the mountains in the south, was flowing with milk and honey; their size had grown with an afflux of every sort of idler and vagabond; and they steered unhandily towards the winter with a mass of baggage and tophamper that simply invited *rastellamenti*. These they accordingly received in very full measure...there was scarcely one formation left in anything which resembled fighting trim'. The Clover mission met with the XII Zone leadership on 5 February at Santo Stefano, which asked it to help in reforming its command structure; subsequently Captain Hastings was tasked to orchestrate this.

The twenty-three years old Hastings had landed some twenty kilometres south of where McMullen and Davidson were waiting for him but they all successfully met up the next day and after recruiting a small band of Partisans as bodyguards, porters and couriers, Hastings set off to find the XII Zone commander, Colonel Marziolo, who he found in a *trattoria* in the small mountain village of Groppallo. His first task was to weld three disparate groups of Partisans together, all of different political persuasions and all badly damaged by the winter *rastrellamenti*. By the beginning of April, Hastings signalled '...it can be said that Piacentino is at last on its feet.' His intelligence collection operation also gathered pace, given the limitations that 'Partisan information was tendentious, highly coloured and inaccurate'. The Insulin mission of Captain Brown and Flight Lieutenant Rippingdale dropped by parachute on 23 March to reinforce Clover and McMullen immediately sent them to Hastings who deployed them in Val d'Arda in support of the Partisans there.

In the far west of Clover's area of responsibility, all was not well. After a heroic but failed attempt to cross into Italy over the French Alps, Captain Robert Bentley had finally crossed the frontier near the French coast on his eighth attempt but had been on the run ever since, hardly surprising given the presence of the German 34th Infantry Division in the area. Forced to spend most of his time in hiding, including a short spell disguised as a monk in Taggia monastery next to the German HQ, he was later able to complete his anti-scorch tasks and perform as liaison officer between the civil authorities and the AMG. Others were not so lucky. Major Campbell and Lieutenant Clark RNVR who had landed neat Frabosa on 9 December had both been captured along with their two radio operators; only Captain Irving–Bell remained at large and managed to get to Lieutenant Colonel Stevens's HQ in the Langhe. He then set off to Savona where he was captured and was replaced by Major Vivian Johnston on 21 March. Not all went well for Johnston either. On 7 April, when returning from making a transmission, his group was ambushed by a Partisan patrol which mistook them for Germans. Corporal Ashurst, Captain Irwin-Bell's W/T operator, and an Italian boy were both wounded in the legs and evacuated by ox cart to San Bartolomeo.

Now half way through February, McMullen took stock and decided to concentrate on the areas of greatest tactical importance to the east of the Scrivia valley rather than worry about the west and in particular to attend to the problem of Genoa itself. By this time, all kinds of equipment had been dropped to the Partisans, the worst of winter had past and the enemy had shown decided signs of having had enough. Consequently, McMullen advised the Zone command to step up their attacks on the enemy's main lines of communication and increase the number of prisoners taken. Although enemy forces remained a threat, they were no longer capable of launching a large scale *rastrellamento* and the series of *puntate* expeditions against the Partisans had little effect. In the three months ending mid-April, the Partisans inflicted nearly 3,000 casualties on the enemy and over 200 Germans were taken prisoner and interrogated. Morale was high.

McMullen was tireless, marching around the Zones, inspecting, listening, arguing; his own ideas of right and justice chimed with Partisan patriotism and morale. He took their cause to his heart, though prudently, and got on famously with Miro. 'In short' as Davidson recalled, 'he liked and was liked in return, and there was no trouble between the CLN and "the representatives of Field Marshal Alexander"'. Many times he had to take considerable personal risks as he went in search of his sub-missions and individual Partisan units. Throughout the duration of his mission, he kept a small diary which he had bought locally. In it, he recorded in pencil the main events of each day, not as a log but as a prompt to memory in years to come.

18 January: Snow a bit thick
19 January: Moved to C [Carrega]. Six feet deep on the passes.
22 January: Tried to ski. Both mine fell off after a brilliant turn.
23 January: Slightly uneasy all day. Nonsense of a battle two hours away. Held up by a battle outside our front door. Lots of firing from our side. A few 'overs' from somewhere. Could see no one. Moved at 1900 hours. Arrived at Var. Slept well on wet concrete.
24 January: Ready to move. Moved up to top [three hours of hell]. Fifteen of us slept in a hole

25 January: Dawn. Continued scares. This is too much. Immense confusion. Basil and I eventually telling them what to do. Moved on down in afternoon. Quite nice to arrive home again! Snowing.

26 January: Snowing

27 January: Snowed up. Afternoon scare – nonsense

28 January: Winds causing great drifts. Roads impassable. Scare – Huns at Daglia. Slept rather uncomfortably in boots. No way out anyway!

29 January: On alert all morning. Huns now at Cantasigna. Lovely day but wind high – drifts continually appearing. Route behind us half opened. Both Basil and I smelt a night attack. So moved in bright moonlight over the hill. Perhaps the most impressive walk I have ever done

30 January: Sure enough attack at 0500 hours. Up early and down the hill. Interrogated two. Basil went back. I rather lazily stayed behind worried about George. All OK. Big success. Slight scare of cavalrymen, so moved after dark. Filthy journey. Blizzard. Lost our way

31 January: Interrogations all day. Basil exhausted. Moved up over top to F [Fascia]. Three hours. Very comfortable house

1 February: Excellent sleep on a straw bed

2 February: Good Heavens! An answer from base. Moved at 1200 hours Three and a half hours to F [Fascia].

4 February: Mistle thrush for dinner

14 February: Heavens Pussy – twins. Hope so and hope you do too!*

19 February: First flowers in the valley. [McMullen could never resist picking wild flowers wherever he found them, irrespective of the bullets flying around about him; he then pressed them in his notebook].

23 February: The first spring song of the chaffinch [McMullen was an avid bird-watcher and by the end of the mission, had recorded sightings of over thirty five different birds]

The Clover Mission had been strengthened on 14 April by the addition of Captain Gordon, Lieutenant Richards RNVR and two W/T operators and a few days later Captain Murphy RAMC appeared having walked from the La Spezia area via Placentino and in the process collected some useful medical intelligence on the way. Around this time, a team of six commandos under Lieutenant Russell dropped with orders from 15th Army Group to carry out specific intelligence tasks including prisoner snatching. McMullen initially sent them to Fontabuona but the enemy were too concentrated there and so he redeployed Russell to Novi Ligure

---

* He received an awkwardly drafted signal to the effect that his wife had given birth to twins and 'was this OK?'!

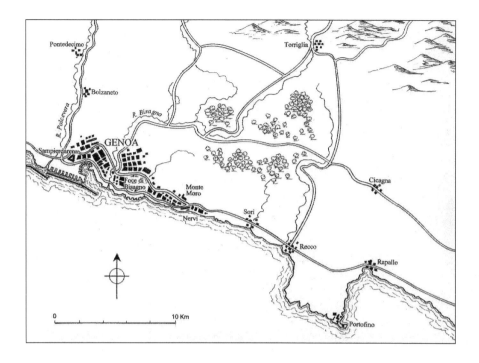

where he arrived in time to take eight prisoners and help the Cichero Division in clearing the valley of enemy,thus saving the tunnels from possible destruction.

'The taking of Greater Genoa from the enemy and the more or less simultaneous liberation of the whole neighbouring territory was an achievement which astonished no-one, perhaps, more than those who carried it out,' wrote McMullen in his post-operational report. He identified several contributing factors, none more debilitating on enemy morale than the long and demoralizing months spent by German troops in Partisan-infested Italy while their homeland was being invaded and overrun. Major General Meinholdt commanding the Fortress of Genoa surrendered himself and all his troops virtually without resistance, thus preventing the destruction of the public services and commercial infrastructure of Genoa. This was in no small part due to McMullen and Davidson who counselled the Partisans at every stage of the negotiations which had begun on 15 April when Meinholdt first contacted the Cardinal of Genoa with a proposal that in exchange for not destroying the city's public services his troops should be allowed to withdraw unmolested by the Partisans. This had come to nothing and by the 23 April when it was visibly clear that the Germans were on the way out*, he again broached the subject with the cardinal, asking for three to four days grace to pull out on the same terms. The cardinal referred this suggestion to the CLN Liguria who responded that they would not treat with the enemy and that afternoon ordered a general insurrection.

The SAP under orders from the Regional command came out in force and the next day Meinholdt threatened to bombard Genoa with his artillery if the CLN did not call off the SAP. When they refused, he held off carrying out his threat which gave time for four small brigades of Partisans to begin their march down from the mountains and infiltrate the city. On 25 April, acting on the agreed plan drawn up by McMullen, the VI Zone command sent units down towards Genoa and directed others to attack in full strength the enemy lines of communications in the Scrivia valley. Late that evening, Davidson set off with the Zone Commissar Attilio towards the city and drove right into the centre without any harassment from the enemy except for sporadic sniping. General Meinholdt had already surrendered at 1930 hours to the Comando Regionale and CLN Liguria but several garrisons had refused to acknowledge his orders.

While the CLN was holding its first full meeting in the San Nicola monastery in the city centre, news came that 1,500 enemy troops had made their way west from the German Naval HQ at Nervi as far as the skyscraper at the Foce di Bisagno, just east of the port, where they blockaded themselves in to await events. Another 2,000 troops in the port made an attempt to break out but were contained. A further 300, surrounded in Sampierdarena, blew up a large ammunition dump, killing scores of civilians, and tried to break out. They were contained by Partisan reinforcements rushed in from Pontedecimo and Bolzaneto. At about 1600 hours on 26 April, Davidson together with Miro and Colonel Farini hurried to the Foce to induce the enemy holding out there to surrender. This they did the next morning at 0900 hours and by the evening of 26 April, only the batteries at Monte Moro and the group at Sampierdarena held out. However, to the consternation of SOE, there was no sign of the advancing Americans on whom they were relying to police the city.

McMullen seized the nettle and drove down to Rapallo that night to find them. During the course of the next morning, American troops from the 92nd Division began to flow into the city, led by McMullen sitting on the bonnet of a Jeep with Colonel MacCaffery, General Almond's Chief of

---

* General Von Vietinghoff had issued his Operation Autumn Mist directive to retreat across the River Po on 20 April 1945

McMullen arrives with US Fifth Army

Staff in the seat behind him. The battle was over. Partisan units took 6,000 prisoners in Genoa itself. Casualties had been kept to a minimum and the anti-scorch programme realized in its entirety, a result beyond the wildest expectations of the Clover mission. The sub-missions had all performed well though Hastings and his Partisans were unable to take and hold the city of Piacenza, where the remnants of a German SS battalion with ten armoured cars had installed themselves. Three US Sherman tanks finally sent them scurrying on their way. Captain Brown had also been involved in orchestrating the attack on Piacenza and after interrogating thirty German POWs, 'went off for some sleep after four days and three nights on Benzedrine and tea.'*In Acqui, Johnston found himself in demand by the Republican General Farina who refused to talk to the Partisans. Wisely he insisted that they were joined by the German General Hilderbrand, who stated that until he received his orders from Corps he was not entitled to make his own decisions. This was to prove costly for the retreating

---

* Report on Insulin mission Piacenza Area

columns were straffed for three hours by Allied fighters and by the time they reached Valenza, half had deserted and the other half surrendered. Johnston entered Savona on 27 April where he remained until handing over to the AMG.

The speed and efficiency with which the Ligurian CLN took over the administration of the province and city of Genoa was no fluke but the result of months of planning, much of it with the assistance of McMullen who had held his first conference with the CLN on 18 and 19 February. Detailed questionnaires were given to the CLN on behalf of AMG which provided demonstrable evidence to the Italians of Allied interest in their plans and activities. A series of further meetings were held which all added to the mutual respect that was so crucial to the right outcome. The McMullen/ Davidson team had an entirely open mind when it came to dealing with the various political shades in Liguria, albeit mostly of a reddish hue. In their report, they wrote that 'the leading personalities...were undoubtedly communists of conviction and long experience, by no means crude hotheads, who understood their absolute need for collaboration with the Allies and with the non-Communist elements among the Italians themselves. Their strength lay precisely in their own wealth of experience, their high standard of discipline and political understanding, and the support of their party.' In particular they singled out Miro, 'a man of great personal charm...of no mean culture and...gifted with an amazing physique. It would have been difficult to have found a better man for the job.'

Both McMullen and Davidson shared the same tenet that 'Partisan warfare is political warfare. Partisan formations, that is, do not fight merely to win the war, they fight to win their particular war. This means that support to any Partisan movement must be based upon a proper and accurate understanding of the political background. Only this will enable a worthwhile estimate to be made of what may, and what may not, be expected of Partisans.'

After liberation, the Clover mission found itself being used as a buffer between the US 92nd Division and the AMG on the one hand and the CLN and Partisan regional command on the other. Demobilization and disarmament of Partisan forces throughout all four provinces of Liguria went smoothly with all un-uniformed and uniformed SAP disarmed by 5 May with the Partisan mountain units shortly following. Killings did take place but were anticipated in view of the last eighteen months of Fascist terror and repression. Members of the Brigata Nere were usually summarily shot. McMullen was far from happy about this new role as assistant to AMG and arranged an interview with Colonel Louis Franck, the senior SOE staff officer whose policy it was. 'In due course I was ushered into his presence...I said my piece mildly but definitely, that we had all been trained and had acted as Liaison Officers to Partisans whom we had encouraged and armed, and having run with the fox, it would be impossible, especially since we had not been trained for anything else, to turn around and then hunt with a new pack of hounds with different objectives. A bad policy and we should all go "to the bad".' Franck said he was inclined to agree and the Clover Mission sailed for the UK on 28 May.

Lieutenant Colonel Peter McMullen: 14 July 1945: Recommendation for MC

Lieutenant Colonel McMullen was dropped by parachute on 18 January 1945 to enemy occupied Italy. His task was to command the British Liaisons Missions operating with the Partisans in the whole of Liguria and to prepare the Partisan forces through these missions for action as required by 15th Amy Group and AFHQ.

Lieutenant Colonel McMullen immediately contacted Partisan elements in the hills behind Genoa and clandestine resistance forces in the towns and cities. By his untiring efforts, his energy and his personality he was able to unify the several Partisan formations in the area and to build up a single organization which carried out fully the tasks allotted it by the Allied Command and contributed largely to the liberation of North West Italy and the rapid advance of the Allied armies.

Lieutenant Colonel McMullen during the whole of his four months in enemy occupied territory, lived with Partisans and identified himself closely with all aspects of their life and activities. In the most difficult country and in appalling weather conditions he made frequent tours of his area in spite of enemy vigilance and counter-Partisan activity. He quickly appreciated that the only way to recover and maintain Partisan morale was to involve them constantly in action with the German and fascist forces and, with this in mind, he personally led them in many attacks against the enemy. It is clear from the reports of his junior officers that at all times and in particular in action or under fire, he conducted himself with great bravery and was a source of inspiration to all his comrades.

He and his mission entered Genoa some twenty-four hours before the arrival of Allied troops and Lieutenant Colonel McMullen personally went out to meet the 92nd US Division and led its commanding general into the liberated city. His presence there in the last stages of liberation and during the first few weeks after gave great encouragement and assistance to the Allied and Italian authorities. The success achieved by the resistance forces in preserving the port of Genoa from destruction was also largely due the untiring and fearless efforts of this officer.

For his arduous period of service in enemy-occupied territory, his leadership under fire and his assistance to Allied and Italian personnel, and for the outstanding results which these qualities enabled him to produce, Lieutenant Colonel McMullen is most strongly recommended for the immediate award of the MC

Revised up to bar to DSO

Lieutenant Colonel Peter McMullen: August 1944: Recommendation for DSO

Lieutenant Colonel McMullen dropped by parachute into Greece on 17 August 1943. Since that date he has held the post of 2i/c to the AMM in the Peloponnese. In that capacity he organized the joint plan of operations for the evacuation from the Peloponnese of the Germans which was expected in October, including attacks on Argos and Araxos aerodromes which were actually attempted. Lieutenant Colonel McMullen personally completed and carried out the attack on Argos aerodrome on the night 5/6 October. The attack involved the support of a covering force of *Andartes* which, however, failed to appear. Notwithstanding this, Lieutenant Colonel McMullen decided to make an attack without this force and successfully destroyed two aircraft and a steamroller. When the charges placed on the first aircraft exploded, Lieutenant Colonel McMullen carried out the placing of the remaining charges under continuous MG fire. He then succeeded in withdrawing his party to safety, despite the minefields which surrounded the aerodrome and the fact that the searchlights were being continually played on his line of escape.

In December, Lieutenant Colonel McMullen attempted to reach Italy by Italian submarine which ground on arrival in Greece. Lieutenant Colonel McMullen took charge of the forty-eight Italian crew and directed their hiding and evacuation in addition to the other members of the party, which took place on the night of 29/30 January 1944 by destroyer.

Lieutenant Colonel McMullen then returned to the Peloponnese by parachute on 2 April. From 13 April to 1 May he assisted in carrying out the duties of HQ under extremely trying conditions of a German drive and in close proximity to them. HQ during that period was moved nine times and was never more than two hours from the Germans. Despite this, HQ continued to function. Twice the location of the HQ was discovered by the Germans. On the first occasion Lieutenant Colonel McMullen witnessed the blowing up of the HQ and immediately the Huns had departed assisted in feeding and re-housing the villagers. On the second occasion, the Germans searched the location thoroughly for hidden stores, over which Lieutenant Colonel McMullen in turn with other members of the station, acted as sentry.

On the various occasions in which Lieutenant Colonel McMullen has been in close contact with the enemy, he has shown complete disregard for personal safety and continued to work without interruption. In addition Lieutenant Colonel McMullen has had to carry out work to maintain good relations with the *Andartes* under the most trying conditions and in the face of open hostilities and threats to his life.

On 15 May, Lieutenant Colonel McMullen took over from Colonel Stevens, commander of the Allied Military Mission.

For his good work during the seven months he has spent in Greece and for his part in the operations on Argos aerodrome, Lieutenant Colonel McMullen is recommended for the immediate award of the DSO.

Awarded

Lieutenant Colonel Basil Davidson: 1947: Citation for Bronze Star Medal

Basil R. Davidson, Lieutenant Colonel, Infantry, British Army for meritorious achievement in connection with military operations in Italy, from 18 January to 2 May 1945. As second in command of an Allied Liaison Mission with Italian Partisans of the Ligurian Province, Lieutenant Colonel Davidson demonstrated great initiative and devotion to duty in operating far behind enemy lines. Parachuted in the vicinity of Genoa in four feet of snow, he immediately assisted in organizing and supervising Partisan activities to coordinate with Allied offensives in the Massa-La-Spetzia area. Despite repeated and determined enemy efforts to capture him, he maintained liaison with Allied troops, gathered and transmitted intelligence information and held clandestine meetings with civil authorities. He raised Partisan morale to the extent that it became an effective fighting force in its actions against the foe during the successful April operations. Lieutenant Colonel

Davidson's untiring efforts and resourcefulness in a position of vital importance to the Allied cause in Italy reflects high merit on the service he
represents. Entered service from London, England.

Awarded

Major Basil Davidson: 22 June 1945: Recommendation for immediate MC

Major [now Acting Lieutenant Colonel] Davidson dropped by parachute
behind enemy lines in the Appennine Mountains of Italy on 18 January 1945
as second-in-command to the Allied Mission responsible for liaison with the
Italian Partisans of Liguria and Emilia.

The Partisans, who at that time were demoralized by the slow Allied advance
and by severe winter conditions, put up little resistance to the constant enemy
attacks and in consequence the mission was continually "on the run" for the
first six weeks, being forced to move daily from place to place. Major Davidson,
by his untiring energy and enthusiasm, did much to inspire the Partisans to
defend themselves and his presence at their first large action at Cartasegna on
23 January 1945 helped greatly to ensure its success. During this period the
mission was twice surprised and forced to withdraw under fire. Major Davidson's coolness and efficiency did much to ensure the safety of the mission.

Later, when the Partisans' morale had recovered, Major Davidson was
instructed to concentrate on intelligence and on anti-scorch plans for the
city and port of Genoa. He carried out both these tasks with great efficiency.
A vast quantity of really valuable intelligence was gathered from prisoners
interrogated by him and from agents organized by him. He made contact
with the CLN of Genoa and at numerous clandestine meetings held in the
outer suburbs of Genoa, Anti-scorch plans were made as a result of which
almost all vital installations in Genoa were saved from destruction.

On 25 April 1945, while the Partisans were still fighting the enemy fortress
troops, Major Davidson moved into the city under fire and remained at the
side of the Partisan military command who finally accepted the surrender of
the entire enemy garrison of 7,000 troops. Allied forces arrived on 27 April
1945 and from then on he acted as adviser to Commander 92 Division on
Partisan matters, helping greatly to ensure public order in the city.

Throughout this period Major Davidson's energy, tact and coolness in all
situations was a magnificent example to the mission and to the Italian Partisans with whom he served and by whom he is held in the greatest respect.
Later, as a Lieutenant Colonel, Davidson was given the freedom of the city of
Genoa. He is strongly recommended for the award of the immediate MC.

Awarded

The sub-missions

Major Stephen Hastings: 27 May 1945: recommendation for immediate MC

Major Hastings, together with his W/T operator and interpreter, dropped by parachute behind enemy lines into the Apennine Mountains of Italy on 19 February 1945. From that date onwards until 29 April 1945 he acted as chief Allied liaison officer to the Italian Partisans in the Piacenza province.

At the time of his arrival the Partisans in this area were demoralized and except for a few scattered groups almost non-existent. Major Hastings at once set to work to organize, train and supply them with arms to form an efficient fighting force under his command. This he did successfully despite frequent enemy attempts to capture him and despite the political and personality conflicts among the various Partisans.

By the beginning of April he had organized three divisions totalling about 4,000 Partisans and had welded them into a unified command. On 25 April 1945 Major Hastings was given orders to attack and capture Piacenza and to seize and hold a bridgehead over the River Po until the arrival of Allied forces. He immediately organized his forces into action and after a three day attack he succeeded in capturing all objectives. Throughout this battle Major Hastings was constantly to the fore, coolly directing and encouraging his forces while under constant MG and mortar fire. During the course of this battle his interpreter was seriously wounded.

This action was a great contribution to the Allied advance and Major Hastings, through his coolness under fire and popularity with the Partisans and his complete disregard of safety, was largely responsible for the determination of the attack and for its successful conclusion. He is strongly recommended for the immediate award of the MC.

Awarded

Captain Basil Irwin: 25 May 1945: recommendation for an immediate MC

Captain Irwin dropped by parachute behind enemy lines in the Apennine Mountains of Italy on 8 March 1945. Since that date until the arrival of Allied troops on 30 April 1945 he commanded a sub-mission to the Italian Partisans in the Ottre Po Pavese.

At the time of his arrival the Partisans were demoralized by a hard winter and were in no way resisting constant enemy patrols throughout the area. By his enthusiasm and leadership under fire in numerous small actions, Captain

Irwin succeeded in organizing the Partisans in his area under common command – no easy matter in view of existing political differences in this area. During this period Captain Irwin gathered much valuable intelligence both from agents organized by him and from personal reconnaissance. The latter included a recce to the Po valley which resulted in valuable information on crossings used by the Germans.

By the beginning of April, the Partisans, directed by Captain Irwin, had cleared the mountain area of the enemy and were carrying out constant attacks on the main roads in the valleys. When called upon for a maximum effort, Captain Irwin on 26 April with his Partisans attacked and captured Voghera and went on to take Pavia and were the first Partisans to enter Milan. By his initiative and drive while under fire during the period, Captain Irwin contributed greatly to the Allied advance and to the quick surrender of the Germans.

Throughout his period behind the line Captain Irwin has shown complete disregard for his own safety. By his tact, judgment and personal popularity he succeeded in organizing the Partisans and had the satisfaction of fighting with them to achieve much more than was asked of him. He is strongly recommended for the immediate award of the MC.

Awarded

Captain Robert Bentley: May 1945: recommendation for immediate MC

Captain Bentley, having volunteered for work with Partisan forces behind the enemy lines, was landed by sea in the Bordighera area on 6 January 1945 on the fourth attempt. His guide was not there to meet him and the party, led by Captain Bentley, had to set off alone through enemy defence posts and seek out a safe house. This they found, but, owing to the close proximity of the enemy, they were obliged to move on the next day. Wearing civilian overcoats over their uniforms they moved by day through the midst of the enemy, relying on a local guide to take them through enemy check points. Immediately after he had established his mission, Captain Bentley contacted Partisan commanders in the area and arranged for supplies to be sent in by sea.

Two attempts were made to get sea sorties into the area but each failed as no contact was made by the craft with the shore party. As supplies were vital, Captain Bentley made the perilous journey back to the coast, making his way again through the enemy positions and road blocks in order that he could personally supervise the next sea sortie; then, returning to the mountains, he made further attempts to organize the Partisans and succeeded in

Basil Davidson

arranging for supplies to be dropped by air. By now the situation appeared better; but it was not to last for almost immediately his party was heavily attacked by the enemy and for many weeks they were continually chased from one place to another. At one stage, when the situation appeared hopeless and their capture imminent, Captain Bentley showed great courage and initiative by ordering his party, now worn out, to cease their flight and he led them into the neighbouring town occupied by the enemy and obtained sanctuary in the local monastery next door to the enemy HQ.

Subsequently the party was able to rebuild the Partisan strength and the latter, reinforced by supplies, were able under his experience and guidance to play a big part in the final liberation of North Italy.

Captain Bentley has shown outstanding courage when faced at times by apparently overwhelming odds, but his bravery and devotion to duty won through and he is strongly recommended for the immediate award of the MC.

Awarded

Steven Hastings, back row, second from left

11

Captain George Paterson, MC and bar

A Canadian citizen, George Paterson should have been in British Columbia in the autumn of 1939, helping with the harvest on his parent's fruit farm; instead, as a student at Edinburgh University, he joined the Royal Engineers on the outbreak of war and after being commissioned on 11 May 1940, volunteered for the Commandos. After passing their tough selection and training course in Scotland, he was posted to No. 2 Commando which started parachute training in June 1940 and was then re-designated the 11th Special Air Service Battalion ["11 SAS"], at that time Britain's only parachute unit.

Towards the end of 1940 at a meeting at Combined Operations HQ in London, a decision was taken based on technical information provided by George Kent and Sons, the civil engineering firm, to destroy the Tragino aqueduct near Calitri in southern Italy and thereby severely damage the Italian war effort. Supplying fresh water to the three major naval ports of Taranto, Bari and Brindisi and to over two million people in major conurbations, the structure crossed high over the valley of the Tragino River and was by all accounts unguarded. Various options were looked at including sea landings and aerial bombardment but finally its destruction was entrusted to 11 SAS in an ambitious combination of a long-range parachute drop and seaborne extraction

Command of the operation (later called Colossus) was given to Major Trevor Pritchard, who immediately called for volunteers: although the whole unit of 350 officers and other ranks stepped forward, only thirty-six were selected. After intensive training in the UK including practicing on a mock aqueduct outside Manchester, the volunteers, known as X Troop, flew to an advanced operating base in Malta. Joining the 11 SAS team were three interpreters, a RAF officer Flight Lieutenant Lucky MC, Rifleman Nasri and the forty-two year old Italian Fortunato Picchi*, the former head waiter at the Savoy Hotel, whose cover was a Free French soldier by the name of Dupont.

---

* After capture, Picchi was interrogated and shot on 6 April 1941; in all likelihood, he was a SOE operative.

The RAF provided eight Whitley bombers for the operation, six of which had been converted to each carry six paratroopers and their equipment. Taking off from Malta at 1830 hours on the night of 10 February 1941, the six aircraft eventually all made it to the general area of the target, but not all the stores were dropped and one aircraft dropped its stick in the wrong valley and they never made it to the objective. Although the piers supporting the aqueduct turned out to be concrete heavily reinforced with steel rather than red brick, enough explosives had been collected on the drop ground to allow a change in the demolition plan. As opposed to blowing up two piers, the charges were concentrated on the destruction of the single western pier, with a hitherto unknown small bridge over the Galistra River about 200 yards away earmarked as an additional demolition target. At 0030 hours on 11 February, the explosives were detonated and the western pier destroyed, causing the aqueduct to crumble and effectively break in half; the Galistra bridge was also successfully blown.

The men of X Troop were now faced with a sixty mile walk through enemy occupied territory to the mouth of the River Sele to rendezvous with a submarine, HMS Triumph, which would then take them back to Malta. Despite travelling in three separate groups, they were all captured over the course of the next few days. Even if they had made it to the coast, they would not have been picked up since one of the two Whitleys conducting the diversionary bombing raid at Foggia had developed engine trouble and ditched in the mouth of the River Sele, where the rendezvous was to occur. Fearing that the pilot's radio traffic had been monitored by the Italians and that the submarine might therefore sail into a trap, the decision was made to abort the pick-up. As it turned out, the damage to the aqueduct was not as serious as anticipated. Nearby reservoirs made good the water supply and the main structure of the aqueduct was repaired in a matter of days. Psychologically though, the raid had been a success, bringing home to the Italian people the unpalatable fact that from now on the Italian mainland was an Allied target, thus forcing them to instigate a system of air-raid warnings that lasted through to the end of the war.

Moving only at night, Paterson and Lee's group covered eighteen miles over two days until they were confronted by a Carabinieri patrol and forced to give themselves up. Initially taken to the military prison in Naples, at the end of February Paterson was moved to PG 78 at Sulmona near Pescara in the Abruzzo. A year later, he together with other Special Air Service officers was moved to PG 27 at San Romano on banks of the River Arno between Florence and Pisa. One of them Tony Deane Drummond managed to escape

which prompted their Italian captors to move them again, this time to PG 5 at Gavi, twenty miles north of Genoa, a forbidding eighteenth century walled fortress high up on the side of a mountain. On every aspect there were precipitous drops while the walls bristled with MG posts and patrolling sentries. In September 1943, news of the fall of Mussolini reached the camp and for a short period, prisoners and guards fraternized. The arrival of a German unit in the next door village put paid to any ideas of escape and within days the prisoners were ordered to assemble to move to Mantua where they were loaded onto box cars bound for Germany.

As the train began its journey north through the mountains, Paterson and some fellow POWs managed to prise open a hole in the wooden walls of the box car and he jumped off the train just as it slowed down to tackle an upwards gradient. Having lost all his clothes in the course of swimming across a river, Paterson was fortunate to find a friendly farmer who handed him on to the village priest who in turn clothed him and gave him shelter. By sheer luck, as he approached Breschia, a cyclist accosted him and having determined that he was English, took him to his home where another escaped English POW, Corporal Jack Harris, was hiding, Their host Luigi then introduced them to the Partisans but their happy-go-lucky approach to life soon became a worry for the two Englishmen and they found a safe house with another Italian family in Breschia from where to plan their final escape to freedom.

As it transpired, after being put in touch with the resistance network run by Guiseppe Bacciagaluppi* and his British wife Audrey Smith in Milan, Paterson and Harris found themselves organizing groups of escaped POWs for onward transmission to Switzerland. It was during this period that Paterson accepted an invitation to spend a weekend with friends in Como but on his return to Milan was caught on the train by the Questura conducting a spot identity check. Having been handed over to and then interrogated by the Gestapo, he was imprisoned in the huge but over-crowded nineteenth century San Vittore prison in the centre of Milan, then under German SS control. In June, Ricci†, his Milan resistance contact, was arrested and joined him in prison. Through the judicious use of hefty bribes, Ricci organized an escape for himself and five others including Paterson. With the help of the Milan Fire Brigade who provided him with a uniform and papers, he reached Como from where he crossed the border into Swit-zerland and arrived at Bellinzona and from there made it to the British Administration Office in Montreux on the shores of Lake Geneva.

Some weeks later, he was summoned to the British Press Office in Berne where SOE officers asked him to consider going back to Italy to assist with a nascent Partisan uprising in Domodossola near the Swiss border. With his fluent Italian and recent firsthand knowledge of the people and the country, Paterson was the ideal choice to replace the original officer who had gone down with meningitis. There was an additional urgency to this request since the four groups of Partisans who were to comprise the uprising, the Green

---

*   Bacciagaluppi was the manager of F.A.C.E., the Italian subsidiary of American Standard
      Electric Corporation.
†   Nino Bacciagaluppi

Domodossola, November 1944

Flames, the *Garibaldini*, Socialists and Royalists, would have to be resupplied with arms and ammunition; furthermore the Allies needed an observer on the spot to report on the eventual political outcome of 'Free Domodossola'. Paterson agreed and immediately recruited as his W/T Operator Corporal Jack Watson, the second in command of his section at Tragino who he had bumped into at the quarantine centre at Bad Losdorf just after he had arrived in Switzerland. Using the new name of Major George Robertson of the Royal Engineers, he and Watson met up with SOE's John Birbeck at Locarno who passed them over at the border to Colonel Attilio Moneta, their liaison officer with the Partisan brigades.

Monetta introduced Patterson to the Brigade commanders – Dionigi Superti of the Socialist Party, Armando 'Arca' Calzavara of the Green Flames and Alfredo Di Dio of the Royalists. The Communist leader, the Russian–trained Vincenzo Moscatelli, was unavailable. During the next two weeks, the Partisans moved south, coming down from their mountain strongholds in the Toce valley and taking out the isolated Fascist detachments who put up little resistance. By the end of September, they started to close in on the town of Domodossola with its 200 strong German garrison. Resistance was short-lived and the commandant hoisted the white flag, surrendering his soldiers, mainly elderly reservists and conscripted Ukrainians, the latter having no qualms about changing sides. For the Partisans, this was a great victory and they set about consolidating their gains. Paterson was worried since the 3,000 lightly armed men who made up the four brigades would be no match for a determined counterattack by seasoned German soldiers. He advocated continuing the advance, using the snowball effect throughout the whole of Northern Italy. Instead, the Partisans set about organizing a local government of 'Free Ossola' under the aegis of Professor Ettore Tibaldi, an administrator sent in by the Italian government in Rome. Problems soon began to multiply, with little money to purchase food and a general shortage of ammunition.

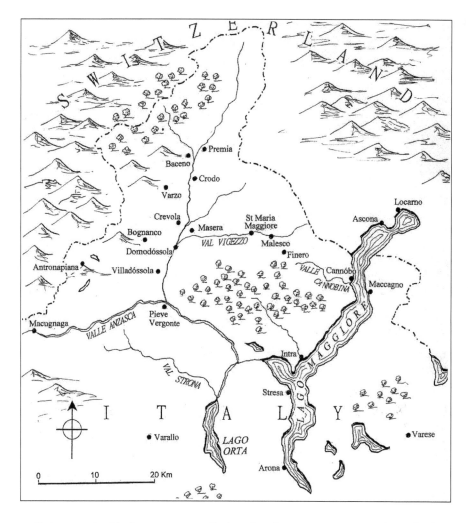

Paterson decided to return to Switzerland to arrange resupply and after meeting up with Birkbeck, was soon on his way back to Domodossola with a list of air drops and 20 million lire which he handed over to the profusely thankful Professor, who was astute enough to know that a government without money is but a short-lived one. However, three day later the first air drop failed to materialize[*] and news quickly followed of a battalion of crack German Alpine troops and Fascist infantry landing near Canobbio after

---

[*] The flight had been grounded by bad weather over Celone. When flights resumed on 12 October, two aircraft made successful sorties, one had to abort and two crashed into mountains with loss of all lives on board.

crossing Lake Maggiore. On 12 October, Paterson went forward with Colonel Moneta to recce the front line at Malesco and found himself in the centre of an intense firefight between the Germans and the Partisans; Di Dio, the Royalist brigade commander, was cut to pieces by machine fire just behind him. The battle went on for two hours and as they tried to extricate themselves still in close contact with the enemy, Moneta was shot dead next to Paterson. After shooting Moneta's assailant, Paterson ran out of ammunition for his Tommy gun and was roughly seized by advancing German troops, angry at the loss of some of their comrades and bent on retribution. On the verge of being shot on the spot, Paterson was only saved by the appearance of an Alpine Corps Sergeant-Major who ordered them to take him prisoner and escort him to the holding cage at Canobbio. He was then collected by the SS and taken back to San Vittore, his former jail in Milan, where, to his dismay, he learnt that German and Republican troops had retaken Domodossola on 14 October. The much-vaunted Free Republic of Ossola had lasted for just forty-three days; it was not until 24 April the following year that Ossola was finally liberated by the resistance.

At San Vittore, Paterson was relentlessly interrogated by the Gestapo about his previous escape. A visit to the Italian prison doctor to tend to his scabies prompted another plan of escape. The doctor who was well disposed towards the Allies suggested taking some pills to fake jaundice which would result in hospitalization and hence a better chance to escape. Unfortunately, just as Paterson was turning the right shade of yellow, he was removed to the Wehrmacht wing of the prison where he was diagnosed with malaria. In his new quarters, Paterson became acquainted with a German Major, a veteran of North Africa and Russia, who was being held on charges of homosexuality. Towards the end of April, they heard far off firing when they were in the exercise yard and with the help of the Major, Paterson made a dramatic escape under the cover of a prison riot. His first action was to head back to Switzerland but after being stopped at the border, returned to Milan where he was sent to the recently arrived Colonel Hedley Vincent of SOE at the villa of Allesandro Pavolini, the head of the Republican Fascist Party who had just been shot after trying to escape by swimming Lake Como. Here he met Major Max Salvadori who knew all about him and told him it was he who had been behind the young Italian doctor who tried to get him out of San Vittore through faking jaundice.

Lieutenant George Paterson: 6 July 1945: recommendation for immediate MC

Lieutenant Paterson after being a POW for some time escaped on 18 September 1943 by jumping off a train north of Verona which was taking him to a PW camp in Germany.

He immediately set about attempting to organize a Partisan group in the Brescia area and during this period he came into contact with an organization responsible for the exfiltration of Allied prisoners of war from North Italy. Lieutenant Paterson volunteered to join this organization in the Brescia area and remained there assisting the passage and safe exfiltration of some hundreds of Allied POWs until the end of November 1943 when both houses which he was using as transit houses for POWs were raided and Lieutenant Paterson's assistant was arrested.

At the beginning of December 1943 Lieutenant Paterson moved into Milan dressed in civilian clothes where he again made contact with the same organization and continued to work for them until 8 January 1944 when he was again taken prisoner and lodged in San Vittore, the SS prison in Milan. On 8 July 1944, after six months in prison, he succeeded in escaping with other members of the organization and made his way successfully into Switzerland disguised as a Milan City fireman.

After a month in Switzerland he made contact with Allied forces and returned to Italy in the Val Dossola area as liaison officer to the Italian Partisans. For the next six weeks he remained in Malesio area, organizing, equipping and training the Partisans and leading them into various skirmishes with the enemy. During this time his courage and leadership together with his past experiences made him almost a legendary figure with his Partisan forces. Under his leadership the Val Dossola was liberated by the Partisans but a German *rastrellamento* immediately took place and Lieutenant Paterson was again taken prisoner on 14 October 1944. He remained a prisoner until 26 April in Milan. On that date he delivered an ultimatum to the commandant of the prison and succeeded in arranging the release of himself and all the remaining prisoners in his ward.

For the past twenty-one months Lieutenant Paterson has shown the greatest courage and ingenuity and a high sense of duty. Totally disregarding his own personal safety, he devoted himself entirely to the furtherance of Allied interest in Northern Italy and is most strongly recommended for the immediate award of the Military Cross.

Awarded

Lieutenant George Paterson: 4 October 1945: citation for MC

Lieutenant Paterson was captured on 12 February 1941 at Calabria, Italy, when returning from a special mission. Subsequently he was imprisoned at Sulmona, Pisa, Padula and Gavi [Camp 5]. In May 1941, Lieutenant Paterson was one of eight officers who escaped from an organized walk; he was, however, recaptured the same day. Almost a year later, at Pisa, he participated in an attempt to break through into an adjacent church; this project was discovered before the officers emerged. Throughout his imprisonment in Italy, Lieutenant Paterson was in secret communication with the War Office.

When the Germans took over Gavi camp at the time of the Italian armistice, they transferred all POWs to Germany. Immediately they had been locked in the train, Lieutenant Paterson and his companions began to break a hole in the side of the carriage. Lieutenant Paterson was the fifth to jump, and although the sentries fired, he was not hit. After swimming a river he continued for another three days until he was exhausted. Friendly Italians then cared for him, and upon his recovery, sent him to a Partisan band near Brescia. Captured by Fascists early in January 1944, he was handed over to German custody. Although for three months escape was impossible because he was isolated, ultimately he was allowed to work in the prison itself [San Vittore]. He and four other POWs bribed one of the guards to loan them the key of the side door; a duplicate key was made and they escaped on 8 July 1944. Lieutenant Paterson made his way to friends, who arranged for his journey to Switzerland.

Awarded

Lett, centre bottom row [Photograph taken behind enemy lines in 1944]

12

Major Gordon Lett, DSO

Captain Bob Walker-Brown, DSO, MBE,
Special Air Service

Gordon Lett was born on 17 November 1910 in a basic hut in a remote village in The Territory of Papua, now known as Papua New Guinea. His father was an English engineer employed to 'open up' this densely forested British possession administered by Australia since 1906; his mother was a pianist and music correspondent for a Sydney newspaper. Following complications after his birth, his mother tragically died and young Lett was brought up by his maternal grandmother in Sydney until being sent to school in England at about the age of 12. He was commissioned into the East Surrey Regiment in 1933, and served with the 1st Battalion which was based at Rawalpindi in India [their summer cantonment was at Kuldana in the Muree Hills]. His appetite for Himalayan adventure whetted by an expedition in the spring of 1937, after a stint in the Sudan in 1938 where the battalion provided the extras to the Korda brothers' film *The Four Feathers*, Lett transferred to the Indian Army and led a second Himalayan expedition in May/June 1939*.

Captured at Tobruk in June 1942, Lett, by a now a Major serving with the Indian Army Service Corps, was interned in Italy, first at Bari, then Camp PG 1 [Chieti] near Pescara and finally at PG 29 [Veano] outside Piacenza. When news of the armistice reached the camp on 8 September 1943, the Senior British Officer Lieutenant Colonel George Younghusband had the good sense to tell the inmates to scatter rather than follow the official line of staying put†, suggesting that each officer took two or three ORs with him. The Camp

---

* On the strength of these expeditions, he was later elected a Fellow of The Royal Geographical Society.

† The order issued to SBOs by Brigadier Crockatt of MI9 and approved by General Montgomery, commander Eighth Army at the time, read: 'In the event of an Allied invasion of Italy, Officers Commanding prison camps will ensure that POWs remain within camp. Authority is granted to all Offciers Commanding to take necessary disciplinary action to prevent individual POWs attempting to rejoin their own units'. Thus some 30,000 out of a total of 68,000 British and Commonwealth POWs were sitting tight when the Germans arrived. They were promptly shipped off to Germany.

Commandant, the pro-British Colonel the Marquese Giancarlo de Medici Castiglione, with a fraternal flourish of his hand, drove off south towards Allied lines, taking two injured POWs with him who were not fit to walk. Clutching a map that he had made in the camp, along with Sergeant Bob Blackmore and Rifleman Mick Miscallef, Lett headed towards Genoa to wait for an imminent Allied landing. After a month of walking over thickly wooded mountains, the little party entered the Rosanno valley where they were given food and shelter by a peasant family. By the end of November, with the Allied armies bogged down south of Rome, Lett and his companions concluded that they little choice other than to stay put and wait developments.

That Christmas three Poles who had escaped from the German Todt labour organization joined Lett's group and before long, he was contacted by Colonel 'Balbi' of the CLN in Genoa who proposed forming an International Brigade to act as a rallying unit for the whole of the Liguria area. Shortly after, Edouardo Basevi, a Lieutenant from a crack Italian Alpini [mountain] Division, established a regular link with the Partisans in Genoa and Lett's fledgling force subjected to a *rastrellamento* on 27 December moved to a new base, 'The Sanctuary', on the 3,000 feet Monte Dragnone. In January, 'a month of strong gales, frost and driving snow', momentum began to build and by February, when it relocated to Torpiana, the 'International Battalion' [Battaglione Internazionale] as it now styled itself consisted of English, Poles, Franco the Sardinian and thirty stalwarts, a group of supporters from Rosanno valley and several others from the Partito d'Azione, many of whom were bent on avoiding the conscription drive of the new Fascist Republic of Salo.

The battalion had by now grown out of all proportion to the scant supplies of arms it had at its disposal; Lett had lost his main arms cache in the December *rastrellamento*. While the threat posed by the enemy was limited to occasional patrols by the Republican Milizia and routine policing by the Carabinieri, it was unrealistic to entertain any idea of the battalion going on the offensive until it had been properly equipped. Lett had managed to get a message through to the Allies about his requirements and it was with great excitement that news of an impending drop was received. After two 'no shows' due to poor weather, a plane finally appeared over the Drop Ground on 14 March. Fires were lit, the pilot flashed his recognition signal but no one had a torch to reply and the plane headed off back to base. The disappointment was palpable; furthermore, the sound of the aircraft has alerted the enemy and on the next day, a large force of Milizia, including German troops for the first time, appeared. Having failed to engage with the Partisans, the enemy withdrew and that evening, two more aircraft appeared

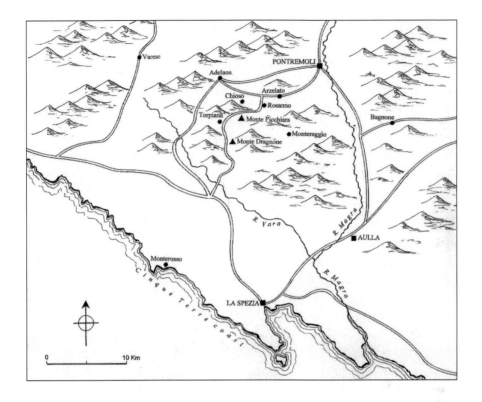

overhead. But with no time to prepare fires, once again Lett and the Partisans watched them fly away without releasing their loads.

In the late spring of 1944, the International Battalion initiated a series of small ambush operations against isolated Republican army vehicles on the country roads near Pontremoli. The battalion now numbered about thirty combatants, including two Yugoslavs, a Peruvian, and a 'somewhat bewildered' Somali who had jumped ship in La Spezia. Major Lett, known throughout the valley as 'Maggiore Inglese', recruited three new members of staff, Italian Air Force Lieutenant Aldo Berti as his Adjutant, Branco the Croat as Intelligence Officer and Italian Army Corporal Nello Sani as a section leader. In April an A Force detachment [Ratberry Three] had arrived to organize the evacuation of thirty escaped POWs in the area, including two senior escaped Allied officers, Colonel Henry Lowry-Corry and Colonel Dicky Richards, who had taken shelter in the Rossano Valley in November 1943. In May, Lett accompanied the party to the Cinque Terre coast, only to witness the operation aborted. It was a long and dispiriting trek back across the mountains to Monte Picchiara. A second attempt in July, in which

Lowry-Corry also participated, likewise failed when the A Force boat came under fire from the enemy garrison at Monterosso.

News of an impending Allied attack on Cassino together with greatly increased Partisan activity – the Partito d'Azione and Communists bands doubled in numbers – raised the tempo throughout the valley. The International Battalion took command of the largest building in Chiesa, the Palzzo degli Schiavi, and in effect became the acknowledged representatives of law and order in the area. A newcomer to the area, escaped POW Lieutenant Geoff Lockwood, was appointed assistant Adjutant and Quartermaster with specific responsibility for liaising with A Force. In addition, six more Poles, four Russians, two Frenchmen, a Belgian and a Dutchman joined up. The International Battalion was now seen as a proper war fighting unit, not as a refuge for deserters and others on the run. Indeed, Lett insisted on billeting escaped Allied POWs on families in the valley and surrounding area at an arm's length from Battalion Headquarters as he was under instruction from A Force that the War Office was anxious that POWs should not become involved in Italian Partisan warfare.

Shortly after a successful attack on the Republican garrison guarding the dam below Monte Picchiara, a second A Force detachment arrived from Monterosso with the news that the International Battalion had been officially recognised by N0.1 Special Forces HQ and were to be known from now on as the Blundell Mission[*]. For Lett, this meant that he had been created a BLO by proxy, a unique achievement. Although this was welcome news, it came at a time when the political tension between the various resistance factions began to increase, partly due to the lavish airdrops of arms and equipment supplied by the OSS. Turf wars became commonplace, from fights on the dropping grounds to the cold-blooded execution of rival commanders. Relations between the Battalion and the Communist Partisans reached a low when a Political Commissar arrived to indoctrinate its members with lessons about Marx and Engels. The situation was resolved when Colonel Fontana, a representative of the CLN, arrived one day in the Orderly Room at the Palazzo and asked Lett to place his forces at his disposal. Given that the CLN was *de facto* the official organ of the Italian government, Lett promptly agreed although he remained concerned about the political infighting.

After relocating his headquarters to Adelana on 1 August, Lett attended the Colonel's first staff conference which had been called to set up the IV

---

[*]   By 1 July 1944, SOE had deployed only four BLOs – two in Venezia, one in Liguria and one in Emilia.

Partisan Zone and it was soon clear that his misgivings were well placed when both the Communists and the Partito d'Azione demanded that he left Rossano in exchange for their protection. Fortunately, unknown to the Partisans, the Special Force W/T team of Alfonso and Bianchi had arrived a few days earlier, so Lett nimbly finessed his way by reminding them that he alone was in radio contact with Allied HQ and thus the arbiter of supplies of arms and equipment. The fact that the meeting broke up acrimoniously was quickly overshadowed by a major *rastrellamento* by German and Republican troops launched in the early hours of 3 August. Soon the villages of Chiesa and Adelana were ablaze. The Partito d'Azione Partisans on Monte Piccheria were driven off, leaving most of their arms and equipment behind. The International Battalion splintered and it was not until early September that it reassembled in the valley though the situation continued to remain tense with another *rastrellamento* executed in Montereggio a few miles to the south.

Around this time, an escaped POW wearing civilian clothes and speaking fluent Italian arrived with a Partisan escort at Fontana's Divisional HQ, claiming to be a British officer. It was Adrian Gallegos of No.1 Special Force, who was on his epic escape from Stalag VII A, a POW camp at Moosburg fifty kilometers north-east of Munich. Lett was initially wary, especially since Gallegos's story was so 'remarkable', and leaving Lockwood to keep an eye on him in Rossano, he checked him out with AFHQ and met up with him a week later.

'I've received a few signals. Do you know anyone called Gerry [Holdsworth], Adrian?'

'Yes... a man called Gerry was my chief in North Africa.'

'There's a signal here from him. "Following for Gallegos stop Congratulations from us all on your escape stop All the best Gerry"'.

Lett's diligence had in fact saved Gallegos's life for just before he had first met him at Divisional HQ, a Partisan runner had come up to him with a message that Gallegos was a well-known spy, an Italian naval commander to boot, and was to be shot immediately.

At the end of October 1944, Colonel Lowry-Corry had finally managed to cross the lines with A Force and the Battalion was now fully occupied with its work as liaison between Partisan formations and the Allied Command, a task made harder by yet another political flare-up caused by a CLN directive from Genoa that political 'commissars' be attached to all Partisan groups. Wisely, Lett retained an independent unit under the command of Aldo to harass the enemy on the outskirts of Pontremoli. In early November, Major Charles Macintosh, the officer in charge of No.1 Special Force Tac HQ in Florence briefed Lieutenant Gambarotta, a twenty one year old Italian veteran of the Stalingrad front, to visit both the Blundell and Parma Missions to obtain reports on their suitability for a forthcoming SAS parachute operation in support of an US Fifth Army offensive for 15 Army Group had just been given C Squadron 2 SAS by SHAFE on the grounds that it 'would be of immense value in bolstering up the Italian patriots". The plan was to drop a force of five officers and twenty-eight men between Genoa and La Spezia and, by a series of aggressive actions, give an impression that a much stronger force was at large to distract the German 148th Division from the imminent US offensive.

An initially suspicious Lett was finally persuaded by Gambarotta that he was bona fide when he produced a bottle of whisky with the words "Major Macintosh said this would satisfy you!" After studying Gambarotta's reports, Macintosh and the SAS decided that Lett's area was the most suitable and on 22 December Lett signalled that he was ready to receive the SAS squadron on 27 December, which gave him time to seal off the area. Despite receiving a message on 26 December that Lett had been murdered, the SAS squadron commander, Captain Bob Walker Brown, determined to go ahead with the operation, for the situation on the ground had taken a dramatic turn for the worse. "There was a danger, we were told, that the entire left flank of the Allied position was liable to crumble," recalled Walker-Brown.

What had happened was that a brilliantly executed attack by German and Italian Mountain troops, Operation Wintergerwitter [Winterstorm], had caused the American 92nd Negro Division on the extreme left flank of the US Fifth Army to give ground. At 0450 hours on 26 December, elements of two German assault battalions, coming out of the darkness, achieved complete surprise when they attacked the American garrison at Sommocolonia; just eighteen defenders managed to disengage and withdraw. Later that morning, 200 men of the Mittenwald Battalion seized the American positions at Bebbio and Scarpello south of Sommocolonia. At 1400 hours the German spearhead reached Barga and its garrison, the 2nd Battalion, 366th Regiment, surrendered the following morning. In the meantime, Axis mortars had opened fire along the whole front to provide covering fire for the move forward of two further columns[†]. The center column in the Serchio valley overcame weak initial resistance and American troops hastily retreated. The town of Fornaci quickly fell.

---

[*]   G3 Sp Ops 4 December 1944.

[†]   East of Serchio river, two German Grenadier battalions together with an attached company from the Italian Brescia Alpine battalion; west of the river, the other Brescia Alpine companies

The all-Italian right column, however, faced a much more vigorous defence. The San Marco had no problems in occupying the village of Molazzano and in pushing back the defenders, but the Regimental HQ Company suffered losses and could not take the village of Brucciano. The Cadelo Group occupied Calomini, but Vergemoli – defended by troops of the US 370th Infantry Regiment, and some Partisan groups – proved harder to capture. A wide minefield, artillery shelling and the intense machine gun and rifle fire stopped the lead Italian platoons and caused heavy casualties. Even intense Axis artillery fire failed to dislodge the Americans from their positions. In the evening of 26 December, the town still was in American hands, although they eventually retreated, leaving a Partisan group as a cover. By 27 December, the surprise offensive was virtually over. It had been a remarkable success. That morning, the German assault column entered Pian di Coreglia, its objective, and some patrols went as far forward as the village of Calavorno, reporting that the enemy was still in full retreat. The other columns had also reached their objectives. Nearly 100 prisoners had been captured, along with many weapons, food and other materials. In these circumstances, the arrival of the SAS was certainly timely but their deployment was not a direct response to the Wintergerwitter offensive which had taken place seventy-five kilometres to their south-east; the line was restored by two brigades of 8th Indian Division while General Mark Clark mulled over 'the bad performance' of the American 92nd.

First to jump was Captain Chris Leng, SOE liaison officer from Tac HQ. Commissioned into 27th Lancers in 1941, Leng had volunteered for special duties in the Middle East the following year when it became apparent to him that his regiment was being sidelined from the real war. A week later, after a cursory interview in Oxford, he was on a troop ship to Cairo where he spent a month learning Serbo-Croat in preparation for deployment in the Balkans. It never materialized and after six aborted drops over the Brenner Pass in the first half of 1944, he was finally designated second-in-command to Lett. Ironically, after a spell in Cyrenaica, Palestine and Syria, his own regiment had landed in Italy in July 1944 and took over in the Upper Tiber valley from the 12th Royal Lancers; from then on, it was rarely out of the front line as an independent armored reconnaissance unit through to April 1945 when it was disbanded in Austria.

After establishing that Lett was indeed alive and well and very much in control of the Drop Ground, the SAS troops followed Leng down with over 300 chutes of men and equipment falling out of the winter sky. Bob Walker

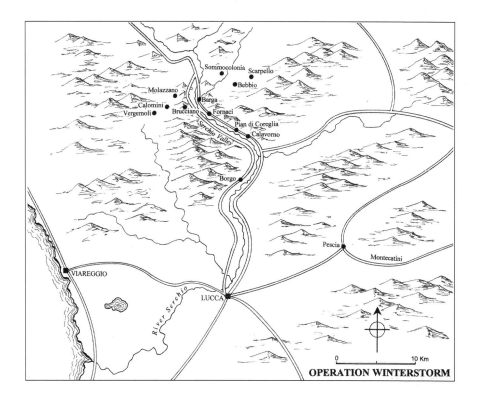

Sommocolonia
Scarpello
Bebbio
Molazzano
Barga
Calomini
Brucciano
Vergemoli
Fornaci
Pian di Coreglia
Calavorno
Serchio Valley
Borgo
Pescia
Montecatini
VIAREGGIO
River Serchio
LUCCA
0   10 Km
OPERATION WINTERSTORM

Brown greeted Lett with the words "The last time we met was in that foul prison camp No 21 at Chieti!" But there was bad news to come. One of the seven US Dakotas that had taken part in the drop returned on a supply run on 30 December and was caught up in turbulence; all seven crew members, including two British aircrew, were killed. This resulted in a temporary ban on the Drop Ground which severely impacted on the ability of No.1 Special Force to resupply Galia and it was only lifted on 2 February. Lett also heard that five out of eight men who he had sent to cross the lines had been killed in a minefield and two were missing.

Bob Walker-Brown had joined the army at the outbreak of the war, initially as a Royal Engineer Territorial Army Reservist. Keen to see active service, he transferred to the Highland Light Infantry in 1941. Wounded and taken prisoner in North Africa in June 1942, he was evacuated to Italy and sent to PG21 at Chieti. Here he joined a tunnelling project and when German guards arrived to evacuate the prisoners northwards after the Italian Armistice was announced, he managed to hide in the partially completed tunnel, emerging after the camp was abandoned. He and two comrades walked down the Apennine ridge for ten days, only to be captured by a German infantry section within sight and sound of the front line. As the firing drew closer, the Germans withdrew, thereby allowing Walker-Brown and his companions to meet up with advance elements of the Eighth Army. Much to his disappointment, he was shipped home to the infantry training centre in Aberdeen as an instructor but not for long. Having got wind that the SAS were looking for volunteers, he managed to transfer to 2 SAS on the strength of his escape experiences and joined 1 Squadron of 2 SAS under the command of Major Roy Farran in the Forest of Chatillon in France in late July 1944. Having successfully attacked the German garrison at Chaumont in conjunction with French resistance fighters, Farran's operation continued with sporadic ambushes of enemy convoys and a concerted mortar attack on the garrison at Langres before the Free French Force under General Leclerc came up from the south.

Operation Galia as the SAS mission was called now got underway and it was not long before Mongol ski troops of the Massa and Parma Military Commands and 285 German Grenadier Battalion moved into the snow-covered mountains in search of the SAS commandos. Lett and Walker Brown had been forewarned of the impending *rastrellamento* and in the circumstances considered that the best form of defence was attack. After all, Allied planners wanted the Germans to believe that elements of 2 British Parachute Brigade, which had recently left Italy for Greece, had returned. Basing themselves in Arzelato, their combined forces attacked on the night of 19 January and in the bitterly cold conditions a vicious game of cat and mouse was played out over the next ten days. Casualties were incurred by both sides but by the time the SAS left the valley at the end of February, they were the clear winners. Lett estimated that over 1,000 Germans had been

SAS with Vickers Heavy Machine Gun

killed, missing or wounded; Walker-Brown's estimate is lower*, citing twenty-two enemy trucks and two trailers destroyed, one truck damaged and 100 to 150 casualties inflicted on enemy forces. But the combined operations of the SAS and Partisans had a much greater psychological effect, far beyond the actual losses inflicted on the enemy: the news that British parachutists were operating alongside the Partisans in the mountains raised morale far and wide; furthermore, it forced the Germans to consider the possibility that bands of Partisans all over the north of Italy might be reinforced by commando units using heavy weapons such as 3 inch mortars and Vickers HMGs. Walker Brown was awarded an immediate DSO for what the citation described as an exceptional 'display of guerrilla skill and personal courage'.

Writing to Macintosh on 14 February 1945, Lett was still raring to get stuck into the Germans. 'You remember some time ago I asked for 500 paratroopers. They sent me thirty-three. Now all I ask is 100 picked men, all commandos if you like, or some commandos and a few infantry, and sabotage specialists. Give me these, and a little time, and I promise you we can take and hold Pontremoli for long enough to make it and the road Cisa/Aulla useless to the enemy for a long time. Give me 200 men of the same calibre and with proper – note the word proper – air collaboration, we will finish the war for you on this front in ten days. Perhaps Fifth Army doesn't want to finish the war?'

After handing over command to SOE's Major John Henderson, Lett himself left the valley on 15 March, crossing the lines at Barga ten days later. It was his first moment on friendly ground for two and a half years. Within two weeks, he was heading north again, this time with a jeep and driver. His instructions were to join the US Fifth Army and when the opportunity offered itself, he was to break through the line and spur the Partisans of the IV Zone into descending on the military port of La Spetzia. As it happened, he teamed up with the Partisan fighter Elio, who had so impressed Major Tony Oldham and Captain Battaglia in Garfagana, and the two of them entered La Spetzia twenty-four hours ahead of the Americans. An Italian naval officer working for the Allies found him there 'heartily sick of all Partisan squabbles and troubles and of having to wait so long for the Allies to arrive'. Lett finished his military service in Italy as Allied Military Governor of the City of Pontremoli, the very place he had helped to save when he relayed positions of enemy troops given to

* Op Galia Preliminary Report

him by the bishop to Allied fighters to conduct pinpoint attacks rather than bomb it indiscriminately.

Gordon Lett was awarded a DSO for his outstanding services to the Italian resistance movement. His achievement had been extraordinary in so many different ways. First, he had welded together a motley collection of different nationalities into a cohesive fighting force behind enemy lines. Secondly, through his leadership and reputation for fair play, he had inspired the population of a whole valley to resist the Axis forces and their proxies. Above all, like Napoleon asked of his Marshals, he was lucky. Captain Mackenzie MacDonald had led a similar existence after walking out of his POW camp in Piacenza in September 1943. Although he had been offered the chance to reach the Swiss frontier, he determined to remain in Italy and became deputy commander of the *Garibaldi* Valnure brigade, complete with red star sewn on his Bersagliari hat. In October 1944, while commanding a small group of Partisans gallantly holding up a German attack, he was killed on the banks of the Nure River near Albarola.

Major Gordon Lett: 12 June 1945: recommendation for immediate DSO

Major Lett escaped from a PW camp at the time of the Italian armistice and shortly afterwards he established himself in the valley of Rossano near Spetzia.

He immediately set about building up the first elements of Partisan resistance in North Italy and at the same time undertook the responsibility of hiding, feeding and evacuating ll escaped allied POWs who reached or were sent to his HQ. During the whole time that he remained in Enemy Occupied territory this officer was instrumental in the successful exfiltration of several hundreds of PWs.

Simultaneously he was slowly and steadily building up resistance elements behind enemy lines. By December 1943, he had formed a small band of English, Poles and Italians which began to take an active part in attacking enemy lines of communication. By May 1944 this and had increased to 150 strong and although poorly armed and badly equipped it began to take more aggressive action against the enemy. During the period May/July 1944, led personally by Major Lett, this band attacked the garrison at Calice castle inflicting many casualties, disarmed the garrison of the power station and dam at Teglia and carried out several small ambushes against German convoys on the main roads.

In August 1944, he was taken over by No.1 Special Force as the senior British Liaison Officer in the area and with increased supplies dropped by air he rapidly built up a most effective and efficient Partisan organization in this area. His fame spread rapidly and Partisan leaders from all over Italy came from as far afield as Milan to consult him on their own local problems. In December 1944 a troop of SAS personnel was dropped by parachute to his reception and this force, with advice and guidance from his HQ, carried out a series of brilliant attacks on the enemy troops in this area.

Despite poor food, squalid living condition and two attempts on his life, and with a heavy price on his head, Major Lett remained in position in Partisan territory for over sixteen months until he was evacuated in January 1945 after a replacement had been sent in.

After he had been evacuated he declined to be repatriated to England and elected to return to work as a forward liaison officer with the troops approaching the Spezia area. On 23 April, while forward troops of 92nd Division were still on the east bank of the river Magra, Major Lett, acting on Partisan information, crossed the river west of Sarzana and drove straight into Spetzia and took control over the town as temporary governor. By this time the forward elements of 92nd Division entered the city that night, Major Lett had the situation under complete control and all public services working normally.

Throughout the past eighteen months, Major Lett has shown conspicuous gallantry and devotion to duty. His work with the Partisan forces is of the highest order and his courage and leadership are amply testified by the Partisan forces with whom he worked. He is most strongly recommended for the award of the immediate DSO.

Awarded

Captain Robert Walker Brown: June 1945: recommendation for immediate DSO

On 27 December 1944, Captain Walker Brown and thirty all ranks were dropped by parachute in the Apennines about 100 miles behind the enemy's lines in the area north of La Spezia. Immediately he began offensive activities against the enemy lines of communication running through his area. Although handicapped by deep snow and very rugged terrain, he marched his men over the mountains, attacking enemy transport columns, mortaring enemy-held villages, mining roads and ambushing marching columns until the enemy was forced to deploy 10,000 troops in a drive through his area to eliminate this nuisance. Captain Walker Brown succeeded in avoiding the enemy net and in preserving his force intact by a display of unparalleled guerrilla skill and personal courage. After the enemy drive was over, he renewed his attacks with undiminished vigour.

In addition to being responsible for the whole of the operation, on 30 December 1944 while commanding an ambush on enemy vehicles travelling along the Genoa-Spezia road, he personally accounted for four of the enemy. On 4 January 1945, despite enemy patrols on the same road, he successfully laid a mine on which a truck was destroyed, twelve Germans killed and eight wounded. In attacks personally led by him a total of sixty Germans were killed or wounded.

During two months behind the lines, Walker Brown's force destroyed twenty-three enemy vehicles, carried out two heavy-mortar attacks on enemy billets and machine-gunned at short range two large columns of marching enemy troops. This magnificent record would not have been possible in the mountains in winter if Walker Brown had not led his men with such vigour, enterprise and complete disregard for personal safety.

When ordered to withdraw, Walker Brown successfully exfiltrated his party intact through enemy lines to safety. It is considered his activities were perfect examples of how guerrilla operations of this sort should be carried out.

Awarded

Op Galia [Walker Brown seated centre]

13

Major Tony Oldham, DSO, MC and bar

After attending Dulwich College where his father was a master, Tony Oldham joined the Supplementary Reserve as a member of the Cameron Highlanders before being commissioned on 1 February 1935 into the Indian Army. Having completed his attachment with the Black Watch in Barrackpore, he joined the Second Battalion 5th Mahratta Light Infantry on the Frontier in 1936 during the troubles with the Fakir of Ipi. A fellow officer remembered him as 'bearing a striking resemblance to David Niven and accentuated it by wearing his peaked cap at an angle, growing a similar moustache and smoking his cigarette through a Dunhill holder'*. The Battalion then moved to Aden and, on the outbreak of war, to the Sudan where it formed part of the 4th Indian Division. Having had a variety of jobs including Transport Platoon [Mules], MTO, QM, signals officer and adjutant, on 20 June 1942, by then 2ic, Major Tony Oldham somewhat to his surprise found himself 'in the bag' at Tobruk along with 35,000 other Allied soldiers[†]. As Churchill told the House of Commons on 2 July, 'The fall of Tobruk, with its garrison of about 25,000 men, in a single day was utterly unexpected. Not only was it unexpected by the House and the public at large, but by the War Cabinet, by the Chiefs of the Staff and by the General Staff of the Army'.

Sent first to Bari Transit Camp, Oldham was then transferred to a senior officers' camp near Piacenza in the Po Valley. Determined to escape, he joined a tunnelling venture and after four months of hard work, on 1 July 1943 the twelve participants lowered themselves into the vertical shaft and waited for the cinema show to start in the courtyard. Unfortunately the air supply had been incorrectly hooked up and after a long delay, Oldham reached the undergrowth just as the film ended. Almost immediately the alarm was raised and within two days he had been recaptured and sentenced to thirty days solitary confinement. It was therefore a pleasant surprise for Oldham, when the Italian Commandant came into the camp on 8 September, shook hands with the senior

---

*   A.E.C. writing in Mahratha Newsletter
†   He was in fact posted as 'missing in action'. His mother had no idea he was alive until the end of the war.

British officer and told him that they were free. These actions were repeated all over the country as Italy's Army and Air Force virtually disintegrated after the armistice with the Allies was publicly proclaimed on 8 September. At 1730 hours that afternoon, Marshal Badoglio announced over Rome radio: 'Italy has been compelled to withdraw from the unequal struggle...Hostilities against the British and American forces will now cease on all fronts.'

Allied POWs had four choices, the priority of which depended on where they found themselves: either stay put and wait for the Allied forces* or head north to neutral Switzerland or move south to cross Allied lines or join the Partisans until the Allied armies arrived in their area of operations. As one of a party of eight which left the camp on 10 September, Oldham made his way slowly south into the Apennines with a view to crossing the Allied Lines. After ten days, it became clear that they had a better chance of getting through if they split up into smaller groups, so Oldham and one OR first headed for the coast to get a boat to Corsica but were soon advised by local people to abandon this plan and changed direction for Florence. Three days into their march, the OR strained a tendon and having found a friendly Italian with whom to leave him, Oldham set off alone. After climbing the Apuanian Alps, he reached Castelnuovo Garfagnana in the Serchio Valley. Here he was befriended by an elderly farmer, Orlando Fiore, and passed onto Signora Maria in Gallicano who housed him in her luxurious villa. Life however was not without danger. On one occasion, he was locked in a clothes closet for two hours while the Carabinieri searched the house. His hostess opened the door of the closet and asked the officer if he wished to see inside; luckily he was tired of his search and declined.

In April 1944, the local authorities requisitioned Signora Maria's villa to house refugees from the cities, thus forcing Oldham into the mountains where he lived in Orlando's barn. By this time he had learnt to read and speak Italian and when he heard that there had been an arms drop in the Apuanian Alps, he set off on the night of 10 June to contact the local Partisan leader, Dr Abdenaco Coli, to see if he could help. The situation he found was fairly typical of the time; the eighty or so Partisans in the area all lived at home and only took up arms when it was convenient for them. Oldham argued that they should join him in the woods and carry out raids as far away as possible from their villages in order to avoid reprisals. About twenty men took him up on his offer and within days they had established a base in a barn high up in the mountains far from any village. Armed with Bren and Sten guns, the *brigata's* first raid was on a large Todt organization store house at Arni where they

---

* The official MI9 directive

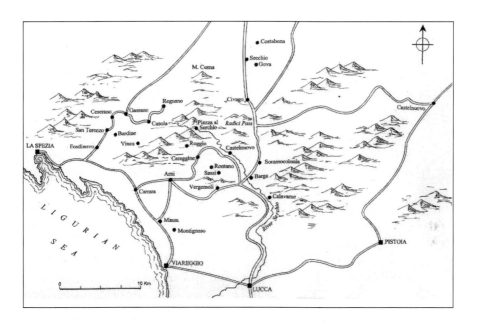

liberated a considerable quantity of food and cigarettes. Soon after they were joined by fourteen deserters from a German Russian Turkestan division, all well armed with German rifles and ammunition.

By now, *La Banda Toni* was about seventy strong and on the morning of 20 June, the anniversary of his capture at Tobruk two years before, Oldham took ten men armed with Stens and rifles down through the woods to ambush the Castelnuovo-Aulla road. As he went forward to recce a suitable site with one escorting Partisan, a column of German vehicles came round the corner of the road – 'it was no use trying to escape so we sat down, hiding our weapons behind our backs and trying to look innocent. The leading truck, which had a machine gun mounted on a swivel in the back, started to slow down and then continued on its way. Twenty-five trucks and an open staff car passed us and then we ran for cover.' When the convoy returned, the Partisans shot up the staff car, killing a colonel and another officer and wounding the two other occupants. In a follow up attack, the Germans lost fifteen killed and twenty-two wounded. Following this engagement, *La Banda Toni* had to reorganize and by 12 July it was down to only forty men as some had left to help with the harvest, others to live at home.

Living in shelters made of branches and leaves, sometimes with a turf roof, Oldham's Partisans began to put out signal fires when they heard the sound of a circling plane. They were soon rewarded and had recovered and distributed two planeloads of arms and ammunition by 14 July. Then on the night of 15/16 July 1944, the SOE Berth/Turdus mission comprised of Captain Roberto Battaglia [Barocci], Lieutenant Bruno Innocenti and Lieutenant Vitaliani dropped into the area of Piola near Careggine, a twenty-five mile error from where it should have been dropped at Ligonchio where the BLO, Major Vivian Johnston, was waiting for them. Within hours, they met up with Oldham and the result of this unscheduled meeting was to have a major impact on Partisan activities in the Garfagnana region.

Partly of English descent – his grandmother, Emma Phipps, came from Wiltshire – Battaglia was born in Rome in 1913. A member of the Partito d'Azione, he fought with the *Giustizia e Liberta* patriots from 1942 onwards, and after the liberation of Rome in June 1944, he transferred to SOE to join the Partisans as a political adviser. Leaving Oldham in situ with Vitaliani, Battaglia set off to find Johnston. The day after he had left, the Germans occupied four villages in Oldham's area and started to improve the track which passed within fifty yards of his camp. There was no option other than to move and after the local men had returned to their homes, Oldham set off north with twenty-four men, arriving three days later at Regnano, a hillside village near Castelnuovo, where he found Battaglia and subsequently Major Johnston.

Fluent in Arabic, Italian and French, twenty-one year old Vivian Johnston had initially been commissioned in the Royal Engineers in October 1942 and posted to the Libyan Arab Army, popularly known as the Sanusi Army. Shortly after Italy had entered the war, a number of Libyan leaders living in exile in Egypt urged their compatriots to organize themselves into military units and join the British in the war against the Axis powers. Five battalions, which were originally destined for guerrilla warfare in the Jabal al Akhdar region of Cyrenaica, were established but because the high mobility of the desert campaigns required a considerable degree of technical and mechanical expertise, the Libyan forces were primarily used for guarding military installations and Axis prisoners. Bored with this outcome, Johnston managed to extricate himself and joined SOE; after a two month stint on the island of Kos, he transferred to No.1 Special Force, dropping into Italy in June 1944.

The three officers – Battaglia, Oldham and Johnston – decided to summon all the main Partisan commanders and their political commissars to a meeting in Regnano on 8 August to thrash out a sustainable *modus operandi* for the coming months. Shrewdly, Battaglia had already had preliminary discussions with the main actors, so it was unanimously decided to unite all the Partisan bands under a new umbrella organisation, the Divisione *Garibaldi* Lunense, with Major Oldham as its military commander and Battaglia as the divisional political commissar. The only exception was the Emilia band which decided to remain as before with their own leaders and with Johnston as their BLO. If they were to confront with any degree of success the considerable enemy forces ranged against them, namely the three Republican Fascist Divisions Mote Rosa, San Marco and Julia and the 148 German Division, Oldham proposed that a formal structure of brigades and battalions should be adopted for practical reasons of administration and operational deployment.

At 0130 hours Oldham was called out of the meeting by an excited Partisan who informed him that the Germans were entering the village. After announcing the news to the assembled delegates, Oldham wrote in his reminiscences 'we all helped to clean up the room. The tables were cleared, every scrap of paper picked up and stuffed into someone's pocket, flasks of wine and glasses disappeared if by magic. In five minutes there was no trace of the meeting. In two minutes more we were all in the woods on our way back to camp.' One officer, Lieutenant Andrea, Johnston's LO, was shot dead while trying to retrieve his W/T set. After hiding in the woods for two days, when enemy patrols passed within twenty yards of their hiding place, Oldham and Battaglia were finally able to come out of their holes and set to work implementing the agreed re-organization of the Partisan bands.

The newly formed Lunense Division now consisted of three brigades. The first or Garfagnana brigade, commanded by Dottore Coli, a close confidant of Oldham since June, numbered around 300 Partisans in total, who were divided into four battalions under command of Marco, Zerbini, Bertagni and Sabatino respectively. Their orders were to sabotage and harass the German lines of communication along the roads Arni-Castelnuovo, Castelnuovo – Piazza al Serchio and Castelnuovo-Passo della Forbici. This they did with aplomb, at one point capturing and holding the village of Le Roccette no less than three times. Other highlights included the destruction of 110 enemy mules and horses of 146th German Division [through putting No 8 shot in their ears]; the destruction of ten enemy vehicles and the seizure of the Passo di Radici by Marco for an entire day; and the further destruction of seven enemy trucks by a sixteen year-old boy, 'Il Rossino', who placed explosives with time pencils in them when they were parked up.

The second brigade, Brigada Carrara, led by Maggiore Contri, was based at Bardine San Terenzo with a fighting strength of about 250 divided into four battalions. Tasked with sabotaging and harassing of the Fosdinovo-Ceserano and Gassano-Casola road networks, the brigade was hampered by the presence of the German 148 Divisional HQ at Ceserano. Any activity was likely to result in high casualties among the civil population. For the 300-strong third 'La Spezia' brigade under Sergeant Major Marini and Domenico, the task of harassing the Fivvizano-Piazza al Serchio and Fivvizano-Casola roads was easier; seven bridges on Fivvizano-Casola road were destroyed.

On 30 August, instructions were received from Tac HQ Fifth Army for an all out effort by the Partisans to support the Allied attack on the Gothic Line but due to poor encoding, no one could make sense of the message until it was resent on 2 September. The next night, all the Partisans in the Garfagnana area swooped down from the hills, attacking roads and blowing up bridges. Their final tally was impressive: 350 German dead, twenty-three bridges destroyed or damaged and about forty enemy vehicles put out of action. Sadly, Marco, the inspirational Partito d'Azione Party commander of the first battalion of the first brigade, was killed, shot by 'an Italian gangster in the pay of the Germans"*. Naturally the enemy reacted and this was the beginning of one of the blackest periods in Partisan history to date. Soon after an officer and sixteen SS storm troopers had been killed by Second Brigade Partisans near Bardine San Terenzo, more than twenty villages were burnt down in reprisal and the entire populations of Bardine San Terenzo and Vinca, nearly 400 old men, women and children, were massacred by SS troops. The savage bloodletting ended with a three-day carnage at Marzabotto at the end of September, one of the worst wartime atrocities in Italy.

Denunciation of Partisans to fascist authorities and spying were an ugly aspect of everyday life in all European resistance movements, Italy being no exception. Oldham, Battaglia and Innocenti had therefore to constitute a Divisional Military Tribunal which in the course of its tenure sentenced twenty spies/collaborators to death; the Divisional Brigades likewise executed about 100. Oldham insisted that scrupulous records were kept of all judicial proceedings. Other crimes like stealing from companions or friendly inhabitants were also punishable by death. Lesser offences merited from two to forty-eight hours tied to a stake with the hands above the head or expulsion from the band after being stripped of all clothes and equipment.

In early October, Oldham and Battaglia set off from their headquarters on Monte Tondo to reconnoitre the Careggine area with a view to linking up with the Allies there. It was clear to Oldham that if the Partisans could synchronize

---

* Battaglia report

a determined and well-planned attack on the enemy's rear with a major assault by Allied forces on the front line, there was a very real chance of facilitating the long-awaited breakthrough of the Gothic Line that had eluded the Allies to date. To achieve this meant expanding the Lunense Division by incorporating other Partisan units into its order of battle and so on 18 October, the two officers held a conference at Forno di Massa with four major Partisan bands, all Communists save the Christian-Democrat Groupo Patriotti; the 4th Apuania Brigade under Dottore Bertolini based at Torsana, the Groupo Patriotti Apuani under Don Pietro based in Forno di Massa, the Brigata Ugo Muccini Liguri under Memmo based in Casette, and lastly the Brigata Ugo Muccini Lunense under the command of Federico at Monte Grosso. Between them, these four formations brought an additional 2,900 men to the Lunense Division, giving it a total fighting strength of approximately 4,000 men. For Oldham and Battaglia, this was an extraordinary achievement within the space of little over two months, particularly in regard to the very real political differences which characterized the Partisan leadership.

In last days of October, Bertagni, the commander of the third battalion of the Garfagnana brigade, launched a daring and opportunistic attack with eighty of his men on the Republican garrison at Castelnuovo. A Fascist officer of the garrison was killed and a long column of carts full of Germans returning from the front was almost completely wiped out, suffering 350 casualties, many caused by mortar fire directed by Germans on the front line who thought that their line had been penetrated. This in turn severely disrupted German movement in the Serchio Valley and a message was sent by courier to advise the Allies accordingly. No response was received and the Americans remained in their original positions.

The strategy of the Lunense Division entered a new phase in November, shifting from mobile operations to the static defence of a specific sector between Arni, Castelnuovo and Montignoso [Massa], an area of twenty-five kilometres long by five to six kilometres deep. The objective of the liberation of the whole of Lunigiana and Garfagnana was by far the most ambitious to date. During the latter part of the month, an additional 300 Partisans from other zones were drafted into the area; Partisans from the upper Serchio valley and from Emilia were deployed in Roggio and Civago to protect the flanks of the liberated zone. If Oldham's Partisans could hold this ground while the US Fifth Army attacked immediately to their front, then a gap could be gorged out of the German defensive line thus facilitating a breakout.

At Tac HQ, Major Charles Macintosh noted on 13 November 1944:

1. 92 [US] Division asked if we could help with Partisans on their immediate front.

2. We explained Major Oldham's position as follows:

(a) He commands the widely scattered and ill-armed Lunense Division of approximately 3,500 men.

(b) He, through Major Davies, has expressed himself capable of co-operating with the regular forces if these were to advance.

(c) He was, at the time (7 November), concentrating some 500 men due East of Castelnuovo. He could concentrate more men of the Apuani Brigade in the area given four days' notice.

(d) His daylight Drop Ground was given by another courier (Lieutenant Bruno).

(e) It was estimated that he might cut the route used by the enemy for the supply of his troops in the Monte Altissomo area for four hours with his present ammunition supply, and that, with more ammunition, he could hold for some twenty-four to forty-eight hours.

3. The information concerning Major Oldham's ground was passed to Base on 6 November.

4. We informed Division that Major Oldham's forces might assist them to the degree shown in paragraph 2 above making the distinction between his possible action armed and his present limitations. We informed them that stores were always ready at Brindisi for operations of this nature and that it might be possible to get a drop through Army. We also told them that we had requested a drop in the usual way but that there were many priorities to be considered...'

Conditions now became really tough. Living in the open at a height of 1,500 metres, the Partisans faced an additional enemy, the snow. Battaglia writes from experience in *The Story of the Italian Resistance* when he states 'the weather gradually worsened. Heavy snow, that scourge of the men of the Resistance, blanketed the ruins of the ravaged countryside and blotted out all signs of life.' Everyone was short of food as Oldham recorded in his post-operational report: 'Garfagnana...by the end of November the district was completely denuded by the enemy of grain, cattle and potatoes and all that remains to the population now is chestnut flour; [the cities of] Massa – Carrara...already starving. No food resources whatsoever in this part and I have seen bare-footed women crossing the snow-covered mountains in order to buy one or two kilos of chestnut flour in Garfagnana.' This flour was used to make *polenta dolce*, a nutritional porridge with a high sugar content poured onto a wooden board and then cut with a string or a peeled willow stick.

At the beginning November, Oldham had sent Lieutenant Innocenti through the Allied lines to organise a supply drop for the Division's final effort to facilitate a breakthrough of the Gothic Line. On 15 November, Innocenti appeared in a Lysander aircraft over Oldham's headquarters and dropped the new Turdus Two plan, signals ciphers and courier codes. Direct contact was then immediately established with Tac HQ Fifth Army. For Oldham, the final fruition of his ambitious plan was now in sight.

The irrepressible Bertagni, 'one of the most courageous officers that the resistance movement has produced"[*], attacked Monte Rocchetta, capturing fifty prisoners and seven machine guns at no cost to his own forces. He passed his prisoners down to the 92nd Negro Division on the other side of the lines but could not convince them to take over this important position which overlooked the greater part of the front. After two days of fierce counter-attacks, the Partisans finally ran out of ammunition and withdrew to Vergemoli where they crossed the Allied lines.

Around this time, Memmo, the Communist commander of the Muccini Lunense Brigade, decided to occupy Carrara to secure the release of captured Partisans who had been denounced by local spies. Having succeeded in occupying the town, he then asked the Lunense Division to come to his assistance, a request which was flatly refused as he had not consulted with it in the first place. Instead he was ordered to limit his activities to the simple exchange of prisoners and then withdraw to the mountains; it was too late for German armoured vehicles had surrounded the town.

Unknown to the Lunense Division, negotiations ensued with the result that an agreement was drawn up between the two opposing forces not to attack each other; the Muccini Lunense Brigade and the Patriotti Apuani who had also become involved agreed to confine themselves to the mountains and the Germans promised to stay within the town and on the roads. German guns trained on Carrara provided the guarantee. As a result of this unauthorized compromise, the Germans were able to move troops away from Massa into the 'liberated zone' of the Lunense Division.

As each day passed, the resupply situation became ever more dire. Ammunition had all but run out and Battaglia estimated that the Partisans had 'half and hour's worth' left. Finally, after two days of no show, the long awaited air drop materialized, including eight Breda 37 machine guns, ten Bren guns, a number of hand grenades, rifles and Sten guns and the all important food. But it was far from perfect: 1,100 pairs of summer underpants floated down from the sky instead of the boots and winter clothing

---

[*]   Battaglia post-operational report

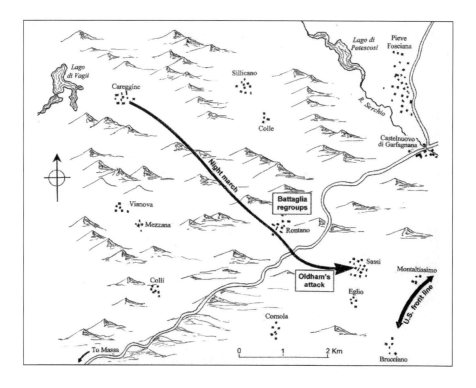

that had been asked for. Furthermore there was no ammunition for the Breda 30s which rendered them useless. It is sanguine to consider that in the third quarter of 1944 (July to September), 10,000 tons of supplies were dropped to Tito's Yugoslav Partisans and a paltry 550 tons to the Italians. Nevertheless, these supplies enabled the Division to continue to implement its plan of attack and its strength was increased by eighty men from the Muccini Brigade Liguria and fifty men from the Muccini Brigade Lunense. On 25 November, when news of the successful arms drop had been confirmed, Fifth Army signalled Oldham, asking him to cooperate in an attack on the enemy by the US 92nd Negro Division in two days time. The Lunense Division was given three objectives over a front of about 1,000 yards, so Oldham quickly drew up plan to invest that part of German front line between Sassi and Monte d'Amina in order to link with the Allies.

Leaving around 500 men to defend the Careggine area, Oldham and Battaglia set off on the moonlit night of 26 November with 200 Partisans. After an hour of good going, it clouded over and started to rain, causing great difficulties on the precipitous track which had become diabolically slippery. By dawn on 27 November, Oldham found himself with only fifty

US 92nd Division at Massa

men, the others somehow having become detached during the appalling long night approach march. None the less, he pressed on and managed to occupy Monte d'Anima by 0730 hours while the rest of the group under Battaglia reorganised at Rontano. Much as he wanted to join Oldham at this crucial stage, it was impossible for Battaglia to come down the side of one bare mountain and up the side of another in full view of German machine gunners. He had to wait until dusk to carry out such a manoeuvre. Oldham's force meanwhile had successfully taken out two German mortar positions but with no sign of the 92nd Division, two companies of German infantry counter-attacked Oldham's position, forcing him to withdraw hurriedly, in the process losing eight men through drowning in the Turrite River. Battaglia's group had attacked a convoy on Castelnuovo-Arni road and it was not until early evening he learnt of Oldham's withdrawal. With their hopes of linking up with the Allies now dashed, both groups quickly realised the necessity of escaping the ever-tightening encirclement by German forces.

By now more or less surrounded in their HQ on the 1,268m Monte Volsci, Oldham and Battaglia came up with a three-pronged strategy to extricate the Division. The Partisans could retain their arms and split up into small groups and continue to harass the enemy. Alternatively, they could cache their weapons and return to their homes, a somewhat unrealistic proposal since most of them were known to the authorities. Finally, they could cross the Allied lines. Given that the Drop Grounds were no longer secure due to the proximity of German troops and the raised level of anti-Partisan operations, there was no choice other than to disperse. Regnano had been reduced to ruins and many civilians executed by the SS. The lack of food and the severity of the winter ruled out continuing operations in the mountains.

What had happened to the much vaunted coordination with the US 92nd [Negro] Division? Clearly it had not gone ahead, leaving Oldham completely exposed and in an untenable position. The official history of the 92nd, states that it 'was expected to launch a major offensive on December 1 in support of the II Corps' renewed attack on Bologna. The attack was rescheduled for Christmas Day due to a predicted German counterattack. When intelligence reports indicated a large German build-up in the northern region of the Serchio Valley, the men of the 371st were transferred to the coastal sector, and elements of the 366th were sent to the valley to support the 370th. Although the Fifth Army never launched its early December assault, it was not a quiet month in the Serchio Valley.' Oldham hints at disagreements with Colonel Sherman of the 92nd Division who was reluctant to get involved. He may have just been realistic since the division's combat performance left much to be desired; in a report* submitted by General Clarke, Fifth Army commander, to Field Marshal Alexander, he highlights the efforts of a 400-strong infantry battalion from the Division which, having launched an attack over 'moderately difficult terrain' at the end of November, finished the assault with just seventy men left although casualty figures were only one killed, fifty-nine wounded and four cases of exhaustion.

With his faithful Turkmens, Oldham returned to Metello where he gave them the choice of staying with Dr. Coli and *Banda Toni* or crossing the line which would have meant being handed over to the Russians. Most elected to stay and after a hazardous night march, Oldham crossed into Allied Lines on the night of 4/5 December over Monte Corchia to Levigliani and then to Viareggio. He was typically apologetic in a note he had sent ahead by courier to Major Macintosh of 1 Special Forces on 29 November. After explaining that it had proved impossible to maintain Partisan forces in large numbers, he was 'terribly sorry that the action of 27 November was a complete failure but we

---

* Clark papers

Germans in action against Partisans

tried our best and now are finished for the moment'. On 9 December, deter-mined to re-enter the fray, he asked Macintosh to send a 'very forceful and tactful' officer to 'the concentration camps of the AMG in Florence to get as many of my old Partisans out of their clutches...and warn them to await instruc-tions as to when and where they may find me.' Furthermore, could A Force be officially informed that he had crossed back over the lines and while Maryland [SOE] was at it, could he have a set of false ID papers? The Americans appar-ently still wanted to use the Partisans on 'the worst part of their bloody front' although with reservations about mixing Negro soldiers with the Partisans. As it transpired, Oldham did not return to lead his Partisans in further attacks and on 14 January reported reluctantly to A [No.1] Allied POW Repatriation camp.

Meanwhile Battaglia had linked up with Major Vivian Johnston and Major Wilcockson at Gova where he received orders to return to base and after an exhausting journey, crossed the lines with Lieutenant Vitaliani on 12 December. En route he picked up the following information about the recently demobilized Lunense division. All the men and arms of 1st Garfag-nana Brigade were safe. A battalion of Alpini and 500 German troops had occupied Careggine after a fierce bombardment and not found a single Partisan. Coli had successfully crossed the lines. The 2nd Carrara Brigade

A SPUR CALLED COURAGE

[Bruno Bacci Bde] was still in position. On 25 November, they had defeated an enemy attack, inflicting fifty casualties. Contri had crossed the lines. The news from the 3rd La Spezia Brigade was less good. Although Marini had managed to cross the lines, twenty villagers had been executed in Regnano as reprisal for Partisan attacks. The remnants of the other three Partisan formations, 4th Bde Apuania, Groupo Patriotti Apuani and Brigata Ugo Muccini Lunense were all under attack by the Germans.

Vivian Johnston was fulsome in his praise of Oldham. In a note of 5 January 1945 to Commander No.1 Special Force, he wrote to express his gratitude to 'the splendid work he [Oldham] performed during his stay in the field.....Working untiringly to form the new Lunense Division...a very disciplined fighting body which gave a good account of itself in ceaseless operations against the enemy...During his stay near the front line, he faced with serenity the lack of food and every other comfort in order to take part in the liberation of the province.' In Battaglia's post-operational report, he attributed one of the main reasons for success to "the personality of Major Oldham, military commander, always the first to sacrifice himself and at points of danger, able to share wholly in the hard life of the Partisans."

Later on, he expanded his view: "There was something in his character that attracted Tony to guerrilla activity – but it was not only this, I don't believe a mature man would take the decision to stay in the area only as a result of a simple impulse or of a sentimental attraction. Certain circumstances had led him to follow this path; first he was exhausted as a result of his escape and for some time had not the strength to continue on is way, he then grew accustomed to and fond of the atmosphere and the feeling in the Garfagnana area; he then felt it his duty to repay hospitality he'd received by using his own military knowledge to help liberate the area and those in it he had grown to care for...In a friendly, cordial way he had come to the division that he would be of more use in enemy territory. He felt the necessity of this war of the people behind the enemy's back and had even helped to make it a thing of importance. Through his affection for the area and its people he had come to love Italy but in a new and special way; not as another nation but as part of humanity that was against the Hun."

At No.1 Special Force Tac HQ in Florence, Major Charles Macintosh summarised the performance of the Lunense Division thus: 'Despite the shortage of arms and other supplies the division, inspired by Oldham, was surprisingly effective; between August and the end of December 1944 it carried out fifty major sabotage actions [including the destruction of thirty important road and rail bridges]; some 1,000 enemy personnel were killed;

mines placed on the Radici Pass helped kill thirty Germans including a General. The Division was to fight several pitched battles and for a glorious but very short time occupied Carrara.'

Released by No.1 Special Force, Oldham was posted to the 3rd Battalion Mahratta Light infantry which had just crossed the River Po and was concentrated in the Trecenta area, east of the Apennines. On leave in March 1945, he married Giuseppina Concherini in Naples, the culmination of a love affair that had begun in 1943 when he first left the POW camp. Wounded in the leg, he was sent by the Partisans to Doctor Ippolito Concherini, who hid him in an attic in one of his properties in Molazzana. Oldham's daughter, Sylvia, recounts that 'as my mother was the bravest and could be trusted to keep her mouth shut, my grandfather had her bring food to my father. They fell in love. She also helped him with the Italian language. After he recovered and went to another location in the region, they still corresponded – individuals would carry love notes in their shoes to my father.' Oldham subsequently returned to India with his battalion and new bride and in 1947 was sent to the Staff College in Quetta but after being hospitalised with suspected TB, he decided to leave the army as a Lieu-tenant Colonel and went to live in Italy. Sadly he encountered much hatred and bitterness there and having been denounced and arrested as a suspected communist and warned that his life was in danger, he emigrated to Canada with his young family.

Major Tony Oldham: 15 January 1945: recommendation for DSO

This officer was captured at Tobruk in June 1942 and after one unsuc-cessful attempt to escape was released by the Italian Military Authorities on 10 September 1943 and immediately forced into hiding in the Garfag-nana area. He at once set about organizing, recruiting and training the patriot forces in this area, and through his ceaseless and untiring energy was successful in building up a substantial Partisan force which became known as the Lunense Division numbering some 4,000 men. From the beginning of June 1944, the forces under his command and at his direction commenced a series of highly successful operations against enemy lines of communication and at least 1,000 enemy were accounted for as killed during the period that Captain Oldham was in command of these forces. His outstanding leadership and ability to face up to every hardship is amply evidenced by the fact that the area in which this Partisan force was organized and led is one of the poorest areas in Italy and had been entirely denuded of food supplies by the enemy, but despite this Captain Oldham succeeded in keeping his forces united, fed and happy until they were finally forced to disband at the end of November on account of the weakness and ill health of his forces caused by starvation.

On 27 November 1944, Captain Oldham personally led a force which was to occupy Monte d'Anima amd Sassi [1005m] in the rear of the Castelnuovo-Massa front in tactical cooperation with units of the Fifth Army. Owing to the difficulties of the terrain and adverse weather, only sixty of the 200 men under his orders for this operation arrived at the assembly point, but despite this and fully realizing that the attacks on these two places were of vital consequence to Fifth Army, he decided to put in his attack with these small forces. The attack on Sassi failed in the face of strong German opposition but Monte d'Anima was occupied by the Partisans and held for four hours until he was compelled to withdraw owing to the failure of the advanced elements of the Fifth Army to make contact and under the severe pressure by the counter-attacks of two German companies supported by heavy mortar fire.

During the whole period that Captain Oldham was operating in enemy occupied territory, he was fully aware of the possibilities of infiltrating through the enemy lines and reaching the Allied forces, but of his own free will he elected to remain and fight with the forces which he had organized, totally disregarding his own safety until his forces were finally forced to disband at the end of November, when he made his way successfully through the Allied lines.

Captain Oldham's outstanding leadership, unfailing courage and devotion to duty during the fourteen months spent by him in enemy occupied territory of his own free will are deserving of the fullest recognition.

Awarded

Captain Tony Oldham: 1 March 1942: recommendation for immediate bar to MC

Before Gazala 22-26 February 1942, Captain Oldham led the party which penetrated the enemy's position to raid the Advanced Landing Ground [ALG] at Martuba. He covered approximately fifty miles across country patrolled by enemy AFVs on the outward journey and reached his objective according to plan. Unfavourable conditions on the first night compelled him to lie up in close proximity to the enemy ALG until the following night. Three enemy aircraft and a bomb dump were destroyed under the noses of the enemy guards. Captain Oldham succeeded in bringing his party back to its unit despite increased enemy patrol activity on the return journey. Such a successful raid called for a high standard of courage, leadership and endurance in its commander.

Awarded

Captain Tony Oldham: March 1941: recommendation for immediate MC

On the morning of 16 March 1941, before Cheren, the enemy, about 150 strong, all Italians, counterattacked Flat Top and effected a lodgement on the East end of the feature. Captain Oldham who had been sent forward, showed outstanding qualities of leadership, duty and initiative. He organized about thirty men of the Battalion's porterage company in his vicinity and personally led them up Flat Top and attacked the enemy in flank with the bayonet, driving them off the hill, killing several and capturing one Italian officer and twelve Italian other ranks.

He himself shot at least one Italian at close quarters and returned covered in blood and brains of one of his assailants.

This prompt and gallant action on the part of Captain Oldham undoubtedly saved a very critical situation and enabled the Battalion to regain control of the vital feature of Flat Top.

Awarded

FM Auchinleck and Oldham 1946

14

Squadron Leader Count Manfred Czernin, DSO, MC, DFC
Major Tom Roworth, MC, Croix de Guerre

The fourth son of the diplomat Count Otto Czernin* von und zu Chudenitz of Dimokur [then in Austria but now in the Czech Republic] and Lucy Beckett, daughter of 2nd Baron Grimthorpe, Manfred Czernin was born in Berlin in 1913. A year later, his parents separated, his father remaining as Counsellor at the Austrian Embassy in St Petersburg and his mother moving to Italy where her grandmother had a house in Rome and her father a villa in Ravello. In 1920 his parents officially divorced, his father gaining custody of his three elder brothers and his mother of him.

Having arranged for him to attend school in England, Lucy Czernin returned to Florence to meet up with her three elder sons and travel with them to Ravello for a holiday. Taking her turn at the wheel, she drove towards Viterbo where they planned to stay the night. At the city gates, they were stopped by a group of Communists who refused to allow the car to pass, despite the fact that their hotel was situated just inside the gates. No sooner had she turned the car around and headed off the way she had come when Communist forces opened fire on the car, instantly killing her fourteen year old son, Jaromir, and seriously wounding his brother, seventeen year old Paul, whose leg had to be amputated. Enrico, her chauffeur, riddled with shotgun pellets, contracted tetanus but fortunately survived. Despite this appalling tragedy, Manfred's family's links with Italy remained as strong as ever and as he continued his education in England, each summer he would return to visit the beautiful Villa Cimbrone in Ravello.

After leaving Oundle School, Czernin was taken on as a trainee manager by the Valentine family who owned a large tobacco plantation in Southern Rhodesia but after a severe bout of malaria he returned to Europe and with the encouragement of his new step-father, Captain Oliver Frost, OBE, MC, a RFC pilot in the First War, he applied for a commission in the RAF and was accepted just after his twenty-second birthday. Having completed his

---

* His elder brother, Ottokar, was the Foreign Minister of Austria-Hungary from 1916-1918

training, he was posted to 57 Squadron in Oxfordshire where he flew two-seater Hawker Hart bombers. A friend at the time commented that Czernin 'liked fast cars and fast aeroplanes – his personality was outside the realms of convention'. Czernin was placed on the Reserve in August 1937 with an 'Average' assessment after 250 flying hours. Somewhat sad at leaving, he retired to Ravello with his mother, whose second marriage had just come unstuck. A trip to America followed and on his return to England, Czernin opened a restaurant called The Hot Dog in Wardour Street in Soho. On the outbreak of war, Czernin was mobilized and posted to No.1 Ferry Pilot's Pool at RAF Hucknall in Nottinghamshire. It was at this time that he eloped with a beautiful debutante, Maud Hamilton, and they married against her parents' wishes.

With only months to go until his twenty-seventh birthday when he would be too old to become a fighter pilot, Czernin managed to fix an interview with Air Vice Marshal Leigh-Mallory, OC Fighter Command's 12 Group, and having successfully been checked out on a Gloster Gladiator biplane, was posted to 504 Squadron to convert to Hawker Hurricanes and then to France with 85 Squadron. Now the shooting war started in earnest and in ten days in May 1940 the Squadron lost nine pilots killed or missing in the course of destroying eighty-nine German aircraft. When the Squadron was withdrawn, Czernin switched to 17 Squadron based at Le Mans, finally returning to England on 19 June. He had five confirmed and two unconfirmed 'kills', a creditable performance for a man now deemed too old to fly fighters.

17 Squadron, now at Debden, spent the next six months fully engaged in the Battle of Britain. Shot down over Suffolk by the German fighter ace Adolf Galland on 17 November, Czernin was up in the air two days later and by the end of the year had notched up fourteen confirmed and two probable kills, and seven damaged enemy aircraft. For the year of 1940, Czernin was one of the top twenty RAF pilots as regards victories and for his ninety-seven operational sorties he was awarded a well-deserved DFC. A contemporary recalled 'the Count was a typical fighter pilot of the time. He enjoyed parties and flying and was good at both. He was to my mind like most Czechs, an individualist in the air rather than a leader.' It was to prove an accurate assessment and over the next two years, Czernin found himself more and more marginalized as a fighter pilot, with a stint as an instructor and then, in March 1942, a posting to Upper Assam in India as Commanding Officer of 146 Squadron before ending up at 224 Group HQ as a Staff Officer Operations.

For the RAF, Czernin's war as a pilot may have been over but the Count had other ideas. Returning to London, he stalked the corridors of the Air Ministry until one day he was spotted by an Air Marshal who took him under his wing and on 17 September 1943 the RAF struck off Squadron Leader M.B.Czernin from its list of operational officers and showed his transfer to Air Ministry Unit [London] for duty in AI 10. In fact, he had joined SOE where he determined to continue the war on his own terms, engaging the enemy at close quarters. His security check raised some issues about his cousin, Hans Czernin, who admitted that a brother was a member of the Nazi party in Vienna, but no problems were encountered about Manfred personally.

Arriving in Italy in November, Czernin underwent the standard SOE courses to prepare him for operations behind enemy lines but it was not until June 1944 that he was selected to jump with his Italian signaller, Piero Bruzzone, into north-east Italy'on a clandestine mission to penetrate into Austria. The first run was aborted when incorrect ground signals were seen. On the next night, 13 June, once more the signals were wrong but this time Czernin told the pilot to drop him and if the landing area proved secure, to make a second approach and drop Piero and the stores. It was a brave decision[†] given the propensity of the Germans to attract Allied aircraft with bogus signals but fortunately proved to be the right one and the pair were escorted by their reception committee, members of *Osoppo* a right-wing resistance group, to the Partisan HQ at the nineteenth century Castle Pielungo in the Friuli region.

Czernin was soon joined by Major Pat Martin-Smith and his W/T operator Sergeant Barker, who were dropped into his area on the night of 18 July. Martin-Smith's task was to act as assistant to Czernin until the first party had been put over the border and then take over the management of the route while Czernin returned to base to report. Almost immediately they were attacked by a strong force of Germans and in their haste to escape both officers lost most of their personal kit and equipment; the castle was effectively demolished. A week later, they moved to Tramonti di Sopra, a small village six kilometres to the west of 6,450 feet Monte Fráscola, an ideal area in terms of DZs and Landing Grounds but over fifty miles by road from the border. Shortly after, having attacked a German MG post at Casiago on 1 August, the mission once again had to flee in the face of an overwhelming German response – '*I Tedeschi vengeno*', 'the Germans are coming' – and travelled non-stop for three days across country to Monte Rosso.

---

* The Op Order of 1 May 1944 also included Sgt Maj MacDowell, R.Sigs as part of the Mission
† He was awarded a MC 'for this courageous action'.

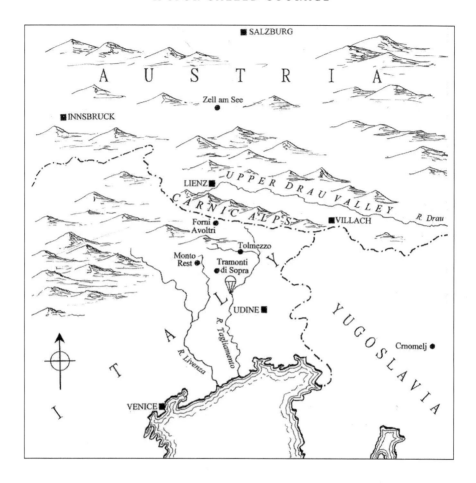

Czernin's main task was to reconnoitre the Italian Austrian border a forty kilometre march away with a view to penetrating into Austria proper*. The idea of using the Carnic Alps as a spring board for Austrian missions had been hatched by No.1 Special Force during a meeting between Major Peter Wilkinson and Commander Gerry Holdsworth to supplement a similar plan which was being rolled out in Slovenia by Wilkinson. Czernin first established two lines across the frontier with the help of an Austrian guide†, Georg Dereatti alias 'Vienna', and identified three other safe passages,

---

*   Darton Op Order 1 May 1944: "To make a reconnaissance of the frontier of the Austrian Tirol with a view to examining the possibilities for infiltrating agents into Austria from North Italy."

†   His first guide disappeared, never to resurface.

which was a major step forward for senior SOE planners. He then asked the local Partisan commanders to send him any Austrian deserters or prisoners and after subjecting them to a screening process, he selected six to work with the mission.

On 12 August, another mission commanded by Major George Fielding was dropped on Czernin's DZ. It included an Austrian, Lieutenant Georgeau, for Czernin to send across the border into Austria, and a party of a further three Austrians under Lieutenant Karmenski. It was decided that Fielding, none of whose team had brought civilian clothes or documents with them except Georgeau, should operate on the Austrian frontier with a group of twenty Partisans with his base in Forni Avoltri [Italy] while Karmenski and his team should sabotage the railway system. Lieutenant Georgeau was despatched by Czernin on 18 August across the frontier with the help of Dereatti, returning ten days later with news that the Austrians he had met in Wetzman were all 'apathetic, lacking in patriotic spirit and ...very frightened of the Nazi machine". However, he re-crossed into Austria ten days later, meeting up again with Czernin's chief guide Dereatti in early October to contact a group of Austrian officers at Villach who had said they wanted to defect. Later that October, Dereatti went back to join Georgeau and set up safe houses in Zell am See and Salzburg. The two of them were spotted in the Upper Drau valley in January but never seen again.

A secondary task was to establish contact with the local Partisans, predominantly Communist-led *Garibaldi* units, and to assist them in sabotage and ambush activities. Two OSS missions in the area[†] were also engaged on this. The first, under Major Smith, arranged supply drops, the second, an all-Italian team of self-professed communists, provided liaison and leadership [one of them became the *Garibaldi* Chief of Staff]. Czernin collaborated with them in several attacks on the railway running through Carnia and as a result his mission was subjected to further anti-Partisan sweeps, on three occasions yet again losing nearly all his kit and equipment.

On 10 October, the Germans launched a major sweep in Carnia and Friuli, capturing two of Fielding's men, Major Smallwood and Sergeant Barker[‡]. Both Czernin and Captain Martin-Smith were engaged in bitter fighting in the area

---

* Fielding report 43/3084
† Czernin post operational report: OSS missions in the Carnia/Friuli area. Captain Hall, the OSS officer who blew up the Cortina railway line, was a member of Smith's mission.
‡ Smallwood had broken his arm and sprained his ankle and Barker, who could have escaped, refused to leave him at the mercy of the Germans.

of the Passo della Mauria; Tramonti fell on 17 October but the Germans with-drew soon after and left a small force of 150 Cossacks to guard it. The mission re-entered it on 20 October and found their DZ intact. Throughout this period, despite repeated requests by both Czernin and Fielding, no stores were dropped to the missions or the Partisans. Among his many adventures was an uncomfortable twelve hours spent half way up a ruined medieval watch tower while a German patrol camped out on the ground floor.

By now, it was essential to exfiltrated Czernin back to Bari so that he could report on the mission's three months in the field and most impor-tantly explain how the lack of supplies was severely constricting their ability to produce results of any kind. The reality was that in three months the two BMMs had only succeeded in getting one SOE-trained operative into Austria in spite of the comparative ease of passage and winter was fast approaching. On the evening of 25 October, Bari signalled that both Czernin and Martin-Smith were to come out. Given the position of various couriers still over the border and that of those in the pipeline, this was unacceptable and it was Czernin alone who left by Lysander on 29 October, in the company of two escaped POWs, Private Brown of the East Yorkshires and Private Clarke of the Sherwood Foresters. They arrived at SOE's new forward HQ in Sienna just in time to hear Field Marshal Alexander's order suspending the dropping of agents into enemy territory until the following spring.

Czernin's mission had been a qualified success. After proving the route into Austria, he had expected to support Fielding's mission; when only one man could go in, that support role fell on Fielding himself, so there was no scope for two Missions. However, there was a need to support the facilities at Tramonti and also a need to continue to recruit Austrians. He had estab-lished six safe houses in Austria, formed a 'courier school' with Martin-Smith where they recruited and trained three internal and five external couriers, and nurtured five contacts within Austria. Dereatti, who he had employed as his chief guide, made no less than seven successful crossings.

However, due to no fault of Czernin, the almost complete failure to drop supplies to the Partisans undermined his credibility [and that of all the other British missions in the area] with the Partisan leadership and also severely compromised his ability to fend off German attacks. As he wrote in his November 1944 report, 'promises made by BLOs in all good faith which for one reason or another are not carried out, tend to damage Allied prestige and shake faith in the Allied promises. This inevitably encourages a dangerously cynical state of mind, particularly open revolu-

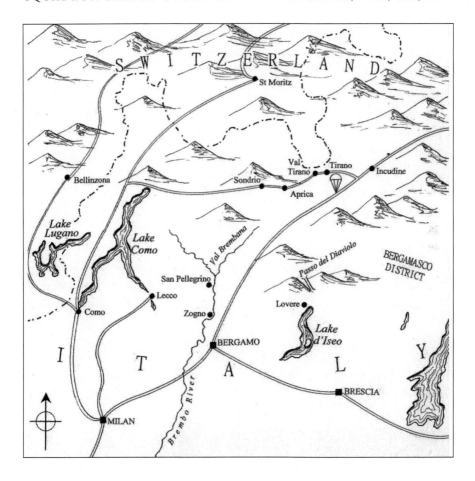

tionary ideas and, consequently, susceptible to pro-Russian tendencies'. Furthermore he was not briefed to sort out the bitter political rivalry between the *Osoppo* and *Garibaldi* Partisans; his successor, Major Tom Roworth, managed to reach a temporary accommodation between the two but this 'unified command' soon fell apart in the face of determined German *rastrellamenti*.

The Partisan groups that remained in the mountains during the winter of 1944 suffered both from the appalling weather and shortage of food. Early in 1945, when several Allied divisions were transferred from Italy to the Western Front, it was apparent to Allied commanders that they would need as much assistance from the Partisans as possible to ensure the success of their final assault on Northern Italy in the spring. To that end, deliveries of food, clothing, arms and explosives began to increase and concurrently British missions were reinforced and increased in number. Much to his delight, after a spell as a Despatch officer and short leave in London*, on 12 March 1945 Czernin and a four man team climbed on board an American Liberator at Sienna airport destined for Tirano just south of the Swiss border. The two Italian officers accompanying him were Old Harrovian Lieutenant Giuliano Mattioli† in charge of anti-scorch activities to protect the dams in the area, and an explosive expert nick-named Moicano. The other two members of the team were British W/T operators.

After an uneventful landing between the villages of Val Tirano and Incudine, the mission set out on its task to co-ordinate the various Partisan bands scattered throughout the Bergamasco District and to unify them under a central command to await orders from 15th Army Group. Being unsure of the whereabouts of the Partisan units and the zone commander General Fiori [who had failed to meet them as planned], the mission decided to make its way south-west towards Bergamo and on that first night set off for the village of Aprica. Arriving there the next morning, despite Mattioli's warnings, Czernin went into the village and soon found himself surrounded by enemy soldiers – 'All that day, with much interest, I watched from a ground floor window German troops parading up and down outside the house'. Unruffled, he returned to the three others and after loading up their mules, they set off to cross the snow-covered 9,000 foot Passo del Diaviolo. The two metre snow proved too deep for the mules, so they were unloaded and with the help of twenty hardy porters hired from the local villages, the mission finally made it over the pass three days later after a final grueling twenty-four hour march through biting cold with no food. The *Giellisti* commander, Beppi Lanfrancchi, met them and took them to his HQ at Lago Nero.

Czernin's area was part of the Lombardy Sector which comprised several groups of Partisans under a Zone Command. The Zone commander who was known as Bassi had around 1,000 Partisans of mixed political loyalties under his command; then came the 600 Olona Group Partisans of the Partito d'Azione under a leader called Marcello; then a 100 strong Green

---

* Always keen to get back to the front, Czernin suggested to Commander Holdsworth and Lt Col Beevor in London that he could be usefully employed flying Mustangs for special drops until the snows cleared when he could be dropped in. [Memo Beevor/Hewitt 10 January 1945]

† This was his fourth mission behind enemy lines.

Loading mules with supplies from drops

Flames group; and finally a 300 strong Communist *Garibaldi* group. All were accorded the status of brigades and in the next few weeks, Czernin and Mattioli toured the district, supplying arms and ammunition to the various groups as well as establishing a permanent base for the mission near Zogno, an enemy garrison town.

Three weeks after the renewed Allied offensive in April 1945, Czernin received the order to clear the Val Brembana and his Partisan forces quickly captured Zogno after a tense meeting with its fascist commander resulted in a bloodless surrender; the same process was repeated at San Pellegrino when the feared *Milizia Forestale* laid down their arms without a fight. The way now lay open to Bergamo where the CLN had already taken part of the town but by the time Czernin arrived with the main force, news came of a large German Panzer column approaching the town. His immediate reaction was to drive as fast as possible to the enemy HQ and demand the immediate and unconditional surrender of Germans and Italian Fascists alike. Coming under small arms fire from both parties, he changed tack and set off to try and stop the column which had the capability of wiping out the Partisan forces. Hurtling down the road in a convoy of three cars, he ran straight into the approaching tanks and had no option other than to drive past them – '...

putting my foot down on the accelerator we got past the whole German column without a shot being fired'. The last car was stopped and its occupants, one of whom was W/T Op Sergeant Williams, taken prisoner.*

Realizing that the game could well be up, Czernin managed to get through to the Panzer commander by telephone at a point of the road where the column had stopped. Informing him that the US Fifth Army were already in Bergamo, he advised him to hoist white flags on his vehicles unless he wanted to be attacked from the land and air. Whether the Panzer officer swallowed this story or not, it had the desired effect of making him change course and the column was later observed escaping northwards by another route. Meanwhile Czernin had reached the advancing Americans who declined his request for assistance in the surrender of Bergamo and headed off towards Lake Como.

Back in Bergamo, the situation looked ominous as sniping between Fascist and Partisans increased. It was time to try another bluff and Czernin got a message through to General Ebeling and Untersturmfuhrer Langen that leading forces of the US Fifth Army had arrived on the outskirts of the town and unless they surrendered within the next two hours, the Americans and Partisans would have no option other than to wipe them out. At 0800 hours the next morning, the German garrison of 3,000 men formally surrendered to the Partisan forces; their signed document was addressed to 'the English Major Manfredi'. With the taking of the town, the whole of the surrounding area was liberated and Allied troops were able to push forward and reach Como on 28 April, cutting off the last German escape route into Austria.

Relieved of his duties when the AMGOT and the US 1 Armoured Division took over control of Bergamo, Czernin headed south to his beloved Ravello and was released from Special Forces on 1 August and then from the RAF on 27 September. His war, in line with his character, had been individualistic, stylish and heroic. Manfred, always conscious of his distinguished 12th century Bohemian lineage, decided from an early stage to fight his own personal war against the Nazis and in doing so, upheld the family tradition of fearlessness, whether on the battlefield or in Partisan politics. In his own way, he proved a master of both.

---

* Czernin later managed to locate the British WT Op NCO in a jail in Bolzano where the Panzer column had dumped him on their way back to Germany.

Squadron Leader Manfred Czernin: 30 October 1945: recommendation for DSO

Squadron Leader Czernin was parachuted behind enemy lines in North West Italy on 21 March 1945. His task was to co-ordinate the various scattered Partisan units into a unified command and with these forces to carry out the directions of 15th Army Group. In order to reach his area of operation in the Bergamasco district, he had to cross the 9,000 feet Passo del Diaviolo which was completely covered with snow six feet deep. He made two attempts to cross the pass but without success. At 0400 hours on 4 April he made a further effort and after marching continuously for twenty-four hours, suffering severely from cold, frost bite and lack of food, he succeeded in crossing the pass. Squadron Leader Czernin immediately commenced to organise the various Partisan forces and by his energy and personality quickly built up a large aggressive Partisan Command. This force, under his direction, went into action on 28 April 1945. He secured the unconditional surrender of three enemy garrisons whilst other forces under his command eliminated or captured the garrisons of three other places. Later the same day, after the whole area had been cleared of the enemy, he, with the Partisan Leader, drove into Bergamo in a car draped with the Union Jack to demand the unconditional surrender of the German Forces. The Germans opened fire and Squadron Leader Czernin was forced to withdraw. He then ordered the Partisans to attack the city and arranged for the underground elements in Bergamo to rise simultaneously. At 0700 hours on 28 April 1945, Squadron Leader Czernin obtained an unconditional surrender from the German General. Throughout this period in the field Squadron Leader Czernin displayed the highest qualities of leadership and by his courage and daring made a noteable contribution to the Allied success in North Italy.

Awarded

Squadron Leader Manfred Czernin: 1 December 1944: recommendation for MC

On the night of 12-13 June 1944, Squadron Leader Czernin and his Wireless Operator were to be dropped into enemy-occupied territory, but the reception signals were not satisfactory and they returned to base. On the following night, the reception was again incorrect. Entirely regardless of his own safety, Squadron Leader Czernin decided to jump with a view to making a personal reconnaissance of the situation. This he did without arms of any description and with the full knowledge that the Germans are constantly arranging bogus receptions for the receipt of Allied personnel and stores. On landing, he found the reception committee to be friendly. Thereupon he flashed a signal to the aircraft which dropped the Wireless Operator and equipment. But for this courageous action, a most vital operation would have had to be postponed at a stage when the time was of the utmost importance to the success of the major plan.

Awarded

Major Tom Roworth: 14 April 1945: recommendation for immediate DSO

Major Roworth was dropped by parachute into North East Italy in September 1944 as the leader of a British Mission. His task was to contact the Partisan forces in the area west of the Tagliamento River and to create a unified force from the various Partisan elements in this area.

He very quickly organized the conflicting elements of these forces into a unified command and under his leadership these forces carried out numerous sabotage attacks and ambushes against the enemy lines of communication. So serious did this threat become to the enemy that a major offensive was launched against the Partisans who were forced to disperse after causing considerable casualties to the enemy.

Although suffering from fever and later with frostbite, Major Roworth quickly re-asembled a large portion of his forces and although driven from the valley and villages he managed to escape capture on numerous occasions. Finally, owing to the constant attacks by the enemy, he was forced to climb and hide on Mount Raut, 6,500 ft above sea level, where he remained for some considerable time in the height of the winter under the most bitter conditions and suffering extremely from frost-bite.

As all Partisan territory was now controlled and garrisoned by the enemy, Major Roworth, fully realizing the risks he was taking, discarded his uniform for civilian clothes in order to be able to descend into the plains and re-organize the Partisan forces. After reaching the Udine, he remained for a period of two months in the valleys, actively engaged in the reorganization of the resistance movement in this area until he was ordered to return to base and exfiltrated by Lysander on 23 February 1945. Always hunted, often sick, and constantly on the move to avoid capture, Major Roworth by his sheer tenacity of purpose and complete disregard of personal safety built up a strong Partisan formation on the plain of Udine, which was constantly harassing and attacking the enemy lines of communication and compelled the Germans to keep large forces in that area.

During the whole of this time Major Roworth was fully aware that his capture in civilian clothing would result in his immediate death, but despite this, and by his outstanding courage and contempt for danger, this officer carried out his mission with great distinction and is most strongly recommended for the immediate award of the DSO.

Awarded

Manfred and Maud, the runaway debutante

15

Major George Fielding, DSO
Captain Pat Martin-Smith, MC

George Fielding came from a similar peripatetic background as Manfred Czernin. Three weeks old when his father was killed at Gallipoli in 1915 serving with the Sherwood Foresters, Fielding was taken by his mother on a trip to Europe soon after the end of the First World War and on arrival in Geneva, he developed a sudden and nasty attack of bronchitis. A local doctor recommended that he was removed from the city as soon as possible and suggested to his mother that the Saanenland on the borders of Germany and France would be an ideal place for him to recuperate. Coincidentally, it was the same area that British POWs escaping from Germany had been interned and since their families had been allowed by the Swiss authorities to join them from England during the war, a lively British community had sprung up in the village of Saanenmöser. Soon installed in the Châlet Bon Accueille, Mrs Fielding decided to make Chateau d'Oex her home and it was here that Fielding spent his school holidays. After attending Shrewsbury School, he joined the Army as an officer cadet at the Royal Military College but his career was short lived after an altercation with a drill instructor who had 'booked' him for 'soot on hat' when it was patently obvious that said soot was coming from a chimney next to the parade ground.

After attending a German course for foreign students at Freiburg University in Baden, through a contact of his maternal uncle who had sought his fortune during the Klondike gold rush, Fielding spent a demanding year in Canada on the edge of the Arctic Circle in the company of professional trappers. From there, he sailed for the Argentine, where his mother's family, the Jewells, had prospered through the good fortune of buying land on which the central station in Buenos Ares was subsequently built. She herself had been born there in 1883. He worked as assistant to the farm manager on one of their *estancias*, establishing his prowess as a pistol shot by winning an orange shooting competition against the *gaucho* foreman, and then became a cattle-buyer in Rosario for Swifts of Chicago before returning to England to enlist. Originally destined for the Gordon Highlanders, Fielding had been befriended by two brothers called Morgan at a London nightclub and persuaded that life

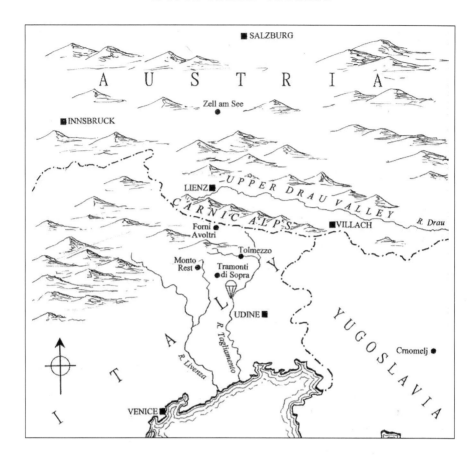

in a cavalry regiment was preferable to 'wearing a skirt'. He was duly commissioned into the 3rd the King's Own Hussars where he was informed that due to their largely drink fuelled exploits, his erstwhile friends the Morgan brothers had been persuaded to resign their commissions.

Soon 'C' Squadron* was despatched to Crete and its sixteen Vickers light tanks distributed in penny packets as armoured reserves. When the Germans invaded the island on 20 May 1941, Fielding found himself in the thick of the fighting along with fellow officer Roy Farran, who was later to become a legendary SAS hero. Shot in the arm by an anti-tank

---

* 'B' Squadron was sent to Java where it was captured in its entirety and its officers and men spent their war as POWs of the Japanese. 'A' Squadron was incorporated into an armoured regiment in 9th Armoured Brigade and lost 47 out of 51 tanks, together with 21 officers and 98 ORs during the Battle of El Alamein.

bullet, Fielding was first treated by Dr Tom Summerville, later immortalized in *The Cretan Runner* as 'senior officer ill', and then given the unenviable task of taking a group of demoralized walking wounded down to the evacuation point on the beach. During the ill-tempered march, Fielding had to constantly chivvy a group of Australians to keep up with the column; one of them clubbed him from behind with a rifle butt, knocking him out cold. Coming to just in time, Fielding made it to the beach and safely embarked for Alexandria, where after a stint as MTO with the 3rd Hussars, he joined the staff of SIME at HQ MEF in Cairo. Feeling he was doing little for the war effort – 'being told to investigate a case of selling One Star brandy in a Three Star bottle is unlikely to win the war' – he replied to a notice board advertisement for special duties and in June 1944, was accepted by SOE. The fact that he lodged at Countess Sophie Tarnowska's Villa Tara on Gezira Isalnd doubtless helped, for his fellow lodgers included SOE luminaries like David Smiley, Paddy Leigh Fermor and Billy McLean.

Fielding's fluency in German made him an ideal candidate for SOE's campaign to penetrate Austria and he was dropped, together with Major Bill Smallwood [also a fluent German speaker], Lieutenant Georgeau [an Austrian] and their W/T operator, Corporal Buttle, on 12 August 1944 to Squadron Leader Manfred Czernin's reception at Tramonti. Their task was to penetrate the East Tirol and Southwest Carinthia and to establish a base and facilities for further penetration at a later date. A second party of three Austrians under command of Lieutenant Karmenski jumped at the same time; they were earmarked for sabotage and demolition activity. To the consternation of Czernin and his second-in-command, Captain Pat Martin-Smith, none of the new arrivals except Georgeau had brought civilian clothes or ID papers with them, 'under the delusion that they could gaily march across the border in British uniform to be joined by a crowd of enthusiastic Austrian patriots'!* The main body was delayed at Tramonti for fifteen days but Czernin managed to get Georgeau, the only one with civilian clothes and ID papers, across the border on 18 August.

Eventually, Czernin arranged for twenty *Osoppo* Partisans under the command of a former Alpini officer, the priest Don 'Aurelio', to escort Fielding's mission to Clavais to the west of Tramonti where they arrived on 24 August. However, it proved too far from the frontier to be practical and so

---

* Martin-Smith draft report Para 11

they moved to Forni Avoltri where they were able to cover two excellent routes into Austria, the Giramondo and Vall'Inferno passes, both of which were unguarded. Mission HQ was installed in the Albergo Sotto Corona, where much to their surprise they discovered a North Country lass called Katie, formerly the Gräfin Donner and now styled Countess Sosic, wife of the harbour master of Naples. Their Partisan escort set up base in the school house at Frassenetto half a mile away and 600 feet further up the mountain. A nearby yet remote village called Sauris was selected as the Drop Ground. The nearest German garrison was a mere seven miles away at Sappada.

Georgeau returned on 26 August and brought with him a new recruit, Rudolph Moser alias 'Henry', a twenty-four year old Wehrmacht NCO deserter. It was agreed that Henry should act as a courier for Fielding across the new route to Forni Avoltri until Georgeau could find an Austrian with the necessary paperwork. Furthermore, if Georgeau was to continue to operate across the frontier, he would need his own W/T operator and one was requested on 27 August. It was now clear from Georgeau's reports that the Austrian people were apathetic, very frightened by the Nazis and appeared to have little patriotic spirit. From now until 10 October, the mission remained put, waiting for promised supplies to be dropped by the Balkan Air Force, the newly formed Bari-based organization responsible for supplying Partisans in Yugoslavia and North East Italy by air.

The activities of the mission were now limited to reconnaissance through lack of any form of supply of arms and ammunition. Major Smallwood crossed over the frontier at the staging post at Birnbaum in an attempt to persuade a farmer to hide an arms cache and to shelter mission members, the latter request being rejected out of hand. Plans were also made to launch a cross-border raid with the *Osoppo* Partisans in order to test the reaction of the local people; would they join the resistance or reject it? Once again, the lack of arms and supplies made the implementation of such a plan a non-starter. Fielding himself crossed the border to Liesing twice, both times to talk to the village priest who was fiercely opposed to the Nazi regime. The recruitment picture was not promising for the German call-up had left behind only males over-sixty, boys under-fourteen or those with disabilities; that said, the priest was of the opinion that if a safe area could be established, it should be possible to attract deserters, particularly from the training and holding regiment at Lienz.

Life in plain clothes was never straightforward. Early in the morning on the day of his arrival in Tramonti di Sopra Fielding went for a stroll in to get a feel for his new surroundings. An Italian, seeing him at such an hour, assumed he must have been to church and greeted him: 'Been to Mass?' to which he, thinking it could do no harm to appear a Catholic, replied: 'Yes'; only to get the answer, 'I don't go, I'm a Protestant from Piedmont'. On another occasion, Fielding and another member of his group were fishing in a river when some German army vehicles appeared. One stopped and an officer approached them to enquire with typical Teutonic attention to detail if they had permits to fish that particular stream. They admitted that they did not and the German officer merely told them that they must go to the town hall and obtain a permit before they fished again. He then got back in his vehicle and left.

Having crossed the frontier at Mauthen, Georgeau had managed to reach Pirkach where he recruited another German as a courier, this time a one-eyed Luftwaffe deserter, codenamed 'Otto', but like Henry, he was without suitable papers. He also contacted Dr Kirschbaumer at Villgraten, an important local figure, who agreed to provide a safe house for him. Based here, there was a real possibility that, provided the required drops of arms and supplies were made, a resistance group could be nurtured in the valley and act as a springboard to a larger movement.

The Italian Partisans were found to be useless at smuggling stores across the frontier, owing to their inadequate training in fieldcraft. It was therefore decided to recruit some British POWs and so Fielding despatched Sergeant Barker, Captain Martin-Smith's W/T operator, to Selva di Cadore near Cortina d'Ampezzo to contact six POWs known to be hiding near the house of a wealthy Jewish businessman. After a hazardous round trip of eleven days, three of which were spent in persuading the POWs that he was not a German plant, Barker returned to Forni Avoltri with his charges, three of whom later left for Yugoslavia.

On 1 October, a German offensive, Operation Waldlaufer, undertaken by Combat Group Schwerdfeger. started in the Carnia region with the aim of clearing the road to Timau and recapturing the barracks at Paluzza; Major Smallwood and Sergeant Barker were located at Forni Avoltri while Fielding and Corporal Buttle were at the Drop Ground at Sauris, waiting for a promised drop by ten aircraft. He quickly crossed the mountains back to Forno and agreed to a plan of action with Smallwood; he, Fielding, would return to Sauris to wait for a single aircraft drop and Smallwood would withdraw with the couriers, Sergeant Barker and their six-strong Partisan bodyguard if directly threatened by the Germans. At dawn on 11 October, Germans were spotted to the north of Forni, prompting Smallwood to leave with Barker for Sauris. After caching their radios and stores except for a B-set and large packs, the two men reached the summit of Monte Tuglia about 1500 hours.

Shortly after they began their descent, Smallwood slipped and in falling nearly thirty feet broke his leg in two places near the ankle. Dragging him to a nearby barn, Barker pressed on into the Val Pessarina where he collected some young *Garibaldini* to help him move the injured Major further down the valley to group of three barns. Here another group of Partisans arrived and set Smallwood's leg in splints. By 13 October, German patrols had arrived in the vicinity of the barns, causing the Partisans to flee and leaving Smallwood with no option other than to give himself up; Barker could certainly had escaped but chose not to leave his badly injured commander alone in such dire circumstances.

At six that evening, they were arrested by a Cossack patrol and by 15 October found themselves at Gestapo HQ in Trieste. Fortunately, their cover story that they had been making a recce with a view to blowing up bridges and roads and assisting British POWs to escape held up well and merely served to confirm to the Germans facts they already knew. With the loss of Smallwood and Barker and the cessation of all Partisan resistance in Carnia, Fielding's BMM, now reduced to one officer and one NCO, with its attendant force of mostly unarmed and ragged Italian Partisans, found itself on its own and the target of intense German patrol activity.

Despite the large numbers of Austrians in Allied captivity, SOE had great difficulty in finding suitable recruits who were prepared to return to Austria to kick start the resistance. John Bruce Lockhart of SIS Bari was experiencing identical difficulties in regard to a paucity of suitable agents and shortage of air support. However, one exceptional individual was identified by SOE, Wolfgang Treichl alias Taggart. An ardent patriot who was determined to liberate his country from the scourge of fascism, Treichl had joined the Afrika Korps with the sole intention of being captured by the British to whom he would offer his services. Along with three other Austrians – Hauber who was to be infiltrated into Austria with him, Second Lieutenant Priestley who was to join Georgeau as his W/T operator and Second Lieutenant Dale who was to join Karmenski – Treichl emplaned on 12 October destined to be dropped to Czernin's mission. A mix up by the pilot and navigator resulted in the team being dropped twelve miles from the DZ into the waiting arms of a German patrol by the Gendarmerie Barracks at Tolmezzo, Field Marshal Kesselring's HQ*. Treichl was shot and killed on landing; Hauber escaped in the darkness and reached Czernin a few days later with Lees and Grant of Karmenski's

---

* According to Hauber, they had been dropped to four fires fifty yards apart in a L shape as opposed to the correct signal of five lights 100 yards apart in a V shape.

party; the other two, Priestley and Dale, were captured but fortunately their story about being British officers was believed and they were treated as POWs rather than handed over to the Gestapo as Austrian spies.

Meanwhile Lieutenant Karmenski and others had arrived from Cadore to add to the already fraught situation confronting Fielding; in addition to the general lack of arms and virtually no ammunition, no one had more than twenty-four hours of rations left at any one time for the Partisan caches, foolishly all stored in the towns, had been burnt by the Germans who had completely cleared the Tagliamento Valley of resistance. In the middle of this critical period, a party of six Austrians arrived from Czernin to be put across the frontier. After a ten day delay due to continuing German operations, Otto and Czernin's chief courier, Dereatti, safely despatched them across the frontier. Lieutenant Hauber, the survivor of the Taggart mission, also arrived around this time and was sent with Karmenski's party to Tramonti which they reached on 29 October..

On the night of 20 October, Fielding returned to Forni to see if the situation there had improved. While asleep in a hay barn, he was woken and warned that his location had been given away to the Germans and having moved to another building some way off, watched at dawn a German patrol surround the barn. After making a reconnaissance of the frontier the next day, Fielding returned to Forni to spend the night in another hay barn and exactly the same chain of events happened. Once more, by moving promptly, he evaded capture. He returned to Sauris despondent and frustrated by the inability of the BMMs and Partisans to respond to enemy activity. Without arms, ammunition, boots and sturdy clothing, they were powerless. In frustration and under relentless pressure from German patrols when the mission's survival depended on the Partisans for food, local intelligence and protection, he sent the Balkan Air Force a message asking that they display 'more of the spirit of the Battle of Britain and less of the Bottle of Bari'. Like many BMMs, he was fed up with making promises to the Partisans about air drops of arms and ammunition which inevitably failed to arrive and therefore undermined the credibility of the SOE mission.

News reached Fielding that Georgeau's W/T operator, Priestley, had been captured by the Germans at Tolmezzo and therefore he decided to return to Forni to warn Georgeau that his codes may have been compromised. Setting out on 29 October, Fielding's first attempt to cross the mountains ended in failure after a six hour slog through thick snow. A second attempt the next day fared slightly better but a mule carrying a load of food fell over a precipice and the rest of the day was spent retrieving it. Yet another attempt had to be abandoned due to avalanches; this time both a man and a mule were lost. A fourth and final attempt got underway the next day, using the low cloud and mist as cover to move below the snowline. Five mules laden with food accompanied the party as it moved out of the Derano valley but as it reached the village below Mione, it found itself surrounded by German troops. Leaving the mules behind, the party managed to escape 'thanks to some very bad shooting on behalf of the mixed force of Germans and Russians', the only casualty being Fielding with a flesh wound to his arm. It was now that he discovered that the Germans had posted a reward of 800,000 Lire for his capture.

During this period, Fielding had been observing 'an extremely bogus and suspicious' OSS Mission headquartered to the East of Comiglians. Consisting of 'Fred', an Italian member of the PCI and his Italian-Egyptian W/T operator, the mission had the same brief as Fielding, namely to open courier lines into Austria. However, convinced that this was a cover for Communist penetration of Austria, Fielding introduced a stooge, codenamed Fuli, through whom he fed suitably edited information to Fred, an arrangement that admirably worked until Fred broke his leg and his W/T operator went off the air due to severe syphilitic symptoms. However, the *Garibaldini* had their own programme based on two 'battalions', the 'Stalin' battalion formed out of Ukrainian, Mongol and Cossack deserters, and the 'Karl Liebknecht' battalion composed of Austrian and German deserters, with the object of eventually sending them to Austria as Communist agent provocateurs. Pat Martin-Smith had information that the Austrian and German contingents were extremely unhappy with their lot, the more so since they had been told they would be shot if they crossed over to the *Osoppo*.

Thus it came as no surprise when five Austrians and two Germans approached Martin-Smith, who immediately arranged for them to be received by Fielding under the formal protection of the BMM. The reaction of the *Garibaldini* was to send their Chief of Staff, Franco, who was also an American OSS officer, to explain that the 'Karl Liebknecht' battalion was actually an OSS creation and would be led in Austria by American officers who were expected any day soon. The seven deserters would have none of it and under the tutelage of Martin-Smith formed two three-man parties ready to be infiltrated into Austria, the first to Klagenfurt and the second to St Polten destined for Vienna. At the same time, he briefed Durreatti to prepare to move to the Salzkammergut to find a base from which the BMM could operate the following spring. The outcome was very different. The leader of the Klagenfurt group appeared to be on the verge of returning to the Wehrmacht and buy his immunity in exchange for betraying the BMM. He was summarily shot by the Partisans in the village mortuary. The next day, the group's Luftwaffe radio operator accidentally blew his brains out when his Sten gun went off in a truck and so the remainder were handed over to Captain Prior, another SOE officer in Tramonti, for deployment as saboteurs.

Fielding finally reached Tramonti on 6 November in time to find that the mission's first drop had arrived the night before; despite a guard and a lock, almost a third of it had been stolen. Ten days later and nearly three months after his original request had been submitted, he was notified that Georgeau's W/T operator, Lieutenant Brenner, was due that night. Dropped at 3,000 feet by the same Polish pilot, who had so carelessly deposited Hauber's party on top of the German HQ at Tolmezzo, Brenner landed half a mile from the nearest fire and after some difficulty in gaining admittance to the Drop Ground, was spirited off by Fielding to the Ampezzo area to get him across the frontier as soon as possible. The area turned out to be crawling with Germans and accordingly Fielding returned with Brenner to Tramonti where he started planning their evacuation. The idea was to exfiltrate by Lysander and after making final arrangements to get a message to Georgeau, Martin-Smith stood vigil on the cold and wet 'Lizzie' field for the next week, only to watch one fly over and then disappear. It later transpired that soon after it was shot down by an American P-40 Lightning. With news of an impending German *rastrellamento*, it became clear that the only way out was by foot and when the drive opened with a combined attack by 1,000 SS Alpenjaeger, a Brigade of Russians and two crack Republican units, the 10th MAS and the San Marco Battalion, the mission left for Slovenia on 27 November on what became an epic 300 mile march.

For the first five days, the mission was compelled to walk around the surrounding hillsides, unable to find a way through the enemy cordon. On the sixth night, after a nineteen-hour walk, they managed to find a gap and the following night crossed the Tagliamento River south of Udine, 'fordable but cold' according to Martin-Smith. Three days later, after crossing the Pontebba railway line to the north of Udine, they reached the First *Osoppo* Brigade in the mountains to the Northeast of the town. The following night they crossed the freezing Natisone River and from there reached the farthest West Slovenian Odred. Their reception by the Slovene Partisans was discourteous and uncooperative; at one point, they were made to stand in a food queue with German deserters. After a tetchy time crossing the River Isonzo, when the Slovene guide refused to accompany them to the bank, the mission arrived at IX Slovene Partisan Corps HQ at Strega [Plannina] where they were welcomed by the BMM and the A Force representative. A further five day march with virtually no food other than chestnuts took them to Slovene HQ at Črnomelj, one leg taking twenty-three and a half hours non-stop marching. On 27 December, they were finally evacuated by air to Bari. However, the airfield at Bari was unusable due to an accident on the runway, so they landed at Foggia, a US airbase. As a truck came to pick up the aircrew, the SOE group made to clamber aboard only to hear the stentorian bark of a sergeant: 'Only US personnel allowed on this truck.' Having walked to the canteen, where coffee, doughnuts and warmth awaited them albeit after a wait of an hour and a half until the Americans opened it at the appointed time, two British officers eyed the Mission's beards and scruffiness, one remarking: 'Rather jungly'. They finally reached Bari in the back of a three-ton truck late the same day.

Once back at No.1 Special Force HQ, Fielding encountered a distinctly frosty reception. Major Charles Villiers gave him a dressing down for losing twenty gold sovereigns and threatened a board of inquiry; Fielding protested that this was a disproportionate response, given that he had been on the run from almost the day he had been dropped. A further reprimand came from a senior airman who berated him for his 'Bottle of Bari' signal. This did not deter him from preparing a swingeing critique of his mission, including the following paragraph on 'Air Support': 'Before the mission left base we were continually assured that during the summer and autumn we would be given air support in the form of drops of supplies and ammunition though the situation might be difficult in the winter. In actual fact the mission received no air support of any kind except during the last week when three drops were received at Tramonti. Many promises were made including one of a drop by ten aircraft to the Italian Partisans, but nothing materialized. These promises were very nearly disastrous for the mission as the temper of constantly disappointed Partisans became very uncertain and perfectly naturally I was held responsible. In fact to outward appearances, we were playing the part of perfidious Albion to perfection. So much for the difficulties at our base in Italy'.

Pat Martin-Smith shared Fielding's view but was more diplomatic in the language he used in his own report: 'Close liaison with the RAF is essential, both before and during an operation, to ensure that it is possible to supply a mission in a given area; it is better to know this beforehand as it is extremely demoralizing for all concerned to discover, after a great build-up of promises of supplies, that the RAF could not, in fact, and never imagined that they could drop into your particular area.' He followed this with a swipe at the Polish pilot who had dropped Treichl and Brenner: 'Pilots other than

British [including British Empire] are extremely hazardous risks; no 'body' should venture into a plane without assuring himself that the pilot is British, and secondly that he has experience of dropping 'bodies' and knows the area to which he is going. This will apply *a fortiori* to Austria'.'

Fielding would not have been amused by Major Tom Roworth's report. Giving among his reasons for bad relations between BLOs and *Garibaldi* units, he identified 'the open anti-communism of Major Fielding and his mission and of Captain Prior who walked around the area in green scarves and alpine hats [uniform of the *Osoppo*]'. He went on to cite the trouble caused by Fielding's acceptance of six German deserters, an act which infuriated the *Garibaldini* who wanted to execute them. Roworth was of course totally ignorant of the fact that the six deserters were all Austrians and that Fielding and Martin-Smith had been desperate to recruit agents to put across the border.

An unrepentant Fielding returned to England on leave where he suffered from a recurrent bout of malaria which his local GP treated with morphine, nearly killing him in the process and thus prevented him from returning to the field before the end of the war.

Major George Fielding: 16 April 1945: recommendation for immediate DSO

Major Fielding was in command of a Mission of four British personnel which was dropped by parachute on the night of 12/13 August 1944 some two hundred miles behind enemy lines to Tramonti, in the Friuli district of North Eastern Italy, charged with the primary task of establishing a base for subversive operations and for obtaining information to facilitate the penetration of East Tirol and South West Carpathia.

After a hazardous march to the North, Major Fielding managed to establish his Mission with the Italian Partisans at Forni Avoltri some fifteen miles South of the Austrian border and immediately set about establishing his courier lines.

Soon after he arrived, the enemy being quickly sensitive to his activities

---

*   To their consternation, the Big Bug mission under Captain Prior was despatched from their aircraft by a Pole who spoke no English and furthermore had failed to hook any of them up.

made repeated and determined attacks with regular troops with the object of clearing his area which on account of his shortages of arms, food and clothing, and the fact that his locally recruited Italian bodyguard became increasingly demoralized through repeated promises of drops which never materialized owing to adverse flying weather, made his position sometimes critical and at all times highly dangerous.

In spite of these difficulties however by his own courage and personality, Major Fielding managed to keep his ragged force together and to continue with his work, and during the period he himself crossed the Austrian frontier disguised as a peasant and made a reconnaissance of the Upper Gail Valley.

On 10 October the Mission was forced to withdraw but Major Fielding returned to the area on 20 October to re-establish the contacts for his courier lines. Next day however, he was betrayed to the Germans, surrounded by the enemy, and wounded and forced to withdraw once more.

The Germans then placed a price of 800,000 lire on this officer's head, an almost irresistible temptation to this poverty stricken district to betray him.

By mid-November the snow had closed the passes for the winter and Major Fielding was ordered to come out via Slovenia. With what remained of his Mission, he successfully accomplished a dangerous and almost impossibly difficult march of 300 miles across mountains which were deep in snow.

That Major Fielding accomplished his task from which extremely valuable information was obtained regarding conditions in Austria and North Eastern Italy was due to his outstanding leadership, resourcefulness and courage for which I have no hesitation in recommending him for the immediate award of a DSO.

Awarded

Captain Pat Martin Smith: 16 May 1945: recommendation for immediate MC

Captain Martin Smith was infiltrated by parachute to the Friulu district of Northern Italy, then some 200 miles behind enemy lines, on 18 July 1944 to act as second-in-command to Squadron Leader Czernin, who was then working to open up a route into Austria between Plocken and Brenner Passes.

Captain Martin Smith himself was given the task of arranging the safe houses and the actual crossings of the frontier by the various parties of agents. To do this he established his base a few miles South of the Austrian frontier.

Between the end of July and the end of November, Squadron leader Czernin's Mission was exposed to repeated enemy attacks and it was due in great part to Captain Martin Smith's resource and leadership that the guerrilla band with whom he was associated with [who were in an extremely low state of morale due to promises of supplies which did not materialize owing to bad flying conditions] were held together successfully.

When the snow closed the passes Captain Martin Smith was ordered to close on Major Fielding who was in the same area and to withdraw with his Mission through Slovenia. This involved a hazardous and almost impossibly difficult march of some 300 miles across the mountains to Slovene HQ and that this march, largely through deep snow, was successful was in no small measure due to Captain Martin Smith's courage and devotion to duty and unfailing cheerfulness under frightful conditions.

Captain Martin Smith's work with the Mission produced much valuable information on conditions in Southern Austria and North Eastern Italy which would not otherwise have been obtained and for his exemplary initiative and devotion to duty through these five months in Reich territory, I have no hesitation in recommending him for the immediate award of the MC.

Awarded

A 'jungly' George Fielding in the mountains

Left – Ross; Right – Tilman

16

Major Bill Tilman, DSO, MC and bar
Captain John Ross MC

Bill Tilman of Everest fame was surely SOE's most famous recruit and one of if not the oldest. Born in 1898 to a prosperous Liverpool sugar merchant, Tilman passed in to the Royal Military Academy at Woolwich in January 1915, taking the 55th place out of 111. However he was destined to be far from mediocre. On 28 July, he was commissioned in the Royal Artillery and the eighteen year old officer arrived in France in January 1916 with B Battery, 161 Brigade, Royal Field Artillery, the men all 'pals' from Scarborough. His first experience of battle was on the infamous Somme front where he served from June to November throughout the First Battle of the Somme, often employed as a Forward Observation Officer with the infantry, a job that exposed him to the greatest of dangers. In January 1917, Tilman was severely wounded in action for which he received an immediate MC from the Corps Commander. Hospitalized for three months, he returned to the front line in May 1917 in time for the Battle of Messines Ridge that June. The following month, he was awarded a bar to his MC for his exemplary defence of Nieuwpoort as acting Battery Commander. In November 1917, Tilman transferred to the elite Royal Horse Artillery and joined "I" battery, part of the mobile reserve of the British cavalry during the German offensive of March 1918. His war ended when he crossed the German frontier in December 1918 to a "little place called Bonn". It had been an extraordinary and in many ways a cathartic experience for the young Tilman and he decided that he had had his fill of soldiering.

In August 1919, having applied for and been granted a square mile of land in the newly formed colony of Kenya, Tilman set sail for Africa and arrived at his property on the south-west edge of the Mau forest when he pitched camp for there was no house. The "African bush of the most prodigious thickness" was soon cleared and the land planted with coffee and a later visit to Kenya by his father resulted in a family investment in a further 2,000 acres. In Africa, Tilman had teamed up with Eric Shipton as a climbing partner and the pair had successively climbed Mount Kilamanjaro and then the 17,000 feet Mount Kenya, where they completed the tricky traverse of the twin peaks of Bation and Nelion. In January 1932, they mounted an expedition to the Ruwenzori Mountains in Uganda – the Mountains of the Moon – where they scaled Alexandra Peak [16,740 feet] and Magherita [16,815 feet]. A very bad fall in the Lake District in England that April resulted in Tilman being told he would never climb again; undeterred, he set off in August on a lone climbing trip to the Alps where he received a letter from a friend telling him that gold had been discovered to the north-east of Lake Victoria. He rushed back out to Africa but the enterprise ended in failure. Restless and irre-pressible, Tilman set off for England, riding from Lake Victoria to the French Cameroons on a bicycle, a journey of over 3,000 miles, and reached home in September 1933.

By now accomplished mountaineers, Tilman and Shipton set out on 6 April 1934 to explore the 25,645 foot Nandi Devi in the Himalayas and the two men became the first people to reach the Nandi Devi Sanctuary. This was followed by an Everest expedition in May 1935 when the two of them climbed seventeen peaks of over 21,000 foot. In April 1936, they went back to climb Nanda Devi and reached the summit on 29 August, having climbed it without oxygen, using nailed boots, iron crampons and wooden shaft ice-axes. Tilman returned to the East the next year, this time without Shipton, and spent a fruitful nine weeks, surveying, mapping and climbing the Karakoram range. With Everest still unconquered, the two set off in 1938 to make an attempt on the summit and by 8 June had reached Camp 6 at 27,200 foot. Conditions deteriorated and the party had no choice but to leave the mountain. Tilman was back the next year, this time in the Assam Himalayas but time had run out for the world was on the verge of war.

Re-enlisting in 32 Field Regiment RA, Tilman found himself back in uniform in France but this time not for long and he, along with thousands of the British soldiers, was rescued from the beaches of Dunkirk in May 1940. A short stint with 120 Battery is Suffolk preceded another overseas posting, this time to Iraq, Syria and finally North Africa, where Tilman commanded a 'Jock column' of 25 pounders in the desperate defence of Mersa Matruh. Repositioned to the Ruweisat Ridge, Tilman took part in the Battle of El Alamein and the subsequent Eighth Army drive through to Tunisia.

At this point in his distinguished military service, at the age of 45, he refused promotion and thus incurred the displeasure of his superior Gunners. Shortly after, he joined SOE and in August 1943, parachuted into

Albania with the Sculpture mission where for the next ten months he tire-lessly travelled across that wild country. Coming out in May 1944 he again courted controversy, this time by endorsing the Communist LNC as the only worthwhile resistance organization in Albania. As a soldier and intensely practical man, Tilman wrote 'although I had been ten months in the country, I was by no means tired of it, but I was tired of the anomalous position in which BLOs were placed.' However, a man of Tilman's stature and experience was an asset that SOE could not afford to waste and in early August 1944 he was offered a job in Italy.

The Simia [Beriwind] mission, composed of Tilman, Captain John Ross, Marini, an ex-Italian submariner W/T operator and Victor Gozzer aka 'Gatti', a former Alpini officer whose role was that of mission interpreter, was primarily charged with making contact with the local Partisans and to coordinate their attacks on bridges and roads during the expected Allied offensive. Ross was considerably younger than Tilman and when war broke out, he had just started his first term at Cambridge reading zoology. After volunteering for service with the Royal Artillery, Ross was posted to an ack ack regiment and saw service in Iraq, Lebanon and North Africa before being posted to the staff of GHQ Cairo. After a year as a Staff Officer, he joined SOE and having completed his training in the Middle East and then Italy, he was picked by Tilman as his Second-in-command. He recalls 'I don't know why he chose me as I was not as tough as the others but we got on well together and I was a reasonable beast of burden and put up with some grim occasions'.

After two aborted drops, one particularly stressful in so much as the team stood by the open hatch to jump for over an hour while the pilot looked for the landing signals, Tilman with Carlyle's two-volume *French Revolution* stuffed in his back pocket and his team finally parachuted on 31 August 1944 into the wooded Alto Piano d'Asiago plateau, high above the Brenta valley; all missed the DZ and landed safely except Marini who sprained his ankle and Tilman who badly jarred his back, the first was unable to walk and the second unable to stand. Ross, although he landed in a tree, was fortunate to walk away uninjured. Another five-strong British mission under the command of the Rhodesian Captain Paul Brietsche jumped with them, again all missing the DZ, and due to wors-ening flying conditions, none of the kit belonging to the two missions followed them down. For the next four months there were no successful resupply drops, either for themselves or the Partisans whom they had come to mentor. According to Brietsche, the BLO running the reception committee, Major John Wilkinson*, was milking a cow when they landed and was heard to exclaim 'Well I warned Base that this was not a body dropping ground!' Wilkinson, a large blonde-haired Royal Artillery officer who communicated in French to the Partisans and fearlessly cycled around in plain clothes, was already a revered figure in the area.

Tilman soon made an impression on his colleagues and the Partisans, who found '*il maggiore con la barba*' tough, utterly reliable and a formidable leader and organizer. His first action was to send Ross and Gatti to contact the *Garibaldi* Nino Nannetti Division†, while still in considerable pain he remained in the Asiago forest with Major Wilkinson, with whom he exchanged W/T operators and scrounged some equipment from. He then set off on 5 September to join the others and they made their way to the Forest of Cansiglio, to the east of Belluno, where the Nannetti Division was based. Half way to their destination, they learnt that a massive German *rastrellamento* in the area had dispersed the Nino Nannetti Partisans, so Tilman decided to backtrack and join up with another Partisan *Garibaldi* brigade, the Gramsci, on a high grassy mountainous plateau called Pietena in Le Vette Feltrine mountains. Here they found 300 Partisans including escaped British POWs and Russian deserters, under the command of Bruno, a man Tilman found rather 'headstrong' and 'something of a fire-eater'. Matters came to a head when the German launched counter Partisan operation on 29 September: Bruno was determined to fight to the last bullet and the last man while Tilman urged him to melt away and come back to the fray another day. Finally, only when surrounded and under mortar fire, Tilman's view prevailed and an order to withdraw was agreed, leaving it up to the Partisans to find a route out of the valley.

Rather than go down into the valley, Tilman typically decided to go up the north face of Le Vette and at the head of a group of sixteen, including all the escaped British POWs, he led them onwards and upwards onto the side of the 7,000 feet mountain. On the night of 1 October, a blizzard engulfed

---

* 29 year-old Royal Artillery Major, John Wilkinson, codename Freccia, had dropped into North Italy with the Beebe Mission on 11 August 1944. Later he moved West to the Trento area and on 8 March 1945 was killed in an ambush near Tonezza. Initial reports merely established that his body had been found along with those of his partisan guide and two Polish escorts but later a German witness came forward and described how he had been callously executed by a German Security patrol after being wounded in the abdomen. After the war, two members of the Fascist Corpo Sicurezza Trentino were tried for his murder but acquitted on lack of evidence.

† Named after an Italian communist who had died fighting in the Spanish Civil War.

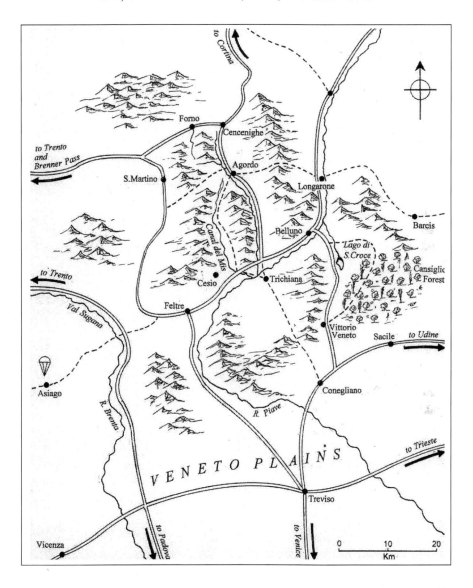

them and then blew throughout the next day, forcing them to spend three nights on a ledge on the bare mountainside. No one ate for seventy-two hours, everyone was stiff with cold and some had frostbite. One of the British contingent slipped, badly cutting his head, and it was only Tilman's heroic efforts to drag him back to the top of a gully that saved his life. Coming off the mountain, they found refuge in a hovel, the residence of the local bird catcher. Ross found it 'a filthy hut but we slept fairly comfortably on a pile of maize husks. Everything was filthy and our young guide who was with us had a headful of lice...some weeks later I found that my shirt, socks and pants were a mass of body lice....I dealt with the lice as well as I could – mainly with a cigarette end'. From then on for the next two weeks they were more or less on the run every day from German patrols, sometimes sleeping in farmhouses, other times in the woods, until finally they reached their original objective, the Forest of Cansiglio and the HQ of the Nannetti Division. Here, in a *malga*, they joined Milo, the new commander, and his headquarters' staff, sleeping in a long hayloft above four cows and living off a diet of small birds elaborately trapped by another 'bird-man'.

The ease which the Germans had managed to defeat comprehensively the Partisan divisions weighed heavily on the CLN and its British advisers; both the Gramsci and Nannetti no longer existed as effective fighting forces. Many *malgas* had been burnt to the ground, Partisans shot and some of them and their supporters hanged. The population was becoming increasingly fearful and thus less sympathetic to the Partisan movement. It was clear to Tilman that a period of quiet was needed to allow time to regroup, re-arm and retrain and that new tactics of operating in small mobile groups must be adopted. Above all, the incessant rain and gales of late October heralded the coming of winter and forced the division to make plans for its survival through to the following spring. It was decided to reduce numbers in the forest to the minimum, to build alternative huts and to procure as much winter clothing as possible. When the first serious snow fell at Cansiglio on 10 November, the mountain environment immediately became hostile: movement for the Partisans was now all but impossible for tracks in the snow revealed their whereabouts to the enemy and shelter became a matter of life or death. The Germans immediately took advantage of this and soon Tilman and Divisional headquarters were forced to move from their *malga* and head deep into the beech forests where they had constructed two twenty-man log-cabins.

These were desperate days. Capt Orr-Ewing reported that 'the month of October is chiefly remembered for its filthy weather and absence of drops. A "fireworks" day was planned for 5 November which, it was hoped, would be general throughout the whole of Veneto, in conjunction with Major Tilman and the plains. It was hoped to raise the morale of the Partisans, which, at this time, was pathetically low. It was planned to block the Val D'Adige in six places, and block all roads leading to it and also roads and railways in the provinces of Vicenza and Verona. However, when no explosive whatever was received, the scheme was naturally abandoned.'

Captain Brietsche, who had escaped from Monte Grappa after his Partisan unit had been attacked by the Germans, had had enough: 'It was in this period that my [Mission] morale was a bit low. We were all completely fed up with the Partisans and considered that they were all useless and not worth working for. They were talking of dispersing for the winter and I foresaw the Missions being left high and dry in the mountains. I took, I admit, a very pessimistic view of things but, on looking back, I think I had very good reasons for doing so. I therefore signalled base for permission to exfiltrate through Yugoslavia and received that permission and details of the route out.' Before leaving, he decided to talk things over with Tilman, who suggested that he should take over his role at the Nannetti division and he, Tilman, would go back to the right of the Piave where he had been before and where there were more mountains for him to climb! Neither Tilman or Ross were impressed by his equivocacy, particularly since their kit and signals equipment had subsequently been dropped to Brietsche on Grappa, an event which he never mentioned to them. Brietsche stayed, only to fall out later with Tilman over a Partisan command appointment.

On 19 November, Tilman set off with Gatti and two guides to Barcis on the other side of the Passo di Cavallo to meet up with the next door mission and discuss arrangements for evacuating the escaped Allied POWs to Yugoslavia. After a punishing journey across the snowbound pass at night, they arrived in Barcis only to find the village burnt down and no sign of Tilman's opposite number. They promptly turned around and when they reached Divisional headquarters at Cansiglio, Tilman set off with Ross to meet an American officer who was with the Tollot Brigade to the west of the Belluno-Vittorio Veneto highway in the hope that he could organize some drops to the Partisans. This time they all managed to meet up and Tilman returned to Cansiglio in time for Christmas but there was no sign of Santa. Despite six attempts to drop supplies in October and November, the last three months of 1944 had been entirely unproductive due to the total absence of successful Allied air drops. Captain Brietsche summed up this period from 15 November to 26 December in his post-operational report: 'This period was one of the worst. There was absolutely nothing to do except wait for aircraft that never came. We had very few arms, were still wearing the clothes we landed in during August, and the food position was foul. To make things more cheerful, sorties were being dropped straight to the enemy. We were in a constant state of alarm and in quite filthy conditions. Snow was about eight feet deep and we did all our man-handling of stores and food at night. It was impossible to carry out any actions against the enemy as we had to spend our time dodging them.' Tilman was equally scathing in his post-Mission report, referring to a 'deplorable records of failure' between 16 October and 28 December when only one of eleven drops had succeeded for whatever reason. 'Not only was navigation very bad but pilots committed the gross fault of dropping their loads regardless of whether correct recognition signals had been exchanged or not'.

It was only finally on Boxing Day that the first drop of arms and ammunition arrived. This freed up Tilman and Ross to move across from the Nannetti to the Belluno Division which, after a series of cross-country marches and overnight stops in cowsheds, they found on 9 January, just as yet another *rastrellamento* was getting underway. Conditions were very different compared to Cansiglio; the Partisans lived in the villages in the day, sleeping out in caves or holes in the ground at night. Due to the Partisans' proximity to German SS HQ and the deep snow, Tilman looked for a more secure Drop Ground in the Forno area to the north east of Belluno. The Fratelli Fenti Brigade who controlled the area was duly warned of the BMM's intention but until it was ready, the mission had to live 'in the strictest seclusion' in a Partisan hideout called 'the cave'. Tilman described the dramatic journey to reach it in *When Men and Mountains Meet*: 'At the entrance to the valley...we began one of the most perilous night walks I have ever indulged in. Across the precipitous valley side a sketchy path, deep in powder snow, pursued its tortuous way, around trees, past jutting boulders and across frozen gullies...We clutched with bare hands at branches, brambles, and glazed rocks until our fingers froze and the sweat of fright and effort dripped from our faces. At midnight we reached a high cliff which overhung slightly. Under two of the best overhangs the Partisans had rigged up a kitchen and sleeping quarters...It was a wild spot. The stream, frozen into silence, lay some 500 feet below, its opposite bank rising abruptly to the rock and snow of Mount Serva 5,000 feet above...Here for three weeks, with three Partisans, we lived like hermits.'

A quick seven hour solo winter ascent of Monte Serva by Tilman made a useful and lasting impression on the Partisans before he left them for the dangerous four-night journey to Forno. Dodging SS patrols and circumventing enemy garrisons and well-defended power stations, Tilman and Ross finally made it to the Val di Gares below the Altipiano delle Pale di San Martino, whose peaks rise to 10,000 feet, where, having first established himself in a small hut underneath an overhang skillfully constructed by two local boys and then mapped out the new Drop Ground, he waited for the promised planes to fly over the narrow valley. On 13 February, after ten days

*John Ross's sketch of Bill
Tilman in the Val di Gares hut*

had passed, the American first plane arrived and four nights later two more made successful drops by delayed-opening parachutes, resulting in substantial deliveries of arms and explosives to the Partisans. Mission accomplished, Tilman and the BMM returned to Rivamonte on 1 March, only to find that intensified enemy activity prevented them from rejoining Divisional HQ. Wisely deciding not to travel in civilian clothes – if caught they would definitely be shot – they were hidden in a coffin-like structure under a load of wood in a lorry and smuggled down the Agordo-Belluno highway past several German block-posts. Ross still often feels the worry he had 'when, at a German block post, a German poked about in the wood above us with a rifle or something – we were very lucky not to be found!"

---

*   Letter Ross/author 17 October 2010

Spring had arrived early in 1945 but this time the Partisans were well prepared, having spent the winter camouflaging and fortifying their positions. Tilman's new hideout with Belluno Divisional HQ was a subterranean bunker hidden under a levelled field sown with potatoes and accessed through a small concealed entrance in a dry stone wall. However, the Nannetti Division was now more or less self-sufficient in arms and ammunition having received over forty drops and the Gramsci Division was well on the mend, so when Major Abba and his second-in-command Deluca of Partisan Zone HQ raised the question of whether a BMM could be attached to it, Tilman agreed to go across with Gatti, albeit reluctantly since he relished the chance to personally go on the offensive with the Partisans brigades and battalions he had so intimately soldiered with throughout the last exacting seven months.

Leaving Ross and Pallino with the Belluno Division, Tilman and Gatti joined Zone HQ in a small farmhouse in the south of the Alpargo district from where they went to Cansiglio to collect their new W/T operator Nicola. What they found was a most remarkable transformation; three separate Drop Grounds were in use, a landing strip to evacuate allied POWs had been prepared and nightly actions against road and railway targets undertaken by well-armed disciplined Partisans. With Nicola safely in tow, they returned to Zone HQ where to his chagrin Tilman described his duties as 'of the nature of a *Maître d'Hotel*, who has to be on view but who seldom does anything so vulgar as work.' Never one to have idle hours on his hands in the mountains, Tilman set to work climbing all the Dolomite peaks within striking distance, an activity at one remove from the Partisans who 'lived among the mountains, sang beautiful songs about them, and liked hearing themselves called mountaineers...would nevertheless have been dumbfounded at the thought of climbing one.'

When the Allied offensive opened in early April, little happened in Tilman's area and it was not until the night of 26 April that Zone HQ heard about the American capture of Verona. By 30 April, all small garrisons south of the River Piave had withdrawn or surrendered but Belluno was full of Germans. While Abba and Deluca opened negotiations with the German General in charge, Tilman went to check the Ponte Nelli Alpi bridge for rumoured demolitions and was nearly killed by an overzealous Partisan machine-gunner who was guarding it. The same afternoon, Tilman made contact with the British advanced guard at Vittorio Veneto and urged them to advance in order to close the Belluno-Longarone road down which the Germans were escaping. Driving down to Veneto on a captured German motorbike, he led the British column comprised of a squadron of 27th Lancers armoured cars and a lorry-borne company of the Rifle Brigade northwards towards Belluno. After a successful skirmish with the retreating Germans, the column advanced to within two miles of the city before meeting stiffer opposition. When Tilman climbed on the leading armoured car to discuss the situation, he found the Squadron Leader shot dead through the heart. By now a battery of 25 pounders of the Essex Yeomanry had arrived from Vittorio and accurate fire began to drop on the German troop and vehicle concentrations. Soon it was all over and on the night of 1 May 4,000 Germans surrendered, followed by the remainder at 1100 hours the next morning.

Tilman was a detached and always curious observer of the Partisans with whom he worked. In his post-mission report, he repeated the conclusions he had reached earlier in Albania: 'There is in my opinion no question that the *Garibaldini* [Communist] formations were the most effective. They were better led, better organized....militarily their faults were mainly due to lack of experience rather than the will to fight...Against all this it must be remembered that the risks they ran once having taken up arms were great.' In his opinion, the Partisans of Northern Italy held high the torch passed down to them by Garibaldi: 'I offer neither pay, nor quarters, nor provisions; I offer hunger, thirst, forced marches, battles and death.' Such was their determination, self-sacrifice and patriotism that they gave their best when asked by Tilman and the other BLOs.

John Orr-Ewing and Christopher Woods, who had worked in the adjoining area to Tilman, concluded that 'looking back over nine months in the field, [we] consider it was very definitely worth going to Veneto. Although we may not have been able to achieve startling results owing to the particularly difficult geographical position of Veneto, yet the arrival of a British Mission, even though initially it brought no drops, showed the Partisans that the Allies took an interest in them and recognized their efforts at throwing off their political tyranny.'

Major Harold Tilman: 18 June 1945: recommendation for immediate DSO

Major Tilman was dropped by parachute North West of Belluno in August 1944 with the object of organizing the Partisan formations in this area which at the time were ill-equipped, untrained and ineffective.

For four months, until the end of 1944, in territory closely controlled by the enemy, and in the face of vigorous conditions of terrain and weather, Major Tilman actively pursued his patient task of creating a military force from a chaotic mass of material. His mission survived two major enemy drives during this period, and he narrowly escaped capture but steadfastly refused to move from his locality in which he could best continue close liaison with his Partisans. In spite of difficulties in obtaining support and encouragement in the form of air supplies, and overcoming political and personal rivalries between Partisan leaders, he succeeded by his energy, tact and personal example in organizing a Partisan division which survived the winter, strengthened in experience and morale and ready for effective cooperation with the Allied armies in the approaching Spring offensive.

In January 1945, having handed over this division to the care of another BLO to build on the sure foundations which he had laid, he moved north west of Belluno to an even more difficult area in the High Dolomites. In the severe winter conditions it was only possible to live in close proximity to enemy garrisons and withdrawal to the mountains in the event of attack was impossible. Major Tilman, with his interpreter, travelled tirelessly throughout this area organizing a second efficient Partisan division, and in March, by concealing himself under a load of wood in a truck on an enemy held road, returned to the neighbourhood of Belluno to coordinate the work of the two divisions by maintaining liaison with the Partisan command for the whole area.

The result of his efforts over a period of eight months may be illustrated by the fact that in the final operations by the Partisans of the two divisions organized under his advice and leadership, a large area was liberated prior to the arrival of Allied troops, some 20,000 enemy troops were captured and 1,800 killed. A vast quantity of material including some 1,500 MT was also taken.

Major Tilman's calm disregard of danger and his capacity for hard physical exertion were an example and an inspiration to all with whom he came in contact and his figure has become legendary among the Partisans throughout the area.

For his devotion to duty, his total disregard for danger and for his own personal safety, and for the courage of the highest order displayed over a period of more than eight months in enemy occupied territory, Major Tilman is most strongly recommended for the award of the immediate DSO.

Awarded

Major Harold Tilman: 20 December 1940: recommendation for DSO

On 18 May, Captain Tilman, when acting as forward observation officer with forward rear guard troops, carried out a boldly led and cleverly executed withdrawal from Assche, near Brussels, when his OP party had been put out of action by the destruction of tanks of his armoured carrier and wireless. He was ably seconded in this manouevre by Captain P.L.Lloyd, with whom he joined forces. This group, composed of two officers and five men, held their position for an hour, inflicting some twenty casualties and only retiring when surrounded. On frequent subsequent occasions, Captain Tilman controlled the fire of his battery with great skill, inflicting heavy losses on the enemy. Throughout these operations, his coolness under fire was an inspiration to the troops under his command.

Downgraded to Second Bar to MC, then finally awarded a Mention in Dispatches

Captain John Ross: 18 June 1945: recommendation for immediate MC

Captain Ross was dropped by parachute Northwest of Belluno in August 1944 to assist in organizing the Partisan formations in this area. At that time their morale was low, they were poorly equipped and trained, and as a military force, they were ineffective.

For four months until the end of 1944 Captain Ross assisted the senior BLO in training and organizing a Partisan division east of the River Piave. In spite of difficult winter conditions, and although the area was closely controlled by the enemy, this task was successfully accomplished. His mission survived two enemy drives and he narrowly escaped capture but he continued his work of encouragement and training unperturbed. When Captain Ross moved back to the area northwest of Belluno in January 1945, he handed over to his successor a Partisan division of vastly improved morale and fighting effectiveness, which came through the winter intact and operated magnificently in support of the Allied armies in the spring offensive.

From January to March 1945, Captain Ross assisted in the organization of a second Partisan division in the area of the Dolomites, northwest of Belluno. No conditions could have been more difficult for Partisan work. The mission was compelled to live in close proximity to enemy garrisons and withdrawal to the mountains in the event of an attack was impossible owing to the severe winter and deep snow. Captain Ross toured his area tirelessly organizing the reception of stores and welding the Partisan elements into an efficient fighting force.

In late March, Captain Ross took over command of this mission and initiated continuous attacks against enemy garrisons and communications. In April, his Partisans successfully held a German attack, inflicting considerable casualties on the enemy. At the end of April, in their final operations, his division liberated many localities before Allied troops arrived, took some 10,000 enemy POWs and killed some 500 enemy, besides capturing large quantities of material.

This magnificent result, from such an unpromising beginning in the autumn of 1944, was due in large measure to the consistently efficient and conscientious work of Captain Ross over a period of eight months in trying conditions and without regard for his own personal comfort or safety. His judgement and advice on military questions were always sound and he was an example of devotion to duty to all Partisans and members of BMMs with whom he came into contact. He is strongly recommended for the award of an immediate MC.

Awarded

Captain Paul Brietsche: 18 April 1945: recommendation for immediate MC

Captain Brietsche was dropped by parachute into the Belluno area in August 1944 and immediately took over command of considerable Partisan forces operating in that area. Despite continuous attacks by the enemy, Captain Brietsche was able to maintain a supply dropping ground in the centre of enemy-patrolled territory. With these supplies he armed and trained over 1,000 men whose actions and engagement over seven months proved a feature of Italian resistance in the North East.

Captain Brietsche throughout has personally led his formation and although twice wounded he refused to leave the area. During the worst winter months and despite the privations of lack of food and clothing, he maintained the morale of the forces under his command at the highest possible level and his personal courage and example were an inspiration to all.

Numerous casualties were inflicted on the enemy by these Partisan forces and , under Captain Brietsche's leadership, they accounted for seventy enemy killed, twenty wounded and seven POWs, and in addition damaged or destroyed some thirty-five vehicles, four railway trucks and a large petrol dump. Sabotage attacks resulted in the blowing up of three bridges, two railway lines, high tension pylons and telephone lines.

Captain Brietsche was in enemy occupied territory for over eight months. At all times he displayed outstanding courage and devotion to duty under very difficult conditions and he is strongly recommended for the immediate award of the MC.

Awarded

17

Major Tommy Macpherson, MC and two bars, Croix de Guerre*

Major Hedley Vincent, DSO

The son of a senior Indian Civil Servant, Tommy Macpherson spent the first three years of his life in India before returning to the family home in Edinburgh to commence his education. An outstanding athlete and impressive scholar, he excelled at Fettes College and it was while waiting for news of his scholarship application to Trinity College Oxford in early 1939 that he signed up as a second lieutenant in The 4th Queen's Own Cameron Highlanders. On being commissioned that June, he found himself an officer in the Cameron Highlanders, a sergeant in the Fettes OTC and a corporal in the school pipe band!

On mobilization, Macpherson was posted as a platoon commander to the 5th Queen's Own Cameron Highlanders, initially at Badenoch and then Tain, and in the chaotic atmosphere of the phoney war became in short succession 2ic HQ company, transport officer, assistant adjutant and intelligence officer. In May 1940, after the fall of France, he volunteered to join the newly constituted No.11 Scottish Commando and on passing selection and completing training, he sailed with two other Scottish commando units to the Middle East where they arrived in March 1941. After much to'ing and fro'ing around the eastern Mediterranean, Layforce, as the commando formation was now known, was deployed in the invasion of Syria which was occupied by pro-German Vichy French forces. It was at the Battle of Litani River that Macpherson got his first taste of action in what turned out to be a costly engagement; 123 commandoes were killed or wounded while a total of 3,500 Allied lives were lost. Shortly after, three days after his twenty first birthday, he was promoted to captain and took over as adjutant of No.11 Scottish Commando.

In the latter part of 1941, Macpherson was ordered to report to the submarine depot ship *HMS Medway* in Alexandria where he was briefed on a top secret mission. The idea was to send two two-man reconnaissance

---

* Two Palms and Star

patrols by submarine to a point off the Libyan coast and for them to go ashore by canoe to find a suitable landing site for a medium size force of commandos*. Furthermore, they were required to investigate the terrain beyond the beach which would involve climbing up the steep escarpment. The operation went smoothly until the second night when the canoeists failed to rendezvous with the submarine despite zigzagging over the pick-up area all night. It was the same story the following night, so having hidden their canoes in a cave, the members of the mission decided to make their way back to Allied lines across country. Macpherson and Corporal Evans followed the coast while the two SBS officers, Captains Ratcliffe and Raven-scroft, headed inland. After an adventurous few days during which Macpherson killed a large Dobermann guard dog with his commando knife and stole bread loaves from inside a tent full of Germans, they were captured by a patrol of twenty Italian cyclists but not before wrecking an enemy tele-phone exchange for the fun of it. When the two men arrived at Derna, they found the SBS officers waiting for them and after interrogation, all of them were shipped to POW camps in Italy.

Initially Macpherson was put in POW Camp PG 43 at Montalbo Castle where he determined to study Italian before attempting to escape. The following summer, the commando and other 'bad boy' prisoners were trans-ported north to Gavi, the gloomy and impregnable castle that housed POW Camp PG 5†. Soon after the Italian armistice was signed in September 1943, the Germans took over the camp and transported the POWs to Alessandria for shipment to Germany by train. A valorous attempt by Macpherson to escape at the railway station was thwarted but, undeterred, he joined forces at Spittal Transit camp in Austria with two New Zealand officers, Colin Armstrong and Alan Yeoman, and the three of them walked out of the camp disguised as French labourers.

After successfully making their way across the border into Italy, they reached the town of Chiusaforte where Macpherson and Armstrong had the misfortune to pass by an inn disgorging a patrol of *carabinieri* and German soldiers. Immediately arrested and taken to guard HQ, they bluffed their way for the next thirty six hours that they were of French-Croatian extrac-tion and on their way to work in the locomotive sheds in Laibach.

---

* This reconnaissance was a precursor to Operation Flipper when Lieutenant Colonel Geoffrey Keyes, the commanding officer of 11 Scottish Commando, was killed leading the raid on Rommel's HQ.
† George Patterson was held in the same camp.

Unfortunately their captors found a letter from his wife on Armstrong which gave the lie to their story and their next port of call was a camp in East Prussia run by the Gestapo before finally ending up at Stalag 20A near Torun on the Polish-German border.

Irrepressible as ever, Macpherson and Armstrong once again turned their attention to escape and having hitched a ride to Gdynia with the king of the local black market whom the camp escape committee kept supplied with Red Cross parcels, they managed to find a ship sailing for Sweden and on arrival in Gotland contacted the British consul who arranged their flight home. Two years to the day after being captured in North Africa, Macpherson was back in Scotland. It had been an incredible journey, one which demanded extraordinary reserves of physical and mental stamina and courage. Both officers were awarded the MC for their magnificent achievement.

Within days of his arrival, Macpherson was ordered to report to Milton Hall in Cambridgeshire. He discovered once there that he was to be part of a three-man SOE Jedburgh team, codename Quinine, to be dropped into France to galvanize the local resistance in assisting the Allied invasion forces under General Eisenhower. Although much of the training was a rehash of his commando days, there was a great deal to learn in coding, running agents and, of course, the all important parachute course at Ringway outside Manchester. Now a Major, Macpherson was teamed with twenty years old French Lieutenant Michel de Bourbon-Parme and a British radio operator, Sergeant Arthur Brown, also twenty. Having completed an arduous final exercise in the Atlas Mountains, the team returned to England and on the night of 8/9 June 1944 was dropped to the French resistance near Aurillac to the north of Clermont-Ferrand. It was the start of yet another exciting chapter in the young Cameron Highlander officer's life.

Over the next weeks, Macpherson was to cut his teeth on the niceties of sabotage and ambushes behind enemy lines, preparing dropping grounds and organizing reception parties and at the same time learning the essential survival skills of how to avoid detection by German Direction Finding vans, keeping constantly on the move and identifying potential traitors and collaborators.. After blowing up a bridge with his little band of Maquis, Macpherson was informed that a German armoured heavy division was making its way along the Figeac-Tulle road, heading towards Normandy. His French hosts implored him to delay it and without further ado the Jedburghs loaded up as much explosive as they could carry and headed to Brenetoux where a gallant band of *Maquis* were engaged in a firefight with the approaching Panzer division at the river crossing.

Realizing that he lacked both the men and firepower to stop the Germans, Macpherson prepared a series of dummy ambushes and obstacles along the road during the hours of darkness. His tactics paid off for the advance of the German armoured column slowed to a snail's pace the next day as they were forced to dismount and clear the obstructions of fallen trees booby-trapped with mines and grenades. In the mean time, Macpherson's *Maquis* sporadically sprayed them with Sten gun fire and then vanished into the woods. Much later, he learnt that his team had stopped none other than the battle-hardened Das Reich SS Panzer division and helped to prevent their timely arrival to reinforce the hard pressed defenders on the Normandy beaches.

A steady stream of recruits became to appear and soon Macpherson was able to expand his operations into neighbouring areas, blowing up railway lines and bridges and the heavily guarded railway viaduct at the Pont du Garabit. The German military garage at Cahors was successfully sabotaged. By late July 1944, the war in France had swung decisively in the Allies' favour and on 15 August when 200,000 American and French troops landed on the coast between Marseilles and Cannes, Macpherson realized that it was only a matter of time before the Germans started to withdraw their garrison troops north to the German border. Therein lay an opportunity and he began to blow up the bridges on the south side of the Massif Central to deny the retreating Germans the cover of the thickly wooded countryside. Soon the garrison of Aurillac capitulated and in a foretaste of what he was to find in Italy, Macpherson through a game of bluff persuaded the commander of a hundred-strong German detachment which was guarding a mined dam to surrender; shortly afterwards he masterfully negotiated the surrender of General Elster's 23,000 German soldiers retreating from Biarritz.

In September 1944, with the liberation of France completed, the twenty four year old Major Macpherson, together with Sergeant Brown, was posted to Monopoli to await further orders. Apart from Michael Lees, no other SOE officer of his age could match him in experience or expertise: as a professional soldier, his knowledge of battle drills and minor tactics was comprehensive and well tested; as a sabotage expert, his French experience was invaluable; as an operative used to living behind enemy lines, he brought both his POW and Jedburgh credentials to the table; his leadership of men in the field was exemplary; and above all, he had established in his own mind a rigorous intellectual model for the successful prosecution of guerrilla warfare which was to stand him in good stead. In addition, he had weathered the nuances of the political divisions within the French resistance and demonstrated a canny acumen of harnessing them to fulfil strictly military objectives.

On the night of 9/10 June, SOE mission Coolant had been dropped into Yugoslavia with orders to make their way across the frontier into Italy and establish relations with the Partisans in the Udine region. From the beginning, it was clear that politics would dominate the agenda since feelings about the post- First World War border still ran high. In 1915, the Italians had been promised in the secret Treaty of London a significant part of Dalmatia and Slovenia if they came into the war against Germany and Austria-Hungary. However, when negotiations started in earnest at the Versailles Conference in 1919, President Wilson's Fourteen Points favoured the newly created state of Yugoslavia and after much acrimonious haggling, the Italians and Yugoslavs finally settled their differences at Rapallo the following year. Italy got virtually the whole of the Istrian Peninsula including Trieste, Zadar, an Adriatic town with a majority Italian population, and a few islands. Yugoslavia got the rest though Fiume became a free state linked to Italy by a strip of land. This last arrangement was nullified when Mussolini annexed it in January 1922. Still smarting from the Italian invasion of 1941, from the Yugoslavian perspective there was everything to play for in trying to occupy as much Italian territory as possible before the cessation of hostilities. The Slovenes had every reason to be aggrieved. Over 35,000 of them were deported by the Italians to Italy and 3,500 killed either as hostages or during round-ups.

Coolant, commanded by Major Hedley Vincent*, made contact with the Italians on 4 July and by early August had established itself with the *Garibaldini* at Stremis to the west of the Isonzo River to oversee the development of Partisan activity [Operation Sermon]. On 12 August, Vincent was joined by two Royal Engineer officers, Lieutenants Taylor and Godwin, whose task was to set up a sabotage and demolition school and train specialist squads of partisans. Vincent himself was engaged on setting up a unified Partisan command to incorporate the brigades of different political complexions into a single division for 'the *Garibaldini* leaders of the left and *Osoppo* commanders of right wing tendencies distrusted and deprecated each other and so retarded the natural development of the war against the enemy'. Although agreement was reached between the two factions, the *Garibaldini* were allowed by Vincent to get the lion's share of the weapons drops.

In early September, he moved the HQ to Forame and started talks with the Slovene IX Corps and the newly constituted Partisan unified command about Italo-Slovene problems in the area. Meanwhile sporadic Partisan

---

* He was recruited by SOE in West Africa [Luanda] to work for Colonel Louis Franck in Operation Postmaster.

Above: Maj Vincent

Left: Cpl Hargreaves

activity which had resulted in 'the liberation' of a number of villages attracted the attention of the Germans and a major *rastrellamenti* was launched in late September. The Mission had to go on the run and it was not until 16 October that it returned to Forame. Vincent tended to see the *Garibaldini* through rose tinted glasses for his report of 23 October stated that '*Garibaldini* brigades...have always fought well and never avoided action or sabotage' is simply not borne out by other BLOs. Macpherson wrote that 'this combined *Osoppo-Garibaldini* unit was militarily almost completely inactive'. It was incredulous for Vincent to say that 'they regard their participation in this war as a crusade against Fascism and its allies rather than an effort to liberate Italy for particular motives'. Shortly after, Vincent left for Yugoslavia and reached Bari on 8 November. His final report to SOE highlighted the Italo-Slovene problems 'which will prove so difficult to solve by Allied intervention at the conclusion of hostilities'.

On the night of 4 November, Macpherson and his WT Operator Sergeant Brown dropped to an *Osoppo* reception near Canebola [Beaverton Drop Ground]. It was not without incident as Macpherson explained in his letter to Captain Alan Clark, his desk officer in Bari: '13 November: Well, we got here. Quite a nice landing, though from God knows what height, as we took some five minutes to come down. The harness slipped off both of us on the way down: I arrived hanging by my hands with the 'box' lodged firmly under my chin and Brown was tied in an extraordinary knot...Our main sorrow was the non-arrival of our rucksacks, which contained all that we really wanted even if nothing else should turn up. No clothes, no chocolate, no whiskey! Thank heaven for morale, Sir, by Gad, Sir!'

His first observation was to prove astute: the *Garibaldini* 'will almost certainly go Slovene – how far they go is the only point that matters.' He soon discovered that under Vincent's watch, Sasso [Mario Fantini], the *Garibaldini* commander, had sent the Slovenes over 15% of all parachuted arms and material in August and September. Furthermore, it later transpired that on 7 October, the *Garibaldini* had signed a deal with the Slovenes placing themselves under the command of IX Corps, thus taking orders only from Tito, a blatant ruse to avoid being subjugated to allied authority through the CLN. They duly decamped at the end of December, the whole *Garibaldini* Division migrating east across the Isonzo River to join their Slovene 'comrafes'. Shortly after, the leaders of the Carnia and Udine *Garibaldini* held a meeting with senior officers of Tito, who gave them a verbal assurance that whatever part of Italy was annexed to Yugoslavia through their efforts would be made into a Soviet republic within a greater Slav

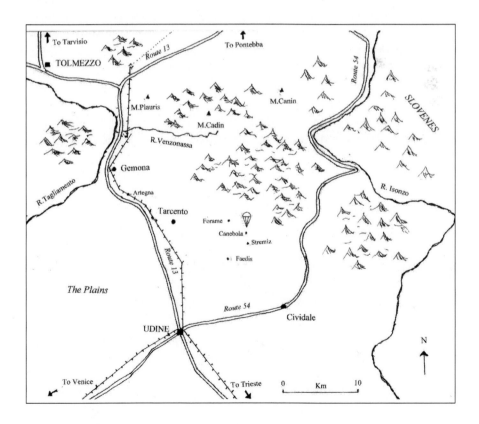

Communist federation and they would get the plum jobs of President, Minister and C in C. So much for Vincent's 'unified command'.

The winter operational plan inherited by Macpherson called for each sabotage squad to derail two trains per week on the Udine-Pontebba line and for the other partisans to mount ambushes on the roads leading North. After Field Marshal Alexander's decision to curtail winter activities by the Partisans, the plan was revised and six squads were given the task of derailing one train per week. However, conditions were far from ideal as Macpherson reported: 'It is snowing hard and bloody cold. We are working hard to fix winter food reserves. I cannot urge strongly enough the need for boots and clothing. It is pathetic to see these boys at work in the snow and ice.' The stock of explosives was alarmingly low when he arrived and it was only after two successful drops in December that they were sufficiently replenished for him to commence sustained operations. Meanwhile training and selection of NCOs had continued apace with limited sabotage operations.

Nevertheless the tally was impressive. In November and December 1944, twenty two trains were derailed, two bridges blown and the railway infra-structure repeatedly damaged. Two actions were of particular note: the derailment of a train on 13 November with the consequent destruction of two Mark III tanks and two 10-ton trucks with ten Germans killed and the devastating Christmas day attack on the Morganti factory in Gemona which had been converted to make spare parts for aircraft.

In early January, Macpherson badly sprained his ankle returning from a recce. 'You just try hurrying over bad country in pitch black with a sprain on you – not fun!' Forced to rely on a slow and stubborn mule to get about, none the less he continued to direct and supervise training and operations. He sent Taylor and Godwin out on 15 January, 'the training side of the job all but complete, the *Garibaldini* gone and the *Osoppo* demobilizing, I can handle the job myself and their presence exposes them to unnecessary unpleasantness as well as, by increasing the size of the party, increasing each difficulty of camouflage.' En route, they were told by the Slovene IX Corps Commissar that '*Osoppo* and Macpherson are in league with the Germans'. They reported on their return to Bari that the *Osoppo* Partisan number were down to three people at Brigade HQ, twenty at Group HQ including the reception party and seven with Macpherson and Brown. In late January, Macpherson sent Corporal Trent and two bodyguards to set up a meeting with the Slovene IX Corps. He made contact as arranged but on the way back he and one of the bodyguards were robbed and murdered by

Lt Ron Taylor and Lt David Godwin

the Slovenes. The other, badly injured, managed to fight his way free and made his way back with the gruesome news.

These remaining *Osoppo* Partisans together with the BMM were ensconced in two log cabins on the slopes overlooking the banks of the Vensonezzo River. Macpherson told Alan Clark on 1 February that 'conditions have become perfectly bloody with 3-4 foot of snow almost everywhere, either so frozen that one can't keep one's foot or so soft that one sinks to the waist. Yesterday I took 13 hours to do as many miles and got frostbite in the bargain....the ankle I damaged a month ago will not heal properly and swells like a balloon at the slightest provocation. However, I get round.' *Osoppo* relations with the Slovenes at this point were dire –'the Slovenes as expected surrounded the *Osoppo* HQ the other day, with lots of malice aforethought and automatic weapons. A fairly sticky battle looked like developing but I managed to persuade the Slovs to be good boys and go home. Their reaction seems now a desire that the Huns clean us up. Last night they left a series of signposts marked *"Alla Brigata Osoppo"* extending from 200 yards from the nearest Cossack garrison to 350 yards from our door. Fortunately our patrol found them first but the game is sure to be tried in other form.'

It came as a considerable blow to Macpherson when Francesco de Gregori ['Bolla'], a former Alpini officer and the inspirational leader of the *Osoppo* on the east of the Tagliamento River, was murdered at Porzûs near Faedis by the *Garibaldini* in early February. In an incident reminiscent of the Glencoe massacre, a group of *Garibaldini* and two Slovenes had arrived at the *Osoppo* HQ in appalling weather and asked for shelter for the night. This was nothing but a pretext to search the camp for Macpherson and when they didn't find him, they killed the majority of the *Osoppo* Partisans whose hospitality they had been enjoying*. Bolla's mangled corpse bore all the hallmarks of the most savage torture. Macpherson had to 'force the surviving leaders out of their mood of passive despair. Their position looks very gloomy. They counted seven enemies – Germans, Russians, Republicans, Slovenes, *Garibaldini*, spies and the winter itself. The Allied armies were still on the wrong side of Bologna, conditions were not permitting drops, their most able leader had been murdered by their "Allies", and their troops had had to be dispersed'. So Macpherson set to work with them, reorganizing and preplanning for the spring. It was the measure of his leadership that they reacted favourably to his exhortations.

During the winter, Macpherson had concentrated on increasing the size and scope of the Partisan organization in the plains, including propaganda, sabotage, intelligence and general military preparedness. It was the beginning of a vast organization of unarmed saboteurs who through simple acts such as destroying office files or watering petrol snipped away at the communications and transportation infrastructure. Railwaymen sabotage squads were also formed in Udine and Pontebba and issued with various types of incendiaries. The fruits of this initiative were impressive. In January and February 1945, the tally was ten derailments [twenty seven wagons], nineteen engines destroyed in situ, thirty one incendiaries planted in goods wagons bound for Germany and the interruption of all traffic on Route 13 for three days by two well sited snow and rock avalanches.

German reaction varied from limited sweeps to a major *rastrellamenti* from 20 to 26 February when 5,000 Germans, 400 Finns and 4,000 Russians were deployed with supporting armour and artillery. Static garrisons were provided by the Russians, 'a heaven-sent reply to the Partisan problem' as Macpherson put it. 'Underpaid, underfed and given the idea that the land was destined from them like Canaan to the Hebrews,..they had to seek their food far and wide and their horse's fodder..they had to do this in protective numbers, so they automatically supplied just the type of provocative, all-persuasive patrols that the enemy wanted.' They were stationed in every hill village with orders to carry out regular patrolling in certain designated

---

* The ringleaders of this massacre were tried and convicted in 1951.

Don Erino D'Agostini and Maj Macpherson, December 1944

areas. On one occasion, Macpherson's mission was caught in a cave 6,000 feet up on Mount Plauris by one such Cossack patrol and were lucky to get away. On another occasion, the Russians regularly used a path 100 yards from the concealed entrance to his hideout.

Fighting the Germans proved doubly difficult since the Slovenes and Slovene controlled *Garibaldini* were equally hostile. The February attacks on *Osoppo* had eliminated an important link in Macpherson's command, intelligence and communications chain and took considerable time and resources to repair. However, the *Osoppo* tally for March proved equally successful with three derailments and eleven wagons destroyed and by implementing Macpherson's idea of utilizing the vast amount of unexploded bombs and ordnance in the area, the Partisans were able to crater the main roads and railways with devastating effect. Ambushes on roads greatly increased during this period as did attacks on electricity pylons, stores, road maintenance and repair equipment and isolated outposts. By April, the momentum created by Macpherson reached its peak with eight derailments, sixteen wagons destroyed, twenty three trucks knocked out, twenty eight pylons blown up and over 190 Germans and Fascists killed or wounded.

Somewhat against the will of the Fascists, the Archbishop of Udine formed a *Guarda Civica* with the task of protecting the population against attacks of every sort. Macpherson and the *Osoppo* successfully infiltrated it and filled its ranks with their own men, who took their orders directly from *Gruppo Osoppo dell'Est*.

During this time, Macpherson had to deal with the strident stipulations of Major Tom Roworth of the Tabella Mission who was operating to the West of the Tagliamento River. Like Vincent, Roworth tended to be too supportive of the *Garibaldini* at the expense of the *Osoppo* – 'the right wing of *Osoppo* has the same idea as the Church and the industrialists who brought about fascism due to hatred and fear of the communists and who will, if the opportunity presents itself, cause another form of authoritarianism probably this time with the Church of Rome as its leader'. In a note to Roworth dated 7 February 1945, having acknowledged receipt of Roworth's unsolicited letters to him of 14 and 29 January, Macpherson noted his remark that 'base has appointed him to define brigade and mission operational areas' but pointed out that 'the former is impossible...no one can predict the areas where each formation will be able to operate in two months – indeed scarcely two weeks hence'. He was adamant that missions should have their own 'natural area' otherwise 'confusion and duplication' result. He then told Roworth that he was strongly against the system of sub-missions under a mission since 'the controlling mission tends to issue impossible or other impracticable orders which arrive after a long delay'.

A case in point was Captain Prior [Big Bug Mission] who Macpherson had met at Christmas – 'he was a very disillusioned man about all his mission...and apparently felt he had been abandoned and decided to go back'. Roworth was vituperative about Prior, almost to the point of accusing him of cowardice and lack of moral fibre; in one letter to Macpherson, he wrote 'I'm afraid Prior was set that his Mission would fail as a sub-mission...I am very disappointed in Prior and pleased with Mosdell.' A more lightly explanation was that Roworth would not brook any criticism or even difference of opinion. For instance, his assessment of the enemy *rastrellamenti* in November 1944 was that 'the enemy did not...succeed in his main intention which was to destroy the partisan movement for the winter in this area.' Prior on the other hand was unequivocal that 'it can be definitely stated that the Germans have completely succeeded in their programme of putting Partisan activity off the map – in this area – for the winter'.

As the Allied advance gathered pace in the spring of 1945, Macpherson's mission entered a new phase. On the morning of 27 April Plan White was activated, cutting all telephone lines between the sea and the Austrian border, and was followed immediately that night by Plan Black, the continuous harassing of all enemy withdrawal routes, especially Routes 13 and 54 to Austria and the Monte Croce Pass. Plan Yellow followed which comprised the Partisans concentrating in given areas to carry out predetermined tasks including Anti-Scorch operations.

The liberation of the city of Udine on 30 April was a model of planning and political expediency. Macpherson had already been in meetings in Gemona with the city's future civilian government; on one occasion, during an air raid, he had cheekily lobbed a grenade into a shelter full of fascist troops and as he ran off, bumped into an Italian officer who shot him at point blank range, the bullet striking his webbing and notebook. He survived; the officer didn't. A potential confrontation between the *Garibaldini* and *Osoppo* was averted when the CLN were persuaded to elect a 'neutral figure' as supreme commander for the operation. Subsequently, the attack went in without a hitch, resulting in the capture intact of the electricity substations, the telephone exchange, the civic buildings and the bridges, all of which had been prepared for demolition. Furthermore, timely intelligence had allowed the Partisans to forestall German attempts to execute the hostages held in the city's jails and to spirit away the Archbishop to safety before a German patrol moved in on his palace. The first Allied armour was thus able to enter the city at 1530 hours without firing a shot.

Macpherson then occupied Gemona and established a defensive perimeter just in time to withstand an enemy counterattack. His position, which had always been nerve wracking, was now critical. About 1,000 Russians and Wehrmacht and 800 SS supported by two heavy tanks came in from the West. A lucky shot fired by the Partisans from a captured gun glanced off the turret of one of the tanks: deciding that the narrow streets were a trap, they withdrew and contented themselves with shelling the town from half a mile away. A local attack forced the Wehrmacht out and the SS spearhead, having captured an *albergo*, proceeded to get drunk. On his way the next day to contact forward elements of the 60th Rifles which had arrived at nearby Artegna, a grenade landed in the back of Macpherson's car which miraculously did not harm the occupants in the front.

By now German troops in Italy had been ordered to surrender but poor communications prevented the message getting through to many units and some were determined to press on back to Germany. So the Partisans continued to block the escape routes and provided anti-sniping clearance patrols to prevent the British advance units from getting bogged down. At the same time, Slovene armed incursions with the connivance of the *Garib-aldini* began to represent a serious threat to the political stability of the region. The Eighth Army commander, General McCreary, asked Macpherson to assist him in maintaining law and order in the border areas and informed No 1 Special Force in Sienna that he was to report directly to him.

The final phase of the Coolant mission began as the AMG took over the liberated areas. In admirably concise yet immensely detailed intelligence Situation Reports, Macpherson, now based in Trieste, warned AFHQ about the 'highly charged situation' in respect of disarming Partisans including the decommissioning of their hidden arms and ammunition dumps and on apprehending Fascists still at large. Always an acute observer of life in the raw, on 21 June he told Lieutenant Colonel Bright, the Allied Provincial Commissioner, that 'a certain commercial spirit has entered into the hiding of arms etc. *Garibaldini* are in some cases selling small consignments of arms and ammo to the Jugs; and Partisans of all sorts are selling vehicle parts to civilians'. Macpherson also observed at first hand the antics of the *Garibaldini* and Slovene Communists to obstruct industry returning to normal conditions.

In August, Macpherson was posted to Sienna for debriefing. Never afraid to speak his mind, the young Major soon realized that his frank report about the situation he had found on his arrival and of the briefing he had been given had been far from universally well received by senior SOE staff

Gen Sir Richard McCreery, Maj Macpherson and Mario Lizzero, Udine 24 June 1945

officers. Likewise, the *Garibaldini* chiefs who had collaborated with the Slovene communists and killed some of their own countrymen were far from happy that Macpherson had revealed their names and aliases. Even Marshal Tito, it later transpired, was irked by his successful contribution to the safeguarding of Italian territorial integrity.

Macpherson's war in Italy had been an outstanding success. Although Lady Luck played a part in keeping him alive, the principal reason for his success was his single-minded focus on sticking to sabotage and avoiding futile skirmishes which provoked savage enemy responses and resulted in serious collateral damage to villages and farms. He was an ardent believer that hit and run tactics were best suited to guerrilla warfare and the ability to melt away to prepositioned hides and food dumps was key to being able to live to fight another day. While his actions may appear carefree almost to the point of recklessness, Macpherson was in fact risk averse and whenever possible every operation was subjected to a detailed reconnaissance and meticulous planning. His attitude was that valuable scant resources, be they men or material, were not to be squandered on vainglorious and futile confrontations with the enemy; they were to be conserved and used surgically to cause the greatest damage at the smallest cost.

A stickler for training and selection of NCOs, he developed the *Osoppo* formations in his region into a motivated and effective fighting force which went on to inflict significant casualties on the enemy and to cause widespread damage to his lines of communication. At the political level, Macpherson made the choice not to ally or associate himself with the Slovene-*Garibaldini* nexus. It was undoubtedly the correct decision for when the war ended, it was the solely presence of the British Eighth Army that frustrated Tito's ambitions to annex Trieste and the Udine region, thus avoiding a bloody civil war.

Major Tommy Macpherson: 26 April 1945: Recommendation for immediate bar to MC

Major Macpherson was parachuted into the Udine area of North East Italy in November 1944 and immediately took over the organization of Partisan operations in the vital Tarvisio line. An attack on his Partisan formations caused the Mission and the Partisans to disperse temporarily. Major Macpherson immediately reorganized his forces and continued with a series of well-planned attacks, including one successful operation against the railway yards in Udine itself, in which Partisans, personally led by him, co-operated with the Air Force in causing considerable damage to vital installations. Eight trains were derailed and their locomotives put out of action. Over fifteen major interruptions of the railway in the area of Tarvisio and Germona were effected.

Major Macpherson's work was done in the face of consistent and forceful enemy interruption and his efforts were further handicapped by the exceedingly delicate situation with the Slovenes.

Throughout the winter and handicapped by injuries received in an earlier action, Major Macpherson carried on with a total disregard of danger and displayed exceptional courage and devotion to duty.

Recommended for the award of a bar to the Military Cross.

Awarded

Major Tommy Macpherson: Recommendation for Bar to MC

This officer was parachuted into the Lot department of France on 9 June 1944, together with a French officer and a radio operator, in order to organize and lead Resistance groups.

Within a few days of their arrival, this party armed a small Maquis and led them into a guerrilla operation against the Das Reich Panzer Division which was moving northwards into the Correze.

First, they demolished a small bridge, thus delaying the enemy's progress for several hours; next, they defended the bridge at Bicteroux for six days against strong enemy attacks. During this action Major Macpherson was always at the most vulnerable point setting a splendid example. Of twenty seven men who took part in these operations, twenty were killed.

The party then organized a Maquis to attack the road and railway from Montauban to Brive, and by 1 July they had entirely eliminated all rail traffic between Cahors and Souillac.

Throughout July Major Macpherson organised ambushes on enemy convoys and with the advance of the Allied Armies from the South, the party engaged in large scale guerrilla operations with great success.

During one of these actions at Livran, 300 Germans and 100 *miliciens* were blocked in a tunnel. After two days they tried to escape from the other side in the train which had stopped in the tunnel. Major Macpherson in conditions of great hazard went into the tunnel and blew up the railway track thus effectively sealing up 400 enemy and the train.

On several other occasions Major Macpherson gave proof of outstanding qualities of gallantry and inspiration to the Maquis.

He is recommended for a bar to the MC.

Awarded

Captain Tommy Macpherson: 10 December 1943: recommendation for MC

Captain Armstrong was captured at Sidi Aziz on 27 November 1941 and was sent to Bari Transit camp and thence to camp 38 [Poppi]. On 20 July 1942 he escaped with Captain Yeoman but was recaptured at Marina di Carrera, having covered 250 miles in three weeks. He was sent to camp 5 [Gavi] in August 1942. On 9 September 1943 the Germans occupied the camp and the POWs were transferred to Acqui and thence to Stalag XVIIIA [Spitaal]. Roll-calls were avoided by hiding in the camp, so that the names of three officers – Captain Armstrong, Captain Macpherson and Captain Yeoman – were not on the list. These three officers contacted the French '*homme de confiance*' and escaped in French uniforms. They reached the Italian frontier but Captain Armstrong and Captain Macpherson were recaptured near Chuisa-forte on 26 September 1943. They were sent to Hohenstein [East Prussia] and thence to Stalag XXI [Thorn, Poland] arriving on 1 October 1943. With the aid of Private Hudson and Sergeant Glancy [who have since reached the UK] Captain Armstrong and Captain Macpherson escaped, arriving in Sweden on 20 October 1943 via Bromberg and Gdynia.

Captain Macpherson was captured near Derna on 2 November 1941 and made two attempts to escape before arriving in Italy. In June 1942 he was sent to Camp 41 [Montalbo] and thence to Camp 5 [Gavi]. On 9 September the Germans occupied the camp and the POWs were transferred to Acqui. Captain Macpherson evaded the guards at the station but was recaptured. He arrived with Captain Armstrong and thenceforth his story is the same as that of Captain Armstrong.

Both these officers displayed great gallantry and tenacity of purpose in continuing their efforts to escape until they were finally successful. I recommend Captain Armstrong for the award of a bar to the MC and Captain Macpherson for the award of the MC.

Awarded

Epilogue

Ballard, Hugh: Returned to Southern Rhodesia and then to Kenya where he farmed with three of his brothers. Died in England in 1983.

Barton, John: Went to Kenya to farm. Died 2009.

Battaglia, Roberto: Became an academic and historian. Died 1963.

Brietsche, Paul: Changed his name to Newton after the war and became a wealthy businessman in the Mediterranean area. Married three times and retired to Devon where he died relatively young.

Cooper, Dick: Published his memoirs in 1957. Died in 1988.

Croft, Andrew: Reorganized Army Junior Leaders and Apprentices and then became Commandant of the Metropolitan Police Cadet Corps at Hendon, introducing adventure training and community service as core activities. Died in 1998.

Czernin, Manfred: Started an airfreight business in South Africa, then switched to the automotive industry, first with the Rootes Group in Paris and then with Renault UK and finally Fiat UK. Died in 1962.

Dallimore-Mallaby, Dick: Lived in Italy after the war where he worked for NATO in Verona. Died in 1981.

Davidson, Basil: Bbecame a prolific journalist/author on post-colonial Africa and confidant of many liberation movements. Died in 2010.

Dodson, Derek: Became a career diplomat and was successively ambassador to Hungary, Brazil and Turkey. Died in 2003.

Farran, Roy: Ater failing to win Dudley and Stourbridge in the 1949 general election, emigrated to Canada to farm. Entered politics, becoming solicitor-general of Alberta from 1975-79. Wrote a number of books, including *Winged Dagger — Adventures on Special Service* (1949), *The Search* (1958) and *Operation Tombola* (1968). Died in 2006, aged 85.

Fielding, George: Tried life as a management trainee with Lever Brothers before buying a farm in the West of Ireland. Later started a Munich-based sporting agency and acquired Rigby's who held the UK concession for the Merkel gun company of East Germany. In his later years, became an accomplished skier in Switzerland and discovered a hitherto latent talent as an artist in his eighties. He died in 2005.

Holland, Charles: Settled in Italy and started Amplifon SpA, now one of the world's largest hearing aids companies. Died ?

Lees, Michael: Became an international businessman, then successful fruit farmer; wrote his SOE memoirs – *Special Operations Executed* – in 1984, followed by *The Rape of Serbia: the British Role in Tito's Grab for Power* in 1990. Died 1992.

Lett, Gordon: Left the army in 1948 and joined the Diplomatic Corps. Later became a NATO lecturer on Psychological Warfare and ended his career at the College of Arms in London when he officiated at the Investiture of the Prince of Wales. Died in 1989.

MacDonald, Buck: Following the war, attended Law School at Dalhousie University, became a Crown Prosecutor and in 1985 was sworn as a Justice of the Nova Scotia Supreme Court. Died in 1995.

MacIntosh, Charles: Returned to Royal Dutch Shell and retired in 1971. Died in 1979.

Martin-Smith, Pat: Became a career SIS officer. After his retirement in 1970, published his SOE memoir *Friuli 44* in Italian. Died in 1995.

McMullen, Peter: Became Chairman of The Hertford Brewery. Died 1983.

Macpherson, Tommy: Joined Mallinsons the timber firm and over the next thirty years became a leading UK and international businessman. Knighted in 1992 for services to industry. Wrote autobiography *Behind Enemy Lines* (2010).

Munthe, Malcolm: Devoted his life to the establishment of a family cultural trust which comprised the Swedish manor house of Hildasholm by Lake Siljan; the medieval Castle Lunghezza, between Rome and Tivoli; and two Jacobean manor houses in England, one outside Much Marcle in Herefordshire, and Southside House in Wimbledon. Died in 1995.

O'Regan, Pat: Joined the FO as a diplomat in 1946. Served in Washington, Moscow and Ankara. Died in 1961.

Oldham, Tony: Left the Army in 1947 and settled in Italy. Later immigrated to Canada where he became a senior manager for the Brooke Bond Company. Widowed in 1981, went to New Zealand in 1988 where he remarried and then settled in Sydney, Australia, where he died in 1992.

Paterson, George: Returned to Canada and became a forestry consultant.

Ross, John: Resumed his medical studies at Cambridge and qualified as a doctor, spending ten years at the London Hospital. He went on to become Consultant General Physician at Hereford Hospital, specializing in renal medicine. Now retired and living in Herefordshire.

Salvadori, Max: Worked for a time with UNESCO and when NATO was formed joined its Paris staff. Then became an academic, settling at Smith College, Massachusetts, where he became Professor of Political Economics. *The Labour and the Wounds* (1954) was his personal record of the twenty-three years he had spent fighting Fascism. Died in 1991.

Stevens, John: Became a distinguished international banker. Later Chairman of Morgan Grenfell and member of the Court of the Bank of England. Died in 1960.

Tilman, Harold: Exchanged mountaineering for ocean sailing in antique British channel cutters. Missing at sea, presumed dead, en route to the Falklands in the South Atlantic in 1978.

Walker Brown, Bob: Joined 22 SAS when it was reformed and later became its second-in-command. From 1961 to 1963 commanded 23 SAS, one of the two Territorial Army units of the regiment. Then served with the Defence Intelligence Staff until his retirement from the Army in 1964. Died in 1989.

Chronology

3 September	Armistice document signed; Marshal Badoglio reassures Germany that Italy will remain on her side

Events during the mainland Italian campaign

1943	
3 September	Eighth Army lands at Reggio [Operation Baytown]
8 September	Terms of Armistice become public.
9 September	Allied landings at Salerno [Operation Avalanche] and Taranto [Operation Slapstick]
11 September	Germans occupy Rome [Operations Axis and Alaric]
	Italian Army issues Directive 44 'to be ready to resist German attack'
12 September	Germans rescue Mussolini [Operation Oak]
14 September	Allied landings in Sardinia [Operation Brimstone]; heavy fighting at Salerno
23 September	Mussolini re-establishes Fascist government in northern Italy
1 October	Allies enter Naples
13 October	Italy declares war on Germany
4 November	French takeover of Corsica completed
22 November	Eighth Army begins offensive on the Sangro River
1 December	German line on the Sangro River broken
23 December	First air drop of war materials to Partisans
1944	
17 January	US Fifth Army offensive along the Gustav line begins; first Allied attack towards Cassino.
22 January	Anzio landings [Operation Shingle]
3 February	First counter attack by Germans at Anzio
15 – 18 February	Allies bomb the monastery at Monte Cassino
16 February	Second German counter attack at Anzio
11 – 12 May	Allied forces open new offensive against Gustav line; River Rapido crossings [Operation Diadem]
15 May	Germans withdraw to the Adolf Hitler Line
18 May	Polish troops capture Monte Cassino
5 June	Allies enter Rome
18 June	French clear Elba [Operation Brassard]
17 July	Allies cross River Arno

18 July	Polish forces capture Ancona
4 August	Allied forces advance into Florence
22 August	Germans withdraw to the Gothic Line
2 September	US troops capture Pisa
4 December	Eighth Army enters Ravenna
1945	
1 April	Allied forces begin offensive in northern Italy
21 April	Bologna captured
26 April	Verona and Genoa captured
28 April	Mussolini executed by Partisans; Allies take Venice
2 May	German troops in Italy surrender

Italian Partisan political parties and military groupings

Note: The Italian word *brigata* [Plural: *brigate*] does not equate to a 2,500 strong British Army *brigade* and has a looser meaning of group or assembly. *Brigate* were typically weak battalions or strong companies, each comprising 200 to 300 men.

Partito Comunista Italiano [PCI] – Communists.
Gruppi de Azione Patriottica [GAP] – Urban active service units
Squadre de Azione Patriottica [SAP] – Strikes and Propaganda
Garibaldi Brigate – Rural active service units whose members were called *Garibaldini*

Partito d'Azione [Pd'A] – Liberal Socialists
Giustizia e Liberta [Justice and Liberty] resistance units called *Giellisti*

Partito Democrazia Cristiana [PDC] – Christian Democrats
Brigate del Popolo – Partisan units
Brigate *Fiamme Verdi* [Emilia only]
Brigare *Osoppo* – 'Green Scarves' Partisans in Friuli area.

Partito Liberale Italiano [PLI] – Liberals

Partito Socialista di Unita Proletaria [PSIUP] – Socialists
Matteotti– Partisan units

Others:
Badogliani – Right wing bands loyal to Marshal Badolglio
Brigate Autonomo – mainly former soldiers of Italian army called *Autonomi*.
Brigate *Fiamme Verdi* or Green Flames – 'non-political' Catholic Partisans
[Lombardy, Brescia, Bergamo, Valle Carmonica, Veneto]
Otto Organization– Prof Ottorino Balduzzi's urban resistance organization in Genoa

Italian Partisan command structure:
Comitato di Liberazione Nazionale – CLN or Committee of National Liberation
Corpo Volontari della Libertà – CVL or Corps of Freedom Volunteers established in June 1944 as a unified command structure of the Partisan movement.
Comitato di Liberazione Nazionale Alta Italia – CLNAI or Committee of the National Liberation of Northern Italy.

Glossary

Italian and German Military and Security Forces

Esercito Nazionale Repubblicano [ENR] or National Republican Army – Made up of four divisions and smaller autonomous units that were organized from Italians servicemen interned by the Germans when Italy surrendered. The RSI included the 'Monterosa' Alpini Division, 'Italia' Bersaglieri Division, 'San Marco' Marine Division and 'Littorio' Infantry Division.

Guardia Nazionale Republicana [GNR] or Republican National Guard – Formed as a new Fascist militia to replace the Black Shirt MSVN from members who remained loyal to Mussolini. They were the primary anti-Partisan security force.

Brigate Nerre or Black Brigades – Formed in 1943 of hardened fascists to support the GNR.

Decima Flottiglia Mezzi d'Assalto, also known as Decima MAS or 10th Assault Vehicle Flotilla – Originally a commando unit of the Italian Royal Army, it was disbanded after the Armistice but led by Commander Prince Junio Borghese, the unit was revived as part of the National Republican Navy with its HQ in La Spetzia. By the end of the war, it had over 18,000 members and it gained a reputation as a savage pro-fascist, anti-communist, anti-resistance force in *rastrellamenti* alongside the German Army.

Milizia Forestale – a Fascist security organization based on the state forests

Carabinieri [Arma dei Carabinieri] – the national gendarmerie of Italy, policing both the military and civilian populations. After September 1943, Carabinieri units in the north of Italy played a prominent role in anti-Partisan operations.

Questura – the headquarters of the Polizia di Stato, dealing with immigration and documentation.

Gestapo – an abbreviation of Geheime Staatspolizei, the official secret police of Nazi Germany.

SD – The Sicherheitsdienst was primarily the intelligence service of the SS and reported to the Reichssicherheitshauptamt [RSHA], as one of its seven departments.

PG – Prigioneri di Guerra or POW camp

General

A Force – A Force was a special services unit created in 1940 by General Wavell to organize by every available means the deception of the enemy high command. The mission of its 'N' section was to train soldiers in escape and evasion techniques. From September 1941 until the end of the war it was led by Lieutenant Colonel Tony Simonds but it was subsumed by MI9 when the latter established its own Middle East section in Cairo under Lieutenant Colonel Dudley Clarke.

AFHQ – Allied Forces Headquarters [Mediterranean]

AFV – Armoured Fighting Vehicle

ALG – Advanced Landing Ground

AMG – Allied Military Government; originally termed AMGOT, Allied Military Government for Occupied Territories.

AMM – Allied Military Mission

Andartes/Antartes – Greek guerrilla fighters.

Anti-scorch – Expression used by Allies to describe plans and operations concerning measures to prevent Germans destroying key infrastructure [electricity, water, telephone network, ports, airfields, railway termini] and industrial plant [factories, stores].

Bari – Italian Adriatic port where SOE HQ was based.

Blind drop – Agents parachuting into hostile territory without a reception committee to meet them.

BLO – A British Liaison Officer attached to a Partisan formation or unit

BMM – A British Military Mission either attached to a Partisan formation or operating independently. Usually consisted of one or two officers, a W/T operator, an interpreter and an Italian LO.

Brindisi – Italian Adriatic port where SOE established various administrative units.

C – initial by which the head of SIS was referred to

Chetnik – In 1941, Yugoslav resistance forces consisted of two factions: the communist-led Partisans and the Chetniks. Based in the Serbian lands, the Chetniks or 'Yugoslav Army in the Fatherland' were a Royalist movement led by Colonel Draza Mihailović. Initially supported by Britain with Military Missions and arms, the Chetniks were abandoned in late 1943 in favour of Tito's Partisans.

DFC – Distinguished Flying Cross awarded to officers for acts of valour, courage or devotion to duty whilst flying in active operations against the enemy.

Drive – see 'Sweep.'

DMI – Director Military Intelligence

DSO – Distinguished Service Order, a medal awarded to officers for outstanding gallant service.

DZ – Dropping zone

EAM – the Communist dominated Greek National Liberation Front.

ELAS – *Ellinikos Laïkos Apeleftherotikos Stratos* or The Greek People's Liberation Army was the military arm of the National Liberation Front [EAM] during the period of the Greek Resistance until February 1945.
FO – the British Foreign Office
Force 133 – original codename for SOE Bari. This later became Force 266, reserving Force 133 for operations run from Cairo.
GOC – General Officer Commanding
GPO – General Post Office
HQ – Headquarters.
ID-Identity
ISLD – see SIS.
LO – Liaison Officer
Lysander –a British army co-operation and liaison aircraft produced by Westland. The aircraft's exceptional short-field performance made possible clandestine missions using small, unprepared airstrips behind enemy lines that placed or recovered agents.
LZ – Landing zone or airstrip
M19 – a department of the British Military Intelligence Directorate, MI9 was set up in 1940 tasked to assist Allied servicemen stranded in Nazi-occupied Europe to return home. These consisted mainly of soldiers who had found themselves cut off after the Dunkirk evacuation and airmen who had been shot down or who had crash landed behind enemy lines. As the war progressed, it expanded its coverage to include all theatres of the conflict where British servicemen were involved.
Maryland – the codename of the SOE radio station in Bari.
MAS – Motoscafo Armato Silurante, Italian MTB
Massingham – the codename of the SOE radio station in Algiers.
MC – Military Cross awarded to officers for bravery.
MEF – Middle East Forces, a British Army Theatre of Operations Command.
MG – Machine Gun
MI[R] – Military intelligence Research, an organization set up in June 1939 in the War Office for the conduct of para-military activities
ML – Motor launch
Monopoli – Italian Adriatic seaside town between Brindisi and Bari where HQ 1 Special Force was based.
MT-Motor transport
MTB – Motor Torpedo Boat
MTO – Motor Transport Officer
NCO – Non-Commissioned Officer e.g. Corporal or Sergeant
OC – officer commanding
Ops – operations
OR – Other Ranks, British Army personnel who are not commissioned officers.

OSS – The Office of Strategic Services (OSS) was the approximate US counterpart of Britain's SIS and SOE with which it co-operated throughout the Second World War and its immediate aftermath.

P- 403 – An American MTB

POW – Prisoner of War

RAF – Royal Air Force.

RAMC-Royal Army Medical Corps

RANKIN – Codename for anticipated period of time between German withdrawal and arrival of Allied forces.

Rastrellamento – literally 'a combing'; a German counter-Partisan tactic of first putting cut-offs/blocking parties in position and then carrying out an intensive sweep over a section of ground known to be occupied by Partisans. Usually launched at very short notice with large troop deployments.

RE – Royal Engineers

RFC – Royal Flying Corps

RN – Royal Navy

RNVR – Royal Naval Volunteer Reserve

RSM – Regimental Sergeant Major

SIME – Security Intelligence Middle East, a section within MEF responsible for protecting British secrets.

SIS – Founded in 1909 as a joint initiative of the Admiralty and the War Office to control secret intelligence operations in the UK and overseas, SIS employed a more discrete approach to its activities than SOE and conducted substantial and successful operations in both occupied Europe and in the Middle East and Far East where it operated under the cover name 'Interservice Liaison Department' (ISLD).

SOE – The Special Operations Executive was formed in 1940 out of a collection of other agencies such as MI[R], a branch of the War Office's Military Intelligence Directorate, Section D of SIS, The Independent Companies (later Commandos) and the propaganda section at Electra House.

SAS – Special Air Service

Section D – Formed in 1938, Section D was an integral though distinct branch of SIS, under the command of Maj Laurence Grand RE. Tasked to cause trouble in German-occupied Europe, it was later merged with SO2 of SOE.

Sweep – An anti-Partisan tactic involving the advance of a large number of troops through a Partisan-held area with the intention of 'driving' the Partisans into ambushes.

TA-Territorial Army

Tac HQ – advanced command and control centre for operations.

USAF – United States Air Force

W/T – Wireless transmitter and receiver.

WT – Weapon training

SOE, SAS and
Partisan Weapons

M1 pack Howitzer: calibre 75mm; could be broken down into 6 mule loads weighing between 73 and 107 kgs; ammunition HE, HEAT, Smoke; range 8,800 metres; rate of fire 3-6 rounds per minute

Beretta SMG: calibre 9mm; weight 3.25 kg; effective range 150-200 metres; 20-40 rounds detachable box magazine

Breda M1930: calibre 6.5mm; weight 10.6 kg; effective range 800 metres; 20 round stripper clips

Breda M1937: calibre 8mm; weight 38 kgs with tripod; effective range 1,000 metres; 20 round stripper clips

Bren Gun: calibre .303; effective range 600 yards; weight 23 lbs; 30 round gravity feed box magazine

British 2″ mortar: weight 10.5 lbs; ammunition HE and Smoke; range 500 metres; rate of fire 8 rounds per minute

British 3″ mortar: weigh 140 lbs; ammunition HE and Smoke; range 2,600 metres

Browning .50 Machine Gun: calibre .50; weight 128 lbs with tripod; effective range 1,500 metres; belt fed

Italian No.35 mortar: calibre 81mm; weight 140 lbs; ammunition HE and Smoke; range 4,300 metres

Luger Pistol: calibre 9mm; weight 2 lbs; effective range 50 metres; 8 round detachable box magazine

Schmeisser Machine Pistol MP 40: calibre 9mm; weight 9 lbs; effective range 100 metres; 32 round detachable box magazine

Sten Gun: calibre 9mm; weight 7lb; effective range 60 metres; 32 round box magazine

Vickers Machine Gun: calibre .303; weight 33-50lbs; effective range 740 metres [indirect fire 4,100 metres]; 250 round canvas belt

SOE Command And Operations In Italy

Note:
1. No orders or decorations are shown
2. This list is by no means comprehensive but shows the main SOE British military missions in Italy. All missions had a code name as did their Operation, Signal Plan[s] and dropping ground.

HEADQUARTERS

LONDON
J Section – Col C.L. Roseberry [see also BRINDISI]
Capt Hugh Seton Watson
Count Julian A Dobrski aka Lt Col Julian Antony Dolbey

BERNE
Jock McCaffery – Assistant Press Attache to Minister David Kelly.
Peter Jellinek
Maj Julian Hall
Maj John Birkbeck
Maj Teddy de Haan [September 1943]
Wilfred van Singer
Francesco Valvassore
Bill Matthey – Austria and Germany desk

ALGIERS ['MASSINGHAM']
Lt Col J.W.Munn
Lt Col David Keswick [November 1942]
Lt Col A. Dodds-Parker

BRINDISI September 1943 to December 1943
Col C.L. Roseberry
Capt Teddy de Haan
Capt Freddy White
W/T Op Sgt Royle
W/T Op Sgt Case

BARI
Maj Gen Billy Stawell HQ SO[M] [March 1944]
Col Louis Franck [GS]
Col David Keswick
Lt Col Jack Beevor
Lt Col Thurston
Maj Peter Lee

MONOPOLI ['MARYLAND']
Comd Gerry Holdsworth, RNVR; commander No.1 Special Force* [from October 1943]
Lt Col Richard Hewitt – 2 i/c
Lt Dick Laming
Lt Comd Hilary Scott, RNVR
Capt Edward Renton
Lt Robin Richards
Fl Lt Christopher Brock
Capt Pat Gibson
Lt Henry Boutigny

Force 139 – Lt Col Henry Threlfall [also at Latiano and Ostuni]
Force 333 – Brig Miles [Torre di Mare]
Rear-Admr M.C. Morgan-Giles RN
Capt Alan Clarke

Tac HQ based in villa between Florence and Fiesole. Attached to US Fifth Army.
Maj Charles Macintosh
Capt James Beatt
Lt Laurence Norris
Lt Furio Lauri – pilot
Capt ER McDermott RE [Liaison unit attached to Eighth Army in December 1944]

---

* By end of war, 1 SF had over 160 officers and 2,000 ORs

SIENNA – HQ 15ᵗʰ Army Group [after September 1944]

Lt Col Richard Hewitt
Lt Col The Hon Bartholomew Pleydell-Bouverie
Major Hedley Vincent

MILAN [1945]

Lt Col Hedley Vincent, commander No. 1 SF Mission
HQ 8ᵗʰ Army – No.6 Special Force
Lt Col Peter Wilkinson
Major Charles Villiers
Capt Edward Renton
Lochead
Major Alex Ramsay
Capt Ted Birkett
Capt John Bennett
Charles Gardner
Sgt Bill Pickering

CORSICA [BALACLAVA] 3 October 1943 to 29 July 1944.

Maj Andrew Croft
Capt Dick Cooper – conducting officer
Lt Paddy Davies, RNVR
Capt Ken Carson,
Sgt Geoffrey Arnold
Lt JL Newton , RNVR
Lt Fisher Howe, US Navy
Lt Comd Pat Whinney [SIS]
Sgt Coltman
Cpl Basil Bourne-Newton
CPO Sam Smalley
CPO Frank Taylor
✞Lt Dow, RNVR* [SIS]
Capt Dickinson
Don Miles
Sgt Collins, Signals section
Harry Coltman
Lt Smith
Sgt Bernard Jones
✞Capt Peter Fowler [A Force]

---

*   Murdered by crew of MAS 541

FIELD MISSIONS UP TO CAPTURE OF ROME

BROW[Sicily]/VIGILANT [Mainland]

Sicily
Maj Malcolm Munthe
Capt Charles MacIntosh
Capt Gilbert Randall
Capt Dick Cooper aka Cavallaro
Capt Massimo Salvadori aka Max Sylvestor
Fl Lt Betts
Sgt Donald Macdonnell
Cpl 'Billy' Beggs
Sgn 'Harry' Hargreaves
Cpl Bill Pickering
Sgt Charlie Borg [Maltese]

Mainland
Salerno unit
Munthe, Salvadori, Macintosh, Hargreaves, Cooper, Beggs and Fraser
Capt Derrick Scott-Job

Naples – Villa Salve
Munthe, Salvadori, Macintosh, Hargreaves, Cooper, Beggs and Fraser
Capt Edward Renton
Lt Comd Adrian 'Gally' Gallegos, RNVR
Basil Evans
Captain Newman
Capt Massimo Salvadori aka Capt Max Sylvester
Capt Dick Cooper
Fl Lt Bewkey
Capt Michael Gubbins
✟ 'Donaldbain'
✟Sgt Morro
Sgt Frank Gee
Lt Simpson Jones, RNVR

Anzio
Maj Malcolm Munthe
✟Capt Michael Gubbins
Maj Massimo Salvadori
'Scouser' Mulvey

Major Pickering
Alberto Tarchiani
Luigi Savilli aka John Saville

Rome
Capt Charles Macintosh

Florence
Capt Charles Macintosh
Lt Henry Fisher
Lt Duckworth

RUDDER
Rome 1943
✝Capt Fabrizioo Vassalli
✝Col Guiseppe Lanza di Montezemolo

NECK
Como and Rome 1943
Lt Dick Dallimore-Mallaby [Monkey]

FIELD MISSIONS AFTER CAPTURE OF ROME

NORTH EAST ITALY

LIVINGSTONE I / CRAYON
July 1943.
Primorsko area
Simcic – Italian Slovene
Bozic – Italian Slovene

LIVINGSTONE II
August 1943 – January 1944.
Gravornico, Primorsko area
✝Maj Neville Darewski
Sgn Leslie Hammond
Sgt Janes Smrke [Canadian Slovene]
✝Maj Stupple [escaped POW]
Capt Ratcliffe [joined at Porozen]

TENNYSON
September 1943
Primorsko area
Sulicoj– Italian Slovene
Crnigoj– Italian Slovene
Corianc– Italian Slovene

BAROGRAPH [PEARL/BAFFLE BLUE/MRS]
1943-1945
Bologna area, then Veneto
Lt Renato Marini
W/T Op Angelo Rocco

CLOWDER
December 1943 –
Carnia area
Maj Peter Wilkinson [Dec 43- Mar 44]
Maj Charles Villiers [dropped 14 May 1944 to HQ IX Partizan Corp]
BLO Owen Reid
Maj William Jones, BLO at Slovene HQ
Capt Davies BLO
✝Maj Alfgar Hesketh Prichard
CSM George Ginger Hughes
Charles Gardner*
Hall
Sgt Catoni [SIS]
2 W/T Ops
Sgt Bill Pickering
Maj James Darton – base
Capt John Wedgwood – base
Betty Hodgson – base

BALLOONET
13 June 1944 – 29 October 1944
Sqn Ldr Manfred Czernin
Sgt Maj D.A.MacDowell, W/T Op [did not drop]
W/T Op Piero Bruzzone
Dropped 18 July 1944:
BLO Capt Pat Martin Smith.

---

*   Born Israel Gold in Birmingham

Sgt Ernest Barker
Dropped 12 October 1944:
✠Wolfgang Treichl aka Taggart
Huber
Priestley W/T Op for Georgeau
Turner aka Dale
All withdraw on 27 November and arrived back at Bari 27 December 1944

COOLANT [Op SERMON]
July 1944 – November 1944
Faedis between River Tagliamento and River Natisone
Maj/Lt Col Hedley Vincent aka Tucker
S/Sgt Donald Macdonnell
Cpl Harry Hargreaves

COOLANT [Op SERMON 1I]
12/13 August 1944-15 January 1945
Dropped to SERMON 1
Lt Ronald Taylor
Lt David Godwin
✠Cpl Mickie Trent* aka Gyurie [Hungarian]

COOLANT
On 4 November 1944, Vincent replaced by
Maj Tom Macpherson
W/T Op Sgt Arthur Brown

HERRINGTON
21March1945 – 2 May 1945
Mortirolo – Bergamo area
Sqn Ldr Manfred Czernin
Lt J.Matthews [Giuliano Mattioli]
W/T Op Sgt J Williams

HAPEVILLE [Op Chariton III]
Dropped 6 April 1945
Capt 'Moicano'
W/T Op Vitaliano

---

*   Murdered by Partisans along with OSS Texas and Mercury Missions.

HOMESTEAD
21 March1945 – 4 May 1945
Mortirolo-Bergamo
Capt RH Pearson
W/T Op Cpl R McSorley

SIAMANG/HARRISBURG
14 April1945 – 4 May 1945
Val Maira and Val Varaita
Lt Paolo Buffa [P.Barton]
W/T Op Diegi [Savona]

BALLOONET VIOLET, a sub-mission of CLOWDER
12 August 1944 – 27 December 1944
Maj George Fielding
Maj William F Smallwood
W/T Op Arthur Buttle
2/Lt Georgeau aka Lt Banks
Lt Karmenski and three Austrians
Lt Martin aka Brenner, W/T Op for Georgeau – dropped 17 November

TABELLA [Op BERGENFIELD/BAKERSFIELD]
19 September 1944 – 24 February 1945
Monte Ioanaz to Tramonti di Sopra
Maj Tom Roworth aka Maj Nicholson
Maj Richard Tolson
W/T Op Cpl Donald Laybourne
LO Cino Bocazzi aka Piave

BITTERROOT/ SCORPIONE
12 August 1944-30 April 1945
Western Veneto Mountains
✝Major John P. Wilkinson [Fresscia]
Capt Christopher M Woods
W/T Op Cpl Douglas Archibald

RUINA/GELA
31 August 1944-30 April 1945
Western Veneto Mountains
Capt Paul Brietsche
Capt John Orr-Ewing

W/T Op Cpl Ball
Lt Giovanni Querze
Costante Armentano-Conte
Joined from Bergenfield 22 Nov 1944:
Maj Richard Tolson.
W/T Op Cpl Donald Laybourne

FLUVIUS
✞Maj Antonio Ferrazza
W/T Op Benito Quaquarellui

GELA BLUE
17 March 1945 – 20 May 1945
Vittorio Veneto/Cansiglio area
Capt AH Lingen

SIMIA
31 August 1944
Dropped with RUINA on Asiago plateau to Nino Nanetti Partisan Division.
Maj Harold Tilman
Capt John Ross
W/T Op Renato Marini aka Antonio Carrisi
Victor Gozzer aka Gatti – interpreter

BIG BUG
12 October 1944 -12 February 1945 [Sub Mission to BERGENFIELD]
Capt Michael Prior
Capt Lionel Mosdell
Cpl Cecil Ridewood

EDENTON BLUE
Capt Richard Dallimore-Mallaby

INCISOR
6/7 April 1945 – 31 May 1945
Vall d'Aosta.
Maj George Morton aka Major Smith
W/T Op Sgt Williams
Sgt Catania ['Lloyd']

EMILIA REGION

BLUNDELL
1943-1944
Maj Gordon Lett
Sgt Bob Blackmore
Rflmn Mick Miscallef
Lt Geoff Lockwood
Lt Chris Leng from 1 SF BLO
Capt George Lloyd-Roberts RAMC
March 1945 Lett replaced by Maj John Henderson and Capt Murphy and Sgt Younger

TURDUS/BERTH
15/16 July 1944 – 4/5 December 1944.
Piola re Careggine.
Capt Roberto Battaglia aka Barocci
Lt Bruno Innocenti
W/T Op Lt Vitaliani
Maj Tony Oldham

FERRET [A Force]
October 1944
Captain Bruno Leoni
Tumiati
Trosa

RUTLAND
Domenico Azzari – later abandoned his mission and moved to Oldham's Lunense Division under the assumed name of Candiani.

COTULLA III
 23 Mar 1945
Maj Vivian R Johnston
✝Lt Andrea aka Guilio Carozze

CLOVER II
2 February 1945
Rooca Bruna – Groppallo.
Maj Stephen Hastings
W/T Op Chalky White

Lt Georgio Insom
Capt Hugh McDermott LO

INSULIN
23 March 1945
San Stephano – Ferriere – Val d'Arda.
Capt Charles Brown
Fl Lt Rippingdale
W/T Op Cpl J.Bradley

SILENTIA
Maj 'Wilky' Wilcockson also Wilcoxson. Withdrew 6 Feb 1945; replaced by Maj
Jim Davies.

EVAPOURATE
Maj John Barton aka Maj Stone
Sgt Charlie Barratt
Gino and Mario Barbera

CISCO
10 February 1945
Cpt Neil Oughtred
W/T Op Sgn Ted Fry

ENVELOPE
15/16 June 1944
Monte Albano; Montefiorino area
Maj Vivian Johnston
W/T Op CQMS Everitt

TOFFEE/ENVELOPE BLUE
27 July 1944 [September 1944]
Frassinoro – Montefiorino – Alpe di Succiso – Grammatica
Maj Jim Davies
Maj 'Wilky' Wilcockson
Maj Charles Holland
Capt G.C. Lloyd Roberts
W/T Op Cpl Frank Hayhurst
W/T Op Cpl Charlie Barratt
Joined February 1945:
Maj Jim Davies

Capt John 'Tiger' Stott
Joined April 1945 in Parma:
Capt John Stewart
Capt Thomas Franklin-Adams

SIHAKA
Bologna
Captain Vito Bilancia

CARIBOU
✠Major Strachan [30 Commando Group] and five ORs

NORTH WEST ITALY

FLAP
7 August 1944
Val Ellero – Marsaglia – Val Stura.
✠Maj Neville Darewski aka Neville Temple
Captain Andrew [Arne] Flygt
Cpl Cromack
W/T Op Bert Farrimond

FLAP II
NW Liguria
Capt Michael Lees
Geoffrey Long [war artist]
Paul Morton [Canadian journalist]
Roberto

SILICA
9/10 September 1944
Cuneo
Lt Col Selby Cope
Capt Rudolf Krzak aka Havel
W/T Op Cpl Williams

PLUMA MISSION
Romano Antonelli

ENVELOPE
2 January 1945

Based at Secchio
Capt Michael Lees
W/T Op Bert Farrimond
Lizza, Italian-born Canadian interpreter
Phil Butler [took over from Lizza]

CLOVER I MISSION
18 January 1945
Monte Antola – Genoa
Lt Col Peter McMullen
Maj Basil Davidson
W/T Op Cpl/Sgt George Armstrong
Lt Wochievevich aka Elio
Later:
Capt J. R.Gordon – 14 April [M 12 Mission]
Lt R.O. Richards, RNVR – 14 April
Capt H.B.M. Murphy– walked up from Spetzia
Cpl Eric Kneeshaw
Cpl E. Evans
Cpl F. Comber
Lt Russell and six commandos

Italian personnel:
Lt Quattrocolo aka Aldo
Malpensi aka Fede
Tattanelli aka Sirio
POWs attached: Bdr McDowell, Bdr Beecroft, Cpl Botha

CLOVER II – A sub mission of CLOVER
Maj S Hastings
W/T Op Sgt Chalky White

SAKI – A sub mission of CLOVER
Capt Robert Bentley in Imperia-Savona area
Cpl James MacDougall

COTULLA III – A sub mission of CLOVER
23 March-20 May 1945 in Savona
Maj Vivian R. Johnston
W/T Op CQMS Everitt

INSULIN – A sub mission of CLOVER
23 March 1945
East of Scrivia
Capt Brown
Fl Lt Rippingdale RAF
W/T Op Cpl Bradley

GENESSE – A sub mission of CLOVER
Voghera
Capt Basil Irwin,
Cpl W.G.Denley
✞Capt Charles Whittaker

FERRULA
Grenoble
Leon Blanchaert {Detachment 11 No.1 Special Force] aka Maj I. Hamilton

CLARINDA
Val d'Aosta
Maj WAF McKenna

CLARION
9 December 1944
Frabosa
Lt Col Duncan Campbell
Lt Clark RNVR
One W/T Op
Capt Basil Irving-Bell
W/T Op Cpl Ashurst

CHARITON
4 February 1945
Maj Max Salvadori [to Milan]
✞Capt John Keany
Capt HB Powell
Capt 'Roccia' [Luigi Cavalieri]
Sgt Bill Pickering
Joined mission 12 April:
Maj Derek Leach
Dropped 28 April:
Maj Richard Lea

BAMON
11 March 1944
Capt Roggerro
Followed by:
Lt Delle 5 August 1944
Lt Bonvicini 21 August 1944

CHEROKEE
16/17 November 1944
Zimone [Biella]. Received by BAMON
Maj Alastair Macdonald
Capt Jim Bell
Lt [later Capt] Patrick Amoore
Cpl Tony Birch

CHEROKEE II
Joined CHEROKEE on 27 December 1944
Capt Burns
Sgt Maj Johns RE
W/T Op Sgt Bell
10 March 1945:
Maj Robert B. Readhead [took over from Macdonald]
18 March 1945:
Lt Mark Terry aka Marco Folchi-Vici
29 March 1945:
Lt Alex Ihnatowicz
30 March 1945:
Capt Leo
Capt Allora
6 April 1945:
Cpl Patrick Fleury
18 April 1945:
Capt John Farran
Cpl Crane
28 Apr1945:
Maj Alan LeBrocq [landed 3 May]
Capt Raymond Neale

FLOODLIGHT/FAIRWAY
August 1944
Accompanied Gen Cadorna , former comd of Arieste Division, when dropped into
N Italy

Maj Oliver Churchill
Capt Cotterel

CORONA MISSION
November 1944
Alba south of Turin
Col John Stevens
Capt Ballard [Operation Excelsior]
Italian W/T Op

PLUMA MISSION
Langhe area in Piedmont
Antonelli

HEDGE/DONUM
31 July 1944
Val Sangone/Val Chisone
Maj Hamilton
Capt Pat O'Regan
WT Op Litturi
WT Op Patane
Lt Ruscelli
Capt Leonard Blanchaert
W/T Op Paradisier [French]
Livio Rivoseachi, interpreter

BANDON MISSION
Maj H. Ballard
W/T Op Sgt Scott
5 May 1945:
Capt Harlow

BANDON II
20 December 1944
✞Maj Adrian Hope
W/T Op Cpl 'Busty' Millard

BANDON III
24 February 1945
Capt W.J. Sayers

W/T Op Sgn Trinchetto

BANDON III
2 April 1945 landed at Vesime
Col John Stevens
Maj Derek Dodson
W/T Op Cpl Lane
Capt Buck Macdonald SAS attached **Corona**
Victor Styles

SAS OPERATIONS in Partisan Zones

Op MAPLE [THISTLEDOWN and DRIFTWOOD]
7 January 1944
Ancona-Urbino/Colle Futa
✠Capt J StG Gunston

Op POMEGRANATE
12 January 1944
Lake Trasimene – Perugia
✠Maj Widdrington
Lt Hughes

Op SPEEDWELL I and II
7 September 1944
NE from La Spetzia
✠Capt Philip Pinckney
✠Capt Pat Dudgeon
Lt 'Tojo' Wedderburn
Lt Anthony Greville-Bell

Op GALIA
27 December 1944 – February 1945
Pontremoli
Maj Bob Walker-Brown

Op CANUCK
January – April 1945
Langhe
Capt Buck [Robert] Macdonald

Op COLD COMFORT [ZOMBIE]
17 February – 31 March 1945
Brenner Pass
✝Maj Ross Littlejohn

Op BRAKE II
31 January 1945
La Spetzia area
Sgt Guscott

Op TOMBOLA
4 March- 24 April 1945
Reggio
Maj Roy Farran
Major Ken Harvey

Op BLIMEY
6 April 1945
Pontremoli
Capt Scott

MI9 IN ITALY
London:
Brig Crockatt
A Force: N Section Algiers [Sept 43]/Taranto, then Bari
Lt Col Tony Simonds [Bari and Cairo]
Asst: Maj JV Fillingham [Bari]
'Squad' Dennis
Boat section: Sub Lt Ian MacPherson RN
Field Escape Section 3: Capt FP Falvey
Field Escape Section 2; Capt Christopher Soames
Western Italy: ✝Capt Peter Fowler
Rome escape organization: Maj SI Derry

CUCKOLD MISSION
Slovenia 1944-45

Typical SOE Officer Kit List for Winter 1943/1944

Clothing worn
Locally manufactured boots or Ammunition Boots
Two pairs of socks
Battledress trousers
Short cotton pants
Short-sleeve wool vest or woollen sweater
Flannel shirt [long sleeve]
Italian or American Wind Jacket
Puttees [short]
Scarf of parachute silk
Beret
Web belt, holster, two ammunition pouches, magazine holder
Water bottle

Spare clothing carried in rucksack*
Spare shirt
Three pairs of socks
One pair gloves
Spare handkerchief
Vest or Sweater
Medical Kit
Shaving kit [razor, soap, spare blades, shaving stick]
One blanket lined with parachute silk
Sheepskin coat
Italian ground sheet

Personal kit
Binoculars
Compass oil

---

*   Usually weighed about 50 lbs

Map case
Campaign knife
Torch including spare battery and bulb
Luminous wrist watch
Message pad AB 153
Two waterproof sacks to fit Battledress pockets
Spoon
Half mess tin
Bowie knife
Waterproof watch holder
Dubbin polish
Towel
Candle
Housewife [needles, buttons and thread]

Personal weapons
Sten Gun 9mm
Semi-automatic pistol Luger 9mm
Two hand grenades [Mills bombs]
For Sten and Luger:
One magazine in Sten gun [32 rounds]
Four spare Sten magazines [128 rounds]
Two packets Luger ammunition [40 rounds]
Loader pull through, oil bottle etc
Knives fighting

Medical kit
Iodine pencil
10 Aspros
Emergoplast plaster dressings
25 No.9 laxative pills
Bismuth Subnitrate or Bismuth Subcarbonate [for dysentery]
Benzedrine carbonate [stimulant]
Streptosil [Sulfanilamide] ointment
Multivitamin tablets

Equipment list for Lieutenant Dick Dallimore-Mallaby ['OLAF']

Compiled from SOE files and Italian police report

1 Watersuit

1 Dinghy

1 Mae West

Italian Clothing [suit provided by BROW] including soft hat, handkerchief, 2 belts, grey tie

1 pullover which could also be used as a reagent when soaked in acid

1 book by Giovanni Papini [pages 185-188 contained negatives of conventional signs]

Copy of *Corriere della Sera* dated 29 June 1943

1 shaving brush containing a signals crystal

1 stick shaving soap

1 tooth brush

1 tin of 'Ideale' dentifrice containing negatives and plans

1 knife attached to sleeve for cutting up dinghy

1 Wallet containing:

Florence ID card No.5930895

Dichiarazione di Riforma [a discharge paper by the Calling-Up Committee of the Province of Florence]

1 second class driving licence [Trieste Prefecture]

Letter from Florence University

A religious picture

A photograph of civilians

6x50 cent stamps

4,300 Lire in small denominations

A tin of milk containing water purification powder

A tin of Vaseline ['Società Boracifera di Larderello-Firenze'] containing photographs of plans

In waterproof bag strapped to inside leg:
1 Torch battery containing:
Spare Trieste ID card No.56031991
Spare Florence ID card No.5953792
Blank Congado [pass for temporary unlimited leave]
Micros of three signal plans
1 Torch battery containing bundle of thirty four 1,000 Lire notes
6 rectangular bricks containing crystals and money were included in waterproof bag
Total money came to Lire 113,000
OLAF also carried an aerial disguised as a clothes line

Bibliography

Absalom, Roger, *Strange Alliance. Aspects of escape and survival in Italy 1943-45*, Leo S.Olschki 1991

Alexander of Tunis, *Memoirs 1940-1945*, Cassell 1962

Atkinson, Rick, *Day of Battle – the war in Sicily and Italy 1943-1944*, Little, Brown & Co 2007

Baerentzen, Lars, *British Reports on Greece 1943-44, JM Stevens, CM Woodhouse, DJ Wallace*, Museum Tusculanum Press, Copenhagen 1982

Battaglia, Roberto, *The story of the Italian Resistance*, Oldhams 1957

Behan, Tom, *The Italian Resistance: Fascists, Guerrillas and the Allies*, Pluto Press 2009

Blaxland, Gregory, *Alexander's Generals, the Italian Campaign 1944-45*, William Kimber 1979

Cabell, Craig, *The History of 30 Assault Unit*, Pen & Sword 2009

Cadogan, Sir Alexander, *Diaries 1938-45, ed D Dilks*, Cassell 1971

Clark, Gen Mark, *Calculated Risk*, Harrap 1951

Cooper, Capt Dick, *The Adventures of a Secret Agent*, Frederick Muller, 1957

Cooper, Capt Dick, *The Man who liked Hell, 12 years in the French Foreign Legion*, Jarrolds 1933

Croft, Andrew, *A Talent for Adventure*, SPA 1991

Davidson, Basil, *Special Operations Europe*, Victor Gollanz 1980

Davies, Tony, *When The Moon Rises*, Futura 1974

Dear, Ian, *Sabotage and Subversion: the SOE and OSS at war*, Cassell 1996

Duggan, Christopher, *The Force of Destiny, A History of Italy since 1796*, Allen Lane 2007

Dulles, Allen, *The Secret Surrender*, Harper and Row 1966

Eden, Anthony, *The Reckoning*, Houghton Mifflin 1965

English, Ian, *Assisted Passage, Walking to Freedom Italy 1943*, Naval and Military, 2005

Farran, Roy, *Operation Tombola*, Collins, 1960

Foot, MRD, SOE: *The Special Operations Executive*, BBC 1984

Forman, Denis, *To Reason Why*, Abacus 1993

Fowler, William, *The Secret War in Italy*, Ian Allan 2010

Franks, Norman, *Double Mission*, William Kimber 1976

Gallegos, Adrian, *From Capri to Oblivion*, Hodder and Stoughton 1959
Gnecchi-Ruscone, Francesco, *When Being Italian was Difficult*, Milan 1999
Hann, Robert, *SAS Operation Galia*, Impress 2009
Hastings, Sir Stephen, *The Drums of Memory*, Leo Cooper 1994
Holland, James, *Italy's Sorrow*, Harper Press 2008
Hood, Stuart, *Carino*, Carcanet 1985
Howarth, Patrick, *Undercover*, Routlege & Keegan Paul, 1980
Hoyt, Edwin, *Backwater War – the Allied campaign in Italy*, Praeger 2002
Jones, Donald, *Escape from Sulmona*, Vantage Press 1980
Kesselring, FM Albert, *Memoirs*, William Kimber 1953
Lamb, Richard, *War in Italy 1943-45, A Brutal Story*, St Martin's Press 1994
Lees, Michael, *Special Operations Executed*, William Kimber 1986
Lett, Gordon, *Rossano*, Hodder and Stoughhton, 1955
Lewis, Laurence, *Echoes of Resistance*, Costello 1985
Macintosh, Charles, *From Cloak to Dagger*, William Kimber 1982
Mackenzie, William, *The Secret History of SOE*, St Ermin's Press 2000
MacMillan, Harold, *The Blast of War*, Macmillan 1967
MacPherson, Sir Tommy, *Behind Enenmy Lines*, Mainstream 2010
Madge, Tim, *The Last Hero: Bill Tilman*, Mountaineers 1995
Martin-Smith, Pat, *Private Memoir*, Imperial War Museum Library
Martin-Smith, Pat: *Friuli 44*, Del Bianco 1991
Mather, Sir Carol, *When the Grass Stops Growing*, Pen & Sword 1997
McCafferty, John, *No Pipes or Drums*, Private memoir, Imperial War Museum
Messenger, Charles, *The Commandos 1940-46*, William Kimber 1985
Morgan, Mike, *Daggers Drawn*, Sutton Publishing 2000
Mortimer, Gavin, *Stirling's Men*, Cassell 2005
Munthe, Malcolm, *Sweet is War*, Duckworth, 1954
Newby, Eric, *Love and War in the Apennines*, Picador 1996
Nicolson, Nigel, *Alex, the Life of FM Alexander of Tunis*, Weidenfeld and Nicolson 1973
O'Donnell, Patrick, *The Brenner Assignment*, Da Capo Press 2008
Oldham, Tony, *Some Experiences of an Escaped POW*, Private papers
Orr-Ewing, John, Private papers, Imperial War Museum
Pickering, William, *The bandits of Cisterna*, Leo Cooper 1991
Riley, JP, *From Pole to Pole, the Life of Quentin Riley*, Bluntisham 1989
Ross, John, Private memoir, Imperial War Museum
Ross, Michael, *From Liguria with Love*, Minerva 1997
Salvadori, Massimo, *The Labour and the Wounds*, Pall Mall Press 1958
Saunders, Hilary St George, *The Green Beret*, Michael Joseph 1949
Smith, Bradley and Agarossi, Elena, *Operation Sunrise, the secret surrender*, Andre Deutsch 1979
Stafford, David, *Secret Agent, The true Story of the Special Operations Executive*,

BBC Books 2000

Stafford, David, *Mission Accomplished, SOE and Italy 1943–1945*, The Bodley Head 2011

Sweet-Escott, Bickham, *Baker Street Irregular*, Methuen 1965

Tilman, Harold, *Where Men and Mountains Meet*, CUP 1946

Tudor, Malcolm, *Special Force, SOE and the Italian Resistance*, Emilia 2004

Warner, Philip, *The SAS: the official history*, Sphere 1983

West, Nigel, *Secret War, the story of SOE*, Hodder and Stoughton 1992

Wilhelm, Maria De Blasio, *The Other Italy: Italian Resistance in World War II*, Norton & Co 1989

Wilkinson, Peter, *Foreign Fields*, IB Taurus, 1997

Windsor, John, *The Mouth of the Wolf*, Hodder and Stoughton, 1967

Woodhouse, CM, *The Struggle for Greece*, Hurst & Co, 2002

Woods, Christopher, Private memoir, Imperial War Museum

Index